TRUE

Newfoundlanders

EARLY HOMES AND FAMILIES OF NEWFOUNDLAND AND LABRADOR

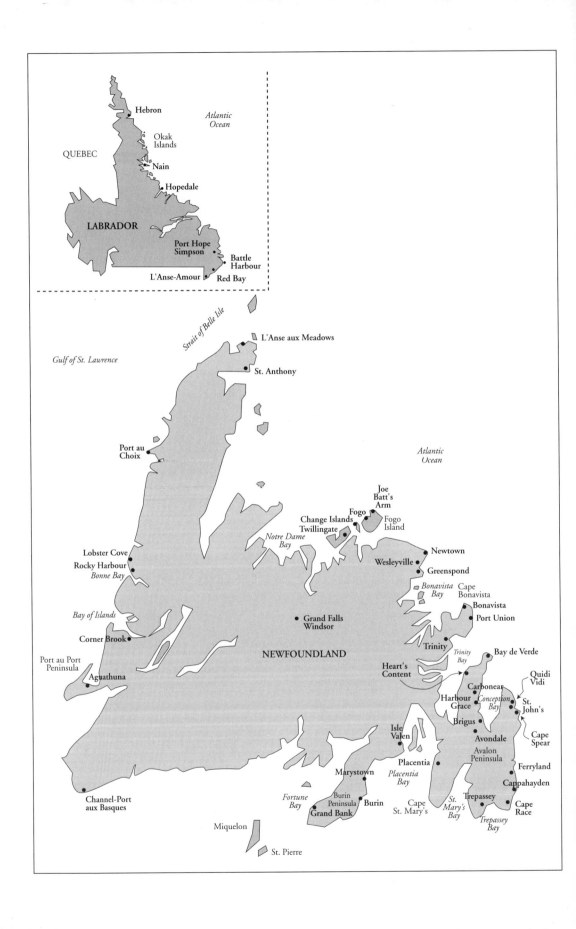

Hebron

Okak Islands

QUEBEC

Nain

Hopedale

LABRADOR

Atlantic Ocean

Port Hope Simpson

Battle Harbour

L'Anse-Amour

Red Bay

Strait of Belle Isle

L'Anse aux Meadows

Gulf of St. Lawrence

St. Anthony

Atlantic Ocean

Port au Choix

Joe Batt's Arm

Fogo

Change Islands

Twillingate

Fogo Island

Notre Dame Bay

Newtown

Wesleyville

Greenspond

Lobster Cove

Rocky Harbour

Bonne Bay

Bonavista Bay

Cape Bonavista

Bonavista

Port Union

Bay of Islands

Grand Falls Windsor

Corner Brook

NEWFOUNDLAND

Trinity

Trinity Bay

Bay de Verde

Port au Port Peninsula

Quidi Vidi

Aguathuna

Heart's Content

Carbonear

Conception Bay

St. John's

Harbour Grace

Brigus

Cape Spear

Avondale

Avalon Peninsula

Isle Valen

Placentia

Ferryland

Marystown

Placentia Bay

Cappahayden

Channel-Port aux Basques

Fortune Bay

Burin Peninsula

Burin

Cape St. Mary's

St. Mary's Bay

Trepassey

Grand Bank

Cape Race

Trepassey Bay

Miquelon

St. Pierre

T R U E

Newfoundlanders

EARLY HOMES AND FAMILIES OF NEWFOUNDLAND AND LABRADOR

MARGARET MCBURNEY AND MARY BYERS
PHOTOGRAPHY BY JOHN DE VISSER

The BOSTON
MILLS PRESS

Published in 1997 by
Boston Mills Press
www.boston-mills.on.ca

Distributed in Canada by
General Distribution Services Inc.
30 Lesmill Road
Toronto, Canada M3B 2T6
Tel 416-445-3333
Fax 416-445-5967
e-mail customer.service@ccmailgw.genpub.com

Distributed in the United States by
General Distribution Services Inc.
85 River Rock Drive, Suite 202
Buffalo, New York 14207
Toll-free 1-800-805-1083
Fax 416-445-5967
e-mail gdsinc.genpub.com

01 00 99 98 97   2 3 4 5

Cataloging in Publication Data

McBurney, Margaret, 1931–
True Newfoundlanders: early homes and families of Newfoundland and Labrador

Includes bibliographical references and index.
ISBN 1-55046-199-0

1. Dwellings - Newfoundland - History.
2. Historic buildings - Newfoundland.
3. Newfoundland - Biography.
I. Byers, Mary, 1933–   . II. De Visser, John, 1930–   . III. Title.

FC2162.M32 1997   971.8   97-930706-6
F1122.8.M32 1997

Photographs by John de Visser
Cover painting, *Wesleyville: Cyril's Kite Over Blackwood's Hill,* by David Blackwood
Cover design by Gillian Stead. Text design by Mary Firth
Edited by Kathleen Fraser
Printed in Canada

Contents

Viking settlement, L'Anse
aux Meadows.

Introduction

Its vast bulk shrouded in fog or outlined in sharp detail by a brilliant sun, Newfoundland is a place of contradictions. By turns harsh, when the sea roils around it, or gentle, when the winds are stilled, its story is told in place names such as Deadman's Cove and Paradise. Visited earlier by Europeans than was mainland Canada, Newfoundland was settled late. Known to mariners around the world, it was populated mainly by English, Irish and French. And though tied by geography to North America, it turned its face toward the British Isles.

The lure of the fisheries is central to the story of Newfoundland and Labrador. For thousands of years before European explorers stumbled on the living wealth around island and mainland, lucrative harvests were being gathered in the waters there — cod that, according to John Cabot, could be scooped out of the water in baskets, and seals, tuna, herring, mackerel and squid.

The abundance in these waters was known of as early as 5500 B.C. (some sources say 7000 B.C.) to Maritime Archaic people — nomadic groups who hunted and fished in Labrador — and their descendants, who moved into Newfoundland in ensuing centuries in pursuit of the seasonal hunt. Burial sites at Port au Choix on the island's northern arm and at L'Anse-Amour in southern Labrador tell something of their existence. About the year A.D. 1000, Viking explorers from Iceland and Greenland reached Labrador and settled briefly at the tip of Newfoundland's Great Northern Peninsula at L'Anse aux Meadows. (There is still some speculation that this forbidding site was the legendary Vinland.) The Beothuk, Newfoundland's native people, were probably descended from the early nomadic tribes, and are believed to have been of Algonkian origin. They lived on the south and northeast coasts of Newfoundland, existing on the abundant resources of land and sea until they encountered Europeans in the sixteenth century. Over hundreds of years they were gradually forced into the interior as their hunting grounds were taken over. The newcomers not only encroached on their territory, they also persecuted the Beothuk and brought diseases to which they had no resistance. (Shawnadithit, the last surviving Beothuk, died of tuberculosis in 1829, at age twenty-eight.)

By the fifteenth century, European explorers seeking a route to the riches of the East had found these fabulous fishing grounds. Basque, French, Portuguese, Spanish and British vessels soon sought out what became known as the world's most prolific fisheries.

Early fishing boat, 1630.

Following Christopher Columbus's discovery of the "Indies" (the continent of North America) in 1492, there was great interest, particularly in Spain and Portugal, in further exploration. John Cabot (Giovanni Caboto), a Venetian of Genoese origin, unable to get support in Spain and perhaps doubting that Columbus had discovered the Indies, sought and received letters patent from Henry VII of England for a voyage of discovery. Relations between Spain and England were fragile. The English king and Cabot were both aware that the new lands to which the explorer would sail had not been granted to Spain by the 1493 Papal Bull, which divided the world between Spain and Portugal. These regions were, in effect, up for grabs.

And so in mid-May 1497, Cabot set sail in the *Matthew*, built in the port of Bristol, with a crew of eighteen or twenty Bristol seamen who, from this westerly coast of England, had experience in ocean navigating. They crossed the Atlantic and on June 24 sighted land at the tip of Cape Bonavista, Newfoundland, where they went ashore. According to Cabot's biographer, R. A. Skelton, the explorer made "a ceremonial act of possession." Then, after another month spent journeying to Nova Scotia and Maine, they returned to England, where Henry VII paid £10 "to hym that founde the new Isle." Cabot was acclaimed. It was assumed that he had found "the country of the Great Khan." But his triumph was short-lived. Conflicting accounts of a voyage the following year suggest that his ship and four others disappeared and were never heard of again.

Jacques Cartier arrived in 1534, making a partial tour of Newfoundland and Labrador (and that was when he described Labrador as "the land God gave to Cain"). When he returned in 1535 he sailed around Newfoundland, finding the passage between it and Cape Breton, proving that Newfoundland was indeed an island.

Then in 1583, bearing a charter from Elizabeth I of England, Sir Humphrey Gilbert sailed triumphantly into St. John's harbour and, although he found Spanish and Portuguese vessels moored there along with the British, claimed Newfoundland and two hundred leagues to the north and south for his queen. According to Gilbert's biographer, David B. Quinn, "The merchants and fishermen assembled before his tent, a rod and turf were cut and delivered to him in virtue of his personal title to the soil, and he proclaimed the land to be the queen's in perpetuity." He followed this proclamation with another, making the Church of England the official religion and forbidding opposition to the queen (this would be treated as high treason) or even disrespect for her majesty. (Offenders were subject to penalties that ranged from having their ships seized to having their ears cut off.) The bystanders, Quinn notes, were "glad to get off so lightly." Historian George M. Story commented that Gilbert "sailed to his death by drowning on the return voyage to England . . . and left Newfoundland as it had been a century before he arrived: a summer fishing station for the maritime nations of Europe. Yet Gilbert's voyage was (if Ireland be excepted) Britain's first overseas colonial effort."

The tales brought home by each explorer's crew were of seas that swarmed with codfish. And so, for the next two and a half centuries, Britain's West Country merchants, familiar with the winds and ways of the Atlantic, took virtual control of the commercial life of Newfoundland. Pursuit of the humble cod led their vessels from Poole and other ports in England's West Country to Newfoundland's shores. Since it was in their interest to discourage settlement, thus preserving for themselves the riches of the cod fishery, and making use of a ready-made naval training facility, they urged the British Crown to support them and persuaded parliament to enact anti-settlement laws. These merchants were, however, adventurous men who risked much, and made and lost fortunes. Many established permanent homes in Newfoundland and eventually assisted settlement by provisioning fishermen in their company stores.

There were no enticements to settle in Newfoundland and Labrador — no offers of free land, no provisioning for a year, no promise of a governor to preserve law and order. Quite the opposite. Harsh measures were the order of the day — houses were burned, and any who chose to stay were forbidden to build within six miles of the shoreline. Deportation was threatened. In 1634 it was decreed that the captain of the first British ship to arrive in a harbour each spring would be admiral and governor of the harbour for that season. This, notes George Story, "gave effective jurisdiction over most of the east coast . . . to the rough, customary justice of the fishing smack and the rum-keg court." Britain's chartered companies along the Avalon Peninsula were their only attempt at official colonization, and they all failed in short order. Wars impeded settlement, lending an instability to certain areas, particularly the west coast, where English-French fishing and settlement rights were in dispute for over two hundred years.

In spite of all this, men wintered over. Land-based fishing operations started up to effect curing of the catch. The earliest settlements were themselves migratory as men moved with the seasonal hunt — from a temporary dwelling by the shore for the summer fishery to another seasonal dwelling inland for the winter's hunt. Gradually these sporadic centres grew. Immigration began and reached its peak during the late eighteenth and early nineteenth centuries. Crews from the West Country vessels stayed; merchants established a permanent residence in Newfoundland or Labrador. There were some for whom conditions in the British Isles were so deplorable that anything would be better; they decided to take their chances in a new land. These settlers were nothing if not tenacious. Many of them were Irish.

The Irish boarded British ships in Cork, Waterford, New Ross and Youghal to work as fishermen and crew for the summer fishery. When permanent settlement began in the eighteenth century, many came as servants and a few as merchants. In the first three decades of the nineteenth century alone, as many as 30,000 to 35,000 Irish immigrated to Newfoundland. They settled

This is Newfoundland.

mainly between St. John's and Placentia on the south shore, with concentrations as well in Conception Bay and on Fogo Island. Eventually the Irish made up nearly fifty percent of the island's population. Their numbers were so great that it became popular to call Newfoundland "John Bull's other Ireland."

The Irish suffered in Newfoundland — particularly as their numbers increased. With centuries of English-Irish antagonism fuelling their distrust, they found more of the same in their new home. Many were tricked and later abandoned by unscrupulous English shipowners (as were English servants as well), treated as rabble by the English establishment, encouraged in their alcoholic excesses, dealt with harshly in the English courts, and forbidden to attend Mass until the official establishment of the Roman Catholic church in 1784. The British accused them of being lazy, untrustworthy and prone to drunkenness. There was sectarian bigotry on both sides. Yet the record is perhaps not as black as has sometimes been painted. The Irish found ample employment, many operating taverns, or working as stonemasons or carpenters or in other skilled trades. Historian Frederick W. Rowe has set out an opposing view: "In fact Irish planters (settlers) and merchants and some fishermen lived in complete amity with their English Protestant neighbours, and were steadfast in their loyalty to British institutions."

As the eighteenth century progressed, life for the people of Newfoundland, although still harsh, became somewhat better. The first of many British naval governors arrived in 1729, albeit only for the summer months and encumbered by the British government's anti-settlement attitude. Local magistrates began to keep some semblance of order during the nine months of the year when there were neither fishing admirals nor king's ships in the harbours. Now St. John's, not initially one of the larger settlements on then island, gradually became an administrative, military, judicial, cultural and commercial centre.

After the Treaty of Paris ended the Seven Years' War in 1763, England annexed Labrador to Newfoundland, creating a vast territory including areas that are now part of Quebec. Then, eleven years later, the British government changed its mind, and Labrador was handed over to Quebec. Finally, in another about-face, Labrador was reannexed to Newfoundland in 1809, the saga producing ongoing territorial claims.

The colony was granted representative government in 1832, with elected and appointed chambers. Responsible government, with full colonial status, arrived in 1855. Religion, ethnicity, and social status played an important part in the politics of the day, and resulted in heated exchanges in the Legislature and occasional violence in the streets. Politics in Newfoundland began and continued with sparks flying, rich in full-blown intrigues, heated rhetoric, and wit laced with a sharp cutting edge.

Throughout the nineteenth century, more and more people arrived, most to work in the cod fishery. In the early years of the century the population numbered about 40,000. By 1891 it had reached 202,000. Gradually sectarian differences eased somewhat. The Roman Catholics in St. John's built the Basilica of St. John the Baptist in 1855, at that time the largest in North America. (The bishop of New York came to the ceremony, then returned to build St. Patrick's Cathedral in New York City.) The Anglican Cathedral of St. John the Baptist was begun in 1849, but the parish traces its roots to 1699, making it the oldest Anglican parish in North America.

The ties between Newfoundland and the British Isles were as strong as the transatlantic cable that eventually joined them. (Some St. John's families were known to send their linens "over home" to be laundered in the right way.) It has been observed that Newfoundland, with the majority of its early settlements facing across the Atlantic and with its more populated southeast coast less than 1,700 miles from the British Isles, grew with its back to North America.

The combination of emigration from West Country Britain and from Ireland accounts largely for the unique dialect that so often identifies a Newfoundlander today. Isolation has helped to preserve its distinctiveness. Words that have a direct connection with a location in the British Isles are still in use. George Story identifies many — fetch (the ghost of a living person), gluam (to snatch suddenly), bang-belly (pancake), figgy-pudden (pudding with raisins), and livyer (an inhabitant or resident). And one custom, an import from the West Country of England, became a flamboyant and sometimes violent part of the Twelve Days of Christmas. Masked men, rigged out in fantastic costumes with elaborate headgear, caroused and roamed the streets carrying sticks or switches with which to batter a fellow reveller. This custom later toned down, becoming a chance to disguise, often in women's clothing, visit the neighbours, challenge them to guess the identity of the caller, and get food and drink in return. This tradition was called Christmas mumming.

There were strong ties with continental Europe and the West Indies as well. The coastlines of Newfoundland and Labrador were dotted with hundreds of harbours, outports that were separated from each other by miles of difficult terrain and accessible to each other most easily by sea. Each had one or more mercantile enterprises with specific links to ports around the world that their vessels frequented. Crews might be more familiar with these exotic ports than those in adjacent bays.

Rum, readily available through trade with the West Indies via Boston, was the most popular tipple. It played an important and particularly destructive role in eighteenth- and nineteenth-century Newfoundland and Labrador, as it did elsewhere. Even the young imbibed. In the early 1800s some 700,000 gallons of rum and spirits were imported to an island with a population of only a few thousand. (Newfoundlanders were assisted in their intake by the many hundreds of transient fishermen from other countries.) Michael Harris, in *Rare Ambition*, describes the scene: "In fact rum arm-wrestled with religion for most of Newfoundland's early history with grog, not God, enjoying the upper hand for more than two hundred years." Legends abound regarding the origins of Newfoundland's infamous "screech." According to Frederick Rowe, this potent drink was so named during the Second World War when military personnel stationed on the island discovered the lure of cheap Demerara rum, brought to Newfoundland in bulk and bottled there. The *Dictionary of Newfoundland English* claims an earlier date, and quotes a bit of doggerel from the September

21, 1904, *Daily News:* "The great unwashed / If he's not squashed / Where rotten rum does flow boys, / 'Tis he will screech upon the beech / To join this Wild West show, boys."

Place names are one of the fascinations of Newfoundland and Labrador. No tedious list of honourable war heroes, but a mellifluous assortment of evocative names — Angel's Cove, Bareneed, Bay D'Espoir, Blow-Me-Down, Breakheart Point, Cape White Handkerchief, Come-By-Chance, Dildo, Famine Point, Famish Gut, Gallows Hill, Gin Cove, Heart's Content, Heart's Delight, Heart's Desire, Little Heart's Ease, Jerry's Nose, Joe Batt's Arm, Paradise, Misery Point, Mistaken Point, Snug Harbour, Wreck Cove and, for the afternoon ritual, Tea Cove, Sugar Loaf and Spoon Cove. Then, when inspiration was lacking one day, Nameless Cove.

The saga of Newfoundland and Labrador is reflected in its buildings, large and small. "Simplicity in style and survival in structure," notes architectural historian Shane O'Dea, "characterize Newfoundland architecture." Compared to neighbouring Nova Scotia, Quebec and New England, "Life in Newfoundland was harsher, living less sophisticated and these differences were manifested in the architecture." Because of their isolation, influences that affected architecture elsewhere were often less apparent here. Houses, however, tended to reflect their builder's origin, and a quick glance indicates their strong cultural links with West Country England and Ireland.

Most early construction was for the fisheries, and so fish flakes and wharves made up the scene by any harbour. Until the early nineteenth century, building a permanent dwelling broke the laws inspired by Britain's anti-settlement policy, and impermanent shelters dotted the landscape until that

The Keneally house,
Carbonear.

time. Most were "tilts," temporary shelters constructed of wooden poles set vertically, sometimes grounded in a trench, with a roof covered in boughs or boards. Variations on these tilts were still being constructed into the twentieth century, and the term came to be used to describe any temporary structure. Evolving from the tilt was the single-storey rectangular dwelling with a steeply pitched roof. A lean to or linhay (a one-storey rear addition) was frequently added later, creating a saltbox, a lean-to addition with a long ancestry. This was succeeded by the two-storey, peaked-roof house with a full, flat-roofed addition. In the outports, the main steep pitched roof was later replaced by the square roof, flatter to conserve building material and easy to repair, a style often called a "Newfoundland house." A building might go through various stages of growth, particularly if it remained in the family over several generations. Wood was the prime building material, so fire was a constant threat, destroying thousands of homes and levelling a town in short order. Fires account in part for the dearth of pre-nineteenth-century buildings remaining today.

Since restrictions against building on and owing land were not lifted until the early nineteenth century, it is not surprising that most permanent building construction dates from that time, and that brick and stone homes did not make their appearance until ownership was secure. Then, as the wealth of the merchants of outport and town grew, it found tangible expression in more flamboyant architectural styles — Gothic Revival, Second Empire and Queen Anne. John de Visser's superb photographs illustrate the rich variety of building styles to be seen and enjoyed today. These display a hard-to-define Newfoundland aspect — a basic, enduring appeal that tells much about their owners. They cast a spell.

There remain throughout the province many other fine nineteenth-century buildings whose history will not be found in these pages. We omitted them, not from lack of interest, but due to space and time restrictions or because they had been altered beyond recognition from the original. We hope that readers will be sufficiently intrigued to seek other fine buildings, for it is always a rewarding task. These buildings are our visible history. We neglect them at our peril.

Another factor contributed to our choice. It has been said that the people of Canada have been left out of Canadian histories. Our selection of buildings, mainly houses, with some public buildings, is made with the stories of their owners in mind — they tell the story of the people of Newfoundland and Labrador. Our interest is in history as seen through their lives — their triumphs, tragedies, heroism and humour. Only a hundred or so buildings have been included. Our cast of characters comes from those whose homes still stand to tell their story. We hope that as you read of the families who lived in them, you will gain insight into the Newfoundland and Labrador that once were, and those remarkable men and women who provided the foundation for what the province is today. Theirs is a story of stoicism and fierce pride. Theirs is a society of survivors.

There are two drawbacks to our method. As we have tied our story to existing buildings and their owners, clearly some important figures have been left out. And since we are dealing with centuries of built history, those houses that have survived are likely to be the well-built homes of the merchant and his family. The fisherman's cottage may have succumbed to a gale long ago. Wherever possible, we have also included simple buildings, even if they are not in prime condition today.

Newfoundland is Canada's youngest province. It joined Confederation on March 31, 1949, after much dissension, contentious argument and rejection had been going on for nearly a century. The last of the British governors, Sir Gordon Macdonald, was a gloomy former union organizer sent by England's Labour government to handle the negotiations. After he left, the defeated anti-confederates enjoyed a measure of satisfaction when the pro-Canadian *St. John's Evening Telegram* was caught by an old journalistic trick — it published a laudatory poem, "Farewell," which praised the recently departed governor. But the first letter in each of its ten lines spelled out the real message: THE BASTARD.

Some time later, when hordes of federal officials descended from Ottawa to facilitate the change of government, a brief exchange took place in an elevator of the Hotel Newfoundland. It summed up the confederation situation for many Newfoundlanders. As a group of weary bureaucrats "from away" stumbled onto the elevator past the operator, one man proclaimed: "They should give this place back to the Indians." The operator was heard to mutter: "We just did."

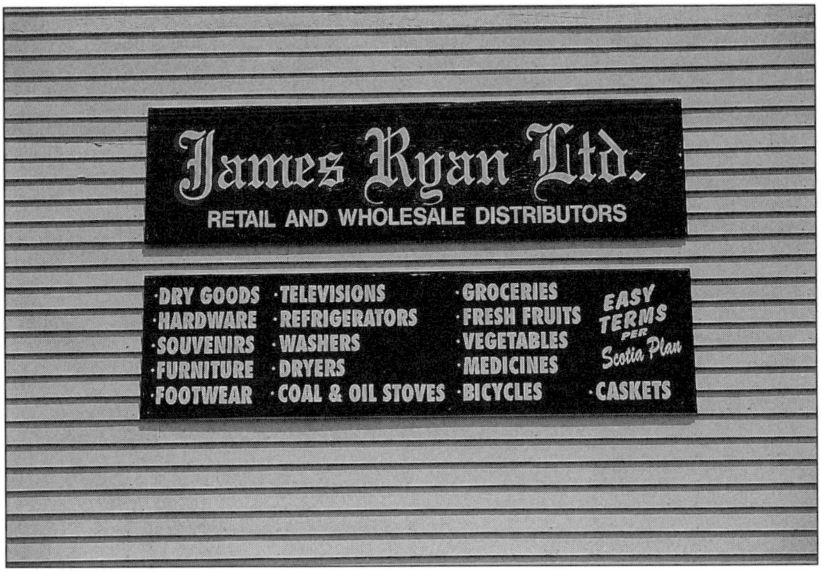
James Ryan Ltd.
RETAIL AND WHOLESALE DISTRIBUTORS
·DRY GOODS
·HARDWARE
·SOUVENIRS
·FURNITURE
·FOOTWEAR
·TELEVISIONS
·REFRIGERATORS
·WASHERS
·DRYERS
·COAL & OIL STOVES
·GROCERIES
·FRESH FRUITS
·VEGETABLES
·MEDICINES
·BICYCLES
EASY TERMS PER Scotia Plan
·CASKETS

The Merchant Fiefdoms of the North

CHAPTER 1

Bonavista

Legend has it that when John Cabot made his historic sighting of the coast of Newfoundland on June 24, 1497, his first words were "O buona vista!" (O happy sight!) The story is apocryphal, but the name stuck, and by 1534, when Jacques Cartier sailed by, he reported that "we reached Newfoundland, sighting land at Cap de Bonnee Vista," suggesting that the name and the coastline were familiar to him.

Cabot, of course, had not made the discovery that preoccupied explorers in the fifteenth and sixteenth centuries. Newfoundland was definitely *not* the northwest passage — a route to the riches of the east — instead the riches lay in the route itself, Newfoundland's prolific waters. But the site was indeed "buona," a flat harbour surrounded by cliffs, beaches and hills. Bonavista was settled in the sixteenth century, and its character became and remained British, a fact that led to many unwelcome visits from the French, Britain's perennial enemy and competitor for the lucrative territories of North America. In fact, Bonavista was the eastern point in the huge territory conceded to the French in 1713 by the Treaty of Utrecht, when the entire northeast coast and part of the west coast became known as the French Shore — a hefty chunk of compensation, considering that the French had just lost the war.

There were other obstacles. The rocks, shoals, and sandbars in the surging seas that surround Newfoundland were ever-present hazards to its seafaring people. Ships making their way along the coast on fishing, sealing or whaling expeditions were often lost in the fog or blown off-course by storms. After three centuries and the loss of thousands of lives, lighthouses finally arrived in Newfoundland, the first at Fort Amherst, near St. John's harbour, in 1813. It was followed by the Cape Spear light in 1836, and one at Harbour Grace Island in 1837.

By the 1840s, Cape Bonavista had become a focal point for the fishery on the northeast coast of Newfoundland and for ships en route to the Labrador fishery. A lighthouse was desperately needed. Tenders were let, and in August

FACING PAGE:
The Bonavista light, high atop a rocky promontory, flashed its first warning to mariners in 1843.

PREVIOUS PAGE:
The Bridge house, Bonavista

1843, newspapers carried the notice that the new Cape Bonavista light would be operating as of September 11, and that its light would "burn at an elevation of 150 feet above the level of the Sea, and will revolve at regular intervals of 2 minutes exhibiting alternately A RED AND WHITE LIGHT."

The lighting apparatus and revolving clockwork mechanism for the Bonavista light came from the famous Inchcape Rock lighthouse off Arbroath, Scotland, where, since 1811, its silvered copper reflectors had illuminated Robert Stevenson's famed engineering masterpiece, the Bell Rock lighthouse. (Stevenson, inventor of the flashing light used in lighthouses around the world, had built twenty-three lighthouses along the coast of Great Britain. Bell Rock, immortalized by Robert Southey in his poem "Inchcape Bell," was the most noted. Stevenson's other claim to fame was his grandson, author Robert Louis Stevenson.)

The new lighthouse needed constant attention to ensure that its light burned and turned continuously, night and day. That became the job of an Irishman, Jeremiah White, and his entire family. The Whites' story paralleled that of many of their countrymen. Conditions in Ireland were harsh in the extreme, and the alternative of life in Newfoundland, although also harsh, promised a living and a home of one's own where, as one immigrant succinctly put it, "dere is nobody to bawl at you."

In the 1820s, White, in search of a better life, embarked for Newfoundland. He and his wife, Mary, settled first in St. John's. But it wasn't until 1842, when word came that tenders were out for a new light at Cape Bonavista, that White applied for and got the job of keeper. After three weeks training at Cape Spear under keeper Emanuel Warr, the Whites — Jeremiah and Mary, their daughter, Johanna, and sons Matthew, Nicholas and Thomas — set off by sea for Bonavista. There the family worked day and night while the lighthouse was being built, and they continued that demanding routine until Jeremiah's death thirty-four years later. Their routine included lighting, tending, watching, and cranking the light all night long. In the daytime they trimmed, filled and polished it — the latter a chore that took three hours each and every day. The Whites' sons carried on for another nineteen years, until 1895.

The light that dominated their existence dominated their home. It was mounted in a stone tower, thirteen feet in diameter, that rose inside the frame two-storey lighthouse. Inside the tower, stairs led up to the lantern. On the ground floor, four rooms (parlour, kitchen, storeroom and bedroom) and a hall were built around the tower, their inner walls following the tower's curve. Probably because tending the light was a twenty-four-hour job for the family, Jeremiah and Mary used the bedroom located on the main floor, next to the workshop, in case of emergency. Bedrooms for the children and an assistant keeper were on the second floor. Two fireplaces added a cheery note to an otherwise spartan and cramped existence — and cramped it was, with two families now living there, Jeremiah's and that of the assistant keeper (a son). Each

SPRING OF THE BIG HAUL:
In Bonavista Bay, in 1843, there were 40,000 seals killed and landed by shoremen; men made wages as high as £120 and women as high as £40; seal bearing ice came in on March 18 and remained jammed on land until March 26.

year the lighthouse inspector reported that the Whites' quarters were inadequate, but it took nine years of such reports before a house was built for them.

The reflector lamps that once shone from Inchcape Rock revolved at Cape Bonavista for fifty-two years. Then a "new" light was installed. Built on the Isle of May, Scotland, in 1816, shipped off in 1837 to the Harbour Grace lighthouse, and then combined with parts from a light at Cape Pine, Newfoundland, it took up its new position at Bonavista in 1895. This recycled light lasted for another sixty-seven years, until the electric light made it obsolete. Today the Bonavista light is a provincial historic site, open to the public during the summer months. It has been restored to 1870, the period when Jeremiah White, then eighty, was still tending his light.

One of the oldest houses in Newfoundland stands near Bonavista harbour. Bridge House was built in 1814 by a Scot, for a Scot. The builder was one Alexander Strathie, a joiner from Greenock, Scotland. His wife, the wonderfully named Tryphena (Fanny) Pottle, bore him nine children. Their great-great-grandson lives in Bonavista today.

The man for whom Strathie built Bridge House was Bonavista merchant William Alexander of Argyleshire. He and his wife, Elizabeth Newell, were parents of three sons and a daughter. Son Robert, born in the Church Street house in 1822, was only six years old when his father died, so he was raised by his mother and then apprenticed to the mercantile firm of J. and W. Stewart, also based in Greenock. By 1861, when Alexander was appointed managing partner in St. John's, the firm was one of the largest in the city. Under his management it continued to grow, exporting huge shiploads of cod to Portugal, Spain and Brazil and thousands of sealskins to Greenock each year. According to his biographer, Melvin Baker, Robert Alexander established an incredible record for the yearly seal catch in 1875, when the firm's vessel *Proteus* brought in over 44,000 seals from two voyages.

Robert Alexander's power extended to local banks and other St. John's companies, and so he was one of that group of St. John's élite locally known as the "Water Street merchants." Politically he was a Conservative. His sole foray into politics was conducted with a dash of Newfoundland patronage. The party was indebted to him for using his considerable influence to smother the flames of the first movement for confederation with Canada, a big issue in the election of 1869. In turn, the influence of the party and like-minded businessmen helped get him elected to the House of Assembly, where he served for only one term, probably due to his failing health. He died in Liverpool in January 1884.

Alexander never married. Melvin Baker notes that, in his will, Alexander left bequests to widows and orphans, to a sailors' home, and to various churches — gestures that the St. John's *Evening Mercury* lauded, adding, with a distinct edge, that this was the "first left by any of the merchants who have made money here."

CATALINA:
Cuttlefish driven ashore during a gale in September 1877 was brought to St. John's and put on exhibition; had tentacles 30 feet long and 5 to 8 feet in girth; body was 9 feet long and its girth was six feet two inches; the circumference of the head was 4 feet; the tail had a span of two feet nine inches.

The *Evening Mercury* was acknowledging a given — that the word "merchant" had pejorative associations that clung to it like seaweed. It was often a derogatory term for the wealthy and powerful, who, it seemed, made money on the backs of working men — merchants such as Ryan, Slade, Lester, and Garland. But the word also carried a grudging recognition that these men provided the jobs that brought organized settlement to Newfoundland and staked fishermen when no one else would. As for the power of the merchants, that was and is visible in what remains of their fishing "premises" and their homes.

These premises, or "rooms," were a visible acknowledgment of an outport merchant's power and influence. But a fishing premises was more than this. It was a community within a community, a complex that made the merchant virtually self-sufficient. James Ryan's Bonavista premises was typical of such a complex and, now restored, illustrates how the highly complicated relationship between fisherman and merchant operated.

James Ryan.

James Ryan epitomized the breed. He was the son of Michael Ryan of Callan parish, Kilkenny County, Ireland, a place noted as the birthplace of Edmund Rice, founder of the Irish Christian Brothers. Ryan was twenty when, in 1833, he immigrated along with thousands of his countrymen to what was called by some "transatlantic Ireland," and by others, the "land of fish." He settled in Bonavista and, local legend has it, operated a tavern, a not unlikely occupation for an Irishman, as his countrymen dominated the publicans' trade. This occupation made him, as James Candow observes in his report on the Ryan premises for Parks Canada, a "central figure . . . often the most important person after the priest." Ryan also operated as a shopkeeper. One trade complemented the other, for a commodity much in demand in both tavern and shop was rum.

Nine years after his arrival in Bonavista, Michael Ryan married Elinor Fleming. Ten children were born to them, seven sons and three daughters, and all but one survived to adulthood. In the story of the Ryan empire, James, the first-born son, was the empire-builder, to be succeeded at his death in that role by Daniel, the second son.

By the time he was fifteen, James was working with his father in the shop and in the tavern. Although rum was popular both places (sold by the glass, half gallon, half pint, and "nag" or "noggin" — a small wooden cask), the store also sold flour, molasses, sugar, tea, coffee, butter, pork, apples, spices, tobacco, soap, thread, buttons, cutlery, shoes, cod jiggers (unbaited, weighted hooks), leather, gunpowder, and squid lines (a strong, light line, about four to fourteen fathoms long, to which a jigger is attached in fishing for bait squid). Payment, notes Candow, "was usually in kind: mainly codfish and cod liver oil, but from time to time hay and seals." Gradually James Ryan steered the course of the business into the local inshore fishery, around Bonavista and Greenspond, then expanded, and with his own vessels, sent men to the Labrador and French Shore fisheries.

Ryan premises, Bonavista.

As the firm grew, its success was visible in the harbour at Bonavista. A mercantile complex took shape, beginning about 1869, as one building after another appeared — three stores; a retail shop cum office; a fish store; a fish storage and packing shop; a salt store to hold the huge quantities needed to cure fish (one end served as a factory where cod livers were rendered into oil); two wharves; two flakes where salted fish were laid on boughs to dry; and barns. There was a retail lumberyard, and shipbuilding facilities; a cooperage where barrels and fish-oil casks were made; a powder magazine; and a tenement house where employees lived. Built nearby in 1877 was a telegraph office, to facilitate Ryan's international dealings. For a while there was a sawmill, and for a short time in the 1890s, a lobster cannery.

As well as this impressive Bonavista complex, Ryan owned over a dozen barter shops, or "adventures," throughout Trinity and Bonavista Bays, where agents for the firm traded supplies for fish during the season. This diversification made sense — if any one area had a poor catch, another area might compensate.

In the midst of the Ryan premises was the merchant's house. Local oral tradition suggests that James Ryan, then nineteen, built the two-and-a-half-storey frame building in 1861. The house was a splendid affair, with nearly 4,000 square feet of floor space. Gable-roofed with a single-storey linhay (a shed-roofed extension), it had central chimneys that allowed for a fireplace in each room. Each of the two upper floors contained four bedrooms. The linhay held a servant's room, pantry, pump room and back porch. Of all the buildings that made up the premises, only the house gave a slight nod to aesthetic embellishments. Treillage on the front porch, and some delicate interior detailing indicated that this was the home of a well-established merchant.

The Ryan house, Bonavista.

James Ryan was fifty-five years old when he married in 1897. Perhaps until then his hard work had precluded other pursuits. His bride was Katharine McCarthy, a Boston woman, born in Carbonear, who was herself thirty-five when they were wed. Both her parents were from families prominent in the Conception Bay area. James and Katharine had two sons, James Edmund and Herbert Felix McCarthy.

Two years after their marriage, James persuaded Katharine's brother, John McCarthy, to join him in the firm, and two years after that, her sister, Margaret, married James's brother, Daniel. So Ryan's was very much a family affair.

Thanks to James Ryan's skillful management, the company survived both the vicissitudes of the fishery and the innate difficulties of running a family firm. In 1894, in the midst of a depression, with many merchants' credit overextended, the banks in St. John's collapsed and with them many merchants. Ryan, always loathe to accept extensive credit, was not among them. But further problems arose. The usual method of operation in the fishery was for a prominent St. John's merchant (in Ryan's case, Bowrings) to advance supplies to his outport partner, who would, in turn, advance these supplies to local fishermen on credit. At season's end the chain reversed itself. The St. John's merchant set a fixed price for the catch, the local merchant weighed and credited it to the fisherman's company account, and the fish were sold abroad, by the St. John's merchant. Suddenly Bowrings cancelled their deal with Ryan. But the astute businessman quickly filled the gap. He went to London and hired a fish broker to take their place.

In 1909 the Ryans, James and Katharine, Daniel and Margaret, moved to St. John's, where they built adjoining mansions on Rennie's Mill Road.

Mrs. James Ryan and housekeeper, at the Ryan house.

James was appointed to the Legislative Council and, notes James Candow, "If it were not for the fact that he was a Roman Catholic, he would undoubtedly have been knighted." He died in 1917 at the peak of his business career and was eulogized as one of Newfoundland's "first and dominant figures." Certainly his generosity and ecumenical spirit were exemplary. He left generous bequests to the Catholic Mount Cashel orphanage, and to the Methodist and Anglican orphanages as well. He also left trust funds to Catholic, Methodist and Church of England ministers in Bonavista, to be given to the "most needy and deserving poor of their congregations." His sisters and brothers were given generous bequests.

The firm continued to be run by family members, including James's brother, Daniel. After Daniel's death, Katharine came into her own. She presided over the business with great acumen. When affairs improved, she gave the employees a bonus (the first they had had in twenty-three years) and then a raise. She virtually ran the business until she was eighty-one, two years before her death. Ryan's was in business until 1978, when it closed its doors after the death of Herbert Ryan in London. The Ryan premises, now restored, were acquired in 1987 by the Historic Sites and Monuments Board in recognition of the East Coast fisheries. They opened to the public in the summer of 1997.

James Ryan, standing by fish flakes.

CHAPTER 2

Fogo Island

Tall tales and romantic legends surround Fogo, the largest of
Newfoundland's offshore islands. Its name, of Portuguese origin — *y do
fogo*, "of the fire" — is possibly a reference to early forest fires, or an allusion
to the smokelike fogs that frequently blanket the island. As elsewhere in Newfoundland, the place names are evocative — the isolation implied in names
such as Seldom Come By and Little Seldom; the hazards associated with Lion's
Den Cove, Wild Cove, and Shoal Bay; or Tilting, which recalls "tilts,"
Newfoundland's first temporary, primitive dwellings. And what of Brimstone
Head, in the hamlet of Fogo? It is said that the Flat Earth Society has solemn-
ly declared it to be one of the Four Corners of the Earth!

FOGO had 258
inhabitants in 1738,
143 wintering there.

Then there is Joe Batt's Arm. Joe Batt was a young Bonavista man who
had been accused and convicted of the theft of a pair of lady's slippers, alleged
to have been stolen from the planter for whom he worked. He was taken to the
whipping post and lashed. Later, still proclaiming his innocence, he and his
supporters took revenge on the planter, burning his fish flakes and otherwise
tormenting him. Yet he knew that spring would bring British vessels and with
them, retribution. He disappeared, seeking safety in a remote and desolate
place. Where better than Fogo Island? Joe Batt gave his name to his small community, and it is still called Joe Batt's Arm, in spite of occasional misguided
efforts to change it to the more mundane Queensville.

Bleak the island may be, but for centuries it was prized by fishing fleets.
It was first used as a summer station by the Beothuk. The Europeans arrived
early in the sixteenth century (Jacques Cartier anchored there in 1534), and
French, Portuguese and Spanish fleets hovered around Fogo for another two
hundred years until permanent settlement began about 1828 at Fogo Harbour.
First to arrive were people from farther south on the coast, where a poor shore
fishery forced a northern migration. Other arrivals were Englishmen from Poole
in Dorset, whose merchants had pretty well cornered the market as far as the

FACING PAGE:
*Brimstone Head, Fogo.
The Flat Earth Society
named it one of the
Earth's four corners.*

northeastern Newfoundland fishery was concerned. The island developed a distinctly Irish flavour as well, thanks to young people from Waterford who were picked up by English fishing ships and brought to Newfoundland as servants.

In spite of frequent attacks by American privateers during the Revolutionary War, the population of Fogo continued to grow, reaching 3,500 by the middle of the nineteenth century, due to the initiative of merchants such as John Slade, who was part of the transition from a migratory to a permanent fishery in Newfoundland.

John Slade was a shrewd and innovative adventurer who made his first recorded visit to Newfoundland in 1748 as master of the trader *Molly*. It was the first of many trips he was to make across the Atlantic. Five years later, in part because of an advantageous marriage, he was able to launch into the Newfoundland trade on his own. He was particularly interested in the region north of Bonavista Bay, an area prolific in codfish and, at the bottom of Notre Dame Bay, rich in timber, furs and salmon runs. He became highly successful, and rich enough that competitors such as Benjamin Lester in Trinity kept a close eye on his business activities; "they hated one another, but they formed a closely knit community for common interest and survival," according to Slade's biographer, W. Gordon Handcock.

Handcock noted that "The ledgers of John Slade and Company from 1783 onwards show that under the credit or truck system the firm was annually staking the ventures of some 90–100 planters in northeastern Newfoundland and employed 150–200 servants directly."

Slade was grooming his only son, John Haiter, to succeed him, but after that young man's death from smallpox in 1772, Slade turned to his nephews — his brother's sons John, David, Robert and Thomas. He also considered adopting a son he had fathered, it was said, by a Twillingate planter's wife. But it was his nephew John (then known as John Slade Jr.) who took over the Newfoundland enterprise and, when the senior Slade died in 1792, became head of the firm. His brothers also became closely involved. By the middle years of the eighteenth century, however, the influence of these West Country merchants was on the wane. John Slade and Company sold out, and another era in the commercial life of Fogo began.

Slade and his competitors had established a pattern — supplying fishermen with necessities, in return for a mortgage on their future catch. At the end of the lucrative summer fishery, the men in each fishing community brought their catch, cured with salt and sun-dried, to the merchant's premises, and from there it was shipped to Europe. Then the fishermen received their pay — but mainly in kind. Barrels of flour and supplies for the winter and for the next sealing season were produced by the merchant and a reconciliation was made. Known as the "truck" system, it was long employed in Newfoundland, and for the most part, the local merchant family in each community felt a responsibility to the men and their families in good seasons or bad. (Although such was

The aptly named Bleak House, Fogo.

not always the case, and not everyone felt grateful — a situation suggested by the adage "A fisherman is one rogue; a merchant is many.") This system lasted until the powerful merchant families in St. John's decided that they wanted a piece of, or to be exact, all of the action, whereupon they promoted legislation to restrict imports and exports. Now each St. John's merchant set up a link with a local merchant family. They took control, stocking the local fishermen and setting the price for fish as a self-appointed marketing board. The West Country aristocracy had been succeeded by the powerful Water Street merchant princes.

John Slade's firm left its mark on Fogo Island's landscape of rocks and ponds. The company house in the village of Fogo still stands, its name, fittingly, Bleak House. Substantial, sturdy and spacious, it bestrides a site that at one time overlooked the vast mercantile complex lying by the shore.

An undated list (written after 1832 but before the business was sold in the 1860s) describes the premises "belonging to and in the occupation of Messrs. R. D. and J. Slade" — the buildings, their construction dates and their value — thus giving us some idea of the extent of the Slade establishment on Fogo alone. It lists the dwelling house, its construction date (1826–27), and a notation stating that it was "substantially built by John King, new shingled in 1832 . . . and in excellent repair." The house had two parlours divided by a centre hall on the first floor, five bedrooms on the second floor, offices on the third floor, and a "Kitchen attached" — probably under a saltbox roof at the rear.

The oldest building on the premises was a nail and grapnel shop, built in 1759, and covered in clapboard in 1801. Also listed were a cooper's shop, and fish, pork, salt and pitch stores, all described as gabled and boarded or

Bleak House.

shingled. There was a fish stage, an oil stage, several large wharves, and a mooring anchor, a cook room, and outbuildings for cows, pigs, and poultry (all of which augmented a too frequent diet of salmon). Eventually, as the Slades' business expanded, a retail store, bookkeeper's house, and office were added.

The business and Bleak House stayed in the family until the 1860s, when the Slades' bookkeeper, John Owen, bought it. Some additions were probably made to the house in his time.

In 1897 both house and business were purchased by another merchant, Henry J. Earle. His grandson, Brian Earle, grew up in Bleak House in the 1930s, during the Great Depression. Although less forbidding, life on the island was then still a challenge for everyone who lived there. Fishermen and merchants alike struggled to survive. He recalled:

> That was in the period of the salt fish days and the whole community was geared to the salt fish industry. The living was completely independent of government. We didn't have welfare. Companies carried the community through the season. Merchants are not supposed to have a very good reputation, but dad would be very worried at the beginning of the season that he would have enough coal in to carry the thing for the winter. We didn't have much meat, mostly seal if we could get it. You had to get the winter supplies in before navigation closed and you didn't get anything more in until the spring. He and the firm on the other side of the harbour had to provide for the whole community. It's an unfortunate thing socially to have it that way. It gives people control of the community that we don't like in this age, but when there was no one else, that was all they could do. Some firms went broke.

My grandfather, Henry Earle, went to Twillingate originally as a teacher. He became a bookkeeper with Owen, and Mr. Owen sent him to Fogo to manage the business there, which was a branch of the Owen business. He became a partner and then he bought the whole thing. That type of operation was the mainspring of the outports. Mother was born in Fogo — a minister's daughter. She went to England when she was four years of age when her father died. She lived there until she was married in Fogo. She was thirty years of age but her background was more England than Newfoundland. . . . As boys we used to work on cargoes of coal and salt coming in — we got ten cents an hour, fourteen cents if we were shovelling. I bought a wooden spoon for my mother to make jam. She was thrilled. . . .

The seasons played a great part in our lives. At the end of December the place would freeze over outside and we would be completely cut off from the outside world. . . . Dad said he was delighted when the thing closed up and he could have a couple of months' peace. People visited more and relaxed. . . . Then, the first of May, the ship men would come on the premises to do repairs — there would be fires on the beach and the whole place came to life, suddenly awakening again. People worked very hard in the summer, getting up at three o'clock in the morning . . . [with] torches on the stages, working late at night. There was never any lost time when "it wasn't fit to be out." When it was raining and blowing they would put on their oilskins and go in the gardens or go off picking partridge berries.

It was a hard life and people put everything they had into it. But there was satisfaction at the end of the season. . . . We were feeding people in other countries with salt fish . . . we were told stories by the sailors who had gone to South America and Europe about how much the fish was valued. The cook was the one the boys would get to know . . . we would get as many stories as we could from him. Everyone owned his own house and piece of land. If they had any success with the fishery at all they would be independent and free. Life in England, where many had come from, was anything but cheerful. Now we look at the Depression years as so hard and devoid of humour, but that is not so. They had good laughs, despite the hardship.

Brian Earle remembered hearing his grandfather tell that when he first came to Fogo Island, Bleak House was used as the manager's house. Apprentices went there for meals, though they didn't always eat in comfort — often in winter the water on the table was frozen on the side away from the fire. But of one thing they could be sure (in fact, it was specified in apprentices' contracts): salmon, so plentiful in Notre Dame Bay, was not to be served more than once a day!

CHAPTER 3

Twillingate

It has been called Newfoundland's Capital of the North. It might also have been called Dorset West, for Twillingate, the most prominent town on the north shore, had a migratory population, not only of fishermen, but of Poole merchants who called the island their second home. Located around a large harbour formed by North and South Twillingate Islands, the settlement was in a key location, positioned to take advantage of the northeast coast and Labrador fisheries and, as well, winter resources of timber, furs, salmon, and a land-based sealing operation.

One building in Twillingate has the history of the town virtually written within its walls. That building, the lovely St. Peter's Church, is a Twillingate landmark. The first St. Peter's was built thanks to the efforts of the first Anglican missionary to be sent to this outpost — an earnest and enthusiastic priest, John Leigh, who arrived in 1816, when he was twenty-seven. His stay was brief, however, for the harsh climate and a bout of scurvy eroded his health. In the summer of 1819, while St. Peter's was being built, Leigh was sent to the less remote Harbour Grace, where later that year, while serving as a magistrate, he sentenced two men to floggings, a punishment so harsh that the resulting uproar led to strident demands for abolition of the surrogate courts. Before he left Twillingate, however, his work evinced a much gentler side of his character. He became involved with the native Beothuk and subsequently urged the Society for the Propogation of the Gospel to help rescue "these poor creatures from their miserable state." He recorded some of their vocabulary and was among the compassionate voices who urged an end to the violent confrontations between the Beothuks and Newfoundland's early settlers.

By this time the resident Anglicans, while acknowledging the existence of another "small dissenting congregation," were hoping that these dissenters would soon see the light and "return to the principles and doctrines of the Episcopal Establishment." Apparently they did. By 1826 that first church, ambitiously built to hold 550, was too small to seat the crowds. And so, just

BANISHMENT:
Thomas Martin, a young Twillingate man, was sentenced on November 11, 1850 to fourteen years banishment for stealing from the shop of Slade, Cox and Co.

FACING PAGE:
St. Peter's Church, built at a cost of £1,000.

Interior, St. Peter's
Church.

eleven years after the first church opened its doors, a new church was built with seating for 880. (Later still it was increased to 1,000. The population of the town had grown to 2,000, a number that the Anglicans split with the Methodists.)

The second St. Peter's was consecrated by the eminent bishop of Newfoundland, Edward Feild, whose arrival in Twillingate on the church ship the *Hawk* was greeted with great enthusiasm by the local Anglicans. Although Feild was known to dislike undue ceremony, he seemed pleased to be greeted so warmly by the townspeople. "Arrived at Twillingate July 1845," he wrote, "welcomed by a splendid display of flags on every side of the Harbour, and discharges of cannon from the establishments of Messrs. Slade and Co., Messrs. Cox and Slade. The Church flag in this settlement is a beautiful St. George's ensign presented by three captains of vessels." Feild was happy to see among the worshippers the "grey heads of many respectable old planters." He described the new building as a "very substantial, capacious, and handsome church, eighty feet by forty-five, with a lofty and characteristic tower at the western end."

About a month after the bishop departed, handsome brass chandeliers arrived, a gift to St. Peter's from John Slade Jr., nephew and namesake of the man responsible for much of the permanent settlement in northeast Newfoundland. The Slade companies, more than fifty years after the death of their founder, were still flourishing. The chandeliers (originally from St. Peter's Church in Poole, Dorset) were among several gifts to the new church — communion plate was donated by the Slades, as were, a year later, two plaques, one bearing the Ten Commandments, the other the Apostles' Creed.

Certainly the Slade family could well afford these generous gestures.

Since the beginning of the Revolutionary War, John Slade had been firmly established in Twillingate with his merchant premises on nearby Fogo Island. By 1845, when the new St. Peter's appeared on the scene, the town was populated with "livyers" (permanent settlers) who, in return for provisioning from the company store, would send cod, harp sealskins, oils, timber and furs back to Poole.

It wasn't the Slades but an act of God that provided the next memorable event in the history of St. Peter's and Twillingate, an event that was brought to mind each time the old church bell rang. The bell itself commemorated the remarkable Great Haul of 1862. In the spring of that year thousands of seals were carried to Twillingate's very doors when the ice on which they lay was driven into the harbour by high winds. Thirty thousand seals were killed in that harvest. The ecstatic citizens agreed that the Great Haul merited official recognition, and so a church bell was ordered. Cast in England, the bell was brought to Twillingate and placed in St. Peter's, the most visible spot in town, where it tolled for the first time in 1863.

In 1884 the chancel of St. Peter's was extended as a memorial to the estimable Edwin Duder, a merchant who brought prosperity to Twillingate, although he never actually lived there. Duder, a Devon native, was a lad of eleven when he and his family arrived in St. John's in 1833. By mid-century he was well on his way to establishing a trading empire. His biographer, historian George Story, suggests that Duder's career exemplified a turning point in Newfoundland's history — when power shifted from the prominent outport merchant families such as the Slades to "St. John's based entrepreneurs, well placed to seize emerging opportunities." Duder owned premises all along the northeast coast to Twillingate where he "supplied the fishermen in exchange for their catch, and owned and managed about 4500 tons of shipping for the period 1840 to 1889." At the height of Duder's power, in the 1870s, he bought out the Slade and Cox premises in Twillingate, thus becoming the owner of one of the largest shipping fleets in the world. By 1888, seven years after Edwin Duder's death, the Twillingate Mutual Insurance Company was offering coverage to 134 ships still owned by the family firm.

The memorial plaque and the chancel in St. Peter's Church were donated by the great man's son, Edwin John Duder. The work was done by Titus Manuel and his son, Alfred — the former worked an astonishing "one thousand, one hundred hours, at fourteen cents an hour." Sixteen-year-old Alfred "spent nine hundred and twenty after school and holiday hours assisting . . . and was paid ten cents an hour." The inscription lauds Duder's firm religious principles and his generosity, while mentioning that he was "not slothful in business" — a singularly dramatic understatement.

But even as Duder's memorial was being built the firm was in decline. The estate had been divided between his two sons, Edwin John (from his first marriage, to Mary Elizabeth Edgar) and Arthur (from his second marriage, to Ann

GREEN BAY DISASTERS [1868]: [A] man named Budgell, with his wife and four children left the upper part of the bay for Tilt Cove; when found next day, the man was frozen to death at the oars of his boat, his wife was dead with her baby at her breast and the three other children were frozen to death locked in each other's arms.

The Ashbourne house —
Queen Anne in the
outports.

Blackler). Arthur died within a year of his father, and as Story explains, "the surviving partner was obliged to pay half of the value of the family firm in cash to his brother's widow." This left the business without adequate capital, and with the crash of the Commercial Bank in 1894, the Duder empire collapsed.

Still standing in Twillingate today is a turreted frame house that dominates the town as the Duder empire once did. Built on land once owned by Edwin Duder, it was sold to Dr. J. Stafford when the firm failed. Originally of two storeys, it gained a third storey, its turret, and considerable dignity in a later addition. It then became the property of the Ashbourne family, who had acquired the Duder business.

Strangely, however, it was not its wealthy merchants, but a woman who, at the turn of the century, brought a degree of international recognition to Twillingate. She was an opera singer, Georgina Stirling, born there in 1867, the daughter of a local physician. Georgina received her musical training in Italy and, in 1893, made her opera debut in Paris. It was an occasion that, according to Henry J. Morgan in *Canadian Men and Women of the Time*, elicited "high encomiums from the musical critics." By 1898 she had become a member of the Grand Italian Opera Concert Company. Like many artists of the day, Georgina felt that a European-sounding name would be more advantageous to her career, and so she chose to call herself (perhaps with a twinge of homesickness) Marie Toulinguet.

For a few short years, the young mezzo-soprano was hailed as "the nightingale of the north," but sadly her career was short-lived. She fell ill while still in her thirties, and gave her last performance in St. John's in 1904. Mlle. Twillingate died in 1934 and was buried in the small cemetery at St. Peter's.

*The last resting place of
Newfoundland songstress
Marie Toulinguet.*

Grand Falls

It was the beginning of the twentieth century, and Germany's stance and policies were becoming more aggressive. British interests, nervous about unstable supplies of newsprint should war become inevitable, looked to North America for a source of supply. Alfred C. Harmsworth (the future Lord Northcliffe) and his brother Harold (to become Lord Rothmere) took action. A representative was sent out in 1903 to assess prospects in Newfoundland. He found them in a location near the Grand Falls. (The name of the falls had at one time been Governor's Falls, after Governor LeMarchant, but the unpopular governor's name was soon dropped in favour of Grand Falls.) Two years later the Anglo-Newfoundland Development Company was incorporated; by 1906 a town was being built; and in October 1909, Lord and Lady Northcliffe arrived for the official opening on a site that, a few years earlier, had been part of Newfoundland's dense interior.

The *Daily News* of October 8, 1909, announced the arrival of the distinguished party in Nova Scotia en route to Grand Falls:

PAPER MILLS AT GRAND FALLS THIS WEEK
Lord Northcliffe and party arrived here by special train late Saturday night and went immediately on board the Bruce. Lord Northcliffe goes to Newfoundland to attend the opening ceremony at the greater paper mills at Grand Falls which have been erected at a cost of seven and a half million dollars, and which comprise two of the most powerful waterfalls in the world, with four thousand square miles of forest attached. These works will give employment, including the logging camps, Lord Northcliffe's railways, and the proposed steamship line, to no fewer than fifteen thousand people. In the management of this concern are many Canadians, the assistant manager being Mr. Woods, of Halifax. The steamship line which he intends to establish will run between Newfoundland and England and will carry not only the paper manufactured in the mills, but also general merchandise, and freight.

[At this point, Lord Northcliffe took the opportunity to express his opinion to the press about the difference between British and American business practices.] "When I was in San Francisco the other day a young reporter put the question to me, 'Are your British great men of business as great as ours?' and I replied, 'Yes, but ours talk less.' And so it is with British and American capital in Canada. The erection of a ten thousand

HURRICANE IN NFLD.: 22 schooners lost in Notre Dame Bay Dec. 12, 1882.

dollar corset plant is more widely boomed by the local Uncle Sams than the purchase of a whole series of municipal or street railway bonds by an English bank."

Grand Falls grew and other businesses opened, including that of Stanley Goodyear. David Macfarlane, a descendant, wrote in *The Danger Tree* of the remarkable Goodyear family. The aristocratic Northcliffes also warranted mention, for the couple's occasional visits to the town brought an aura of excitement and glamour to the hardworking residents. Lord Northcliffe and his lady would arrive like visiting royalty, spend a few days in their Grand Falls home, then set off again on their travels.

They arrived on the train from St. John's or from Port aux Basques, on their way to or from New York or Washington or Boston, where they spent time with the Vanderbilts and the Astors, Thomas Edison, and Mark Twain. In Grand Falls, the men who shook Lord Northcliffe's hand were shaking the hand of a man who had shaken the hand of President Roosevelt and the hand of the King. The Lord and Lady kept servants and a butler at their Grand Falls home — a stately three-storey log residence that had been built according to plans provided by Mark Twain when Northcliffe had expressed admiration for the famous writer's own house during a visit; on a more modest scale, and without the picturesque logs, the design was repeated in many of the finer houses in town — the Goodyears' among them.

CHAPTER 4

Trinity

Settling in Newfoundland was like rowing against the tide. The situation was summed up in a now historic remark made in the British House of Commons in the late 1700s: "The island of Newfoundland has been considered . . . as a great ship moored near the Banks during the fishing season, for the convenience of English fishermen."

The men and women who carved out a living on the island did so in spite of (and certainly not because of) the powerful interests represented by the vessels that were at home in the island's waters. Those entrepreneurs, most of whom came from England's West Country, sent their capital — their ships and men — in search of codfish. They sailed to Newfoundland's fishing grounds, one of the world's most abundant, and took what they wanted from seas that teemed with marine life. Then they left, taking their substantial profits with them. It was a system that worked well for them, and they wanted it kept that way. Permanent settlement would have meant that profits stayed in Newfoundland.

England "actively discouraged" settlement, a policy that meant continual harassment for prospective settlers. Constantly threatened with deportation, they were prevented from cutting wood and were forbidden to build a house within six miles of the sea. George Story, in his essay "Fishermen, Hunters, Planters, and Merchants," notes that "West Country fishermen . . . twice burned down the houses and premises owned by the settlers between Cape Race and Cape Bonavista." As for law and order, it lay in the hands of the first ship's captain (then known as the "fishing admiral") to enter a harbour each spring. In spite of all this, by the mid-1600s there were two or three thousand tenacious settlers living in tiny fishing villages scattered along the coast.

By 1737, when a young English lad named Benjamin Lester left his home in Poole to work in the Newfoundland fishery, several thousand additional permanent settlers had preceded him. Lester's father, Francis, the former mayor of Poole, had just died, so the boy, then thirteen, was heading across the Atlantic to work for his uncle, John Masters.

WARDEN, THOMAS: J.P. at Trinity was accused, in 1757, of assaulting a man and his wife; complainants were found to be disorderly persons and were fined £5, while Mr. Warden was ordered to build at his own expense "a cage for the punishment of disorderly persons."

FACING PAGE:
The restored Garland store.

Benjamin Lester.

Thanks to his family's connections, young Benjamin knew a fair amount about Newfoundland. Poole was a city of merchants and shipowners whose influence and wealth stretched across the Atlantic to control the Newfoundland fishery. These merchants were linked with Newfoundland through ties of business and marriage — and few families had connections more enmeshed than the Lesters and, on Benjamin's mother's side, the Taverners.

Benjamin's mother, Rachel, was the daughter of William Taverner, one of three brothers who, as surveyors, sea captains, privateers (those who carried a government commission authorizing them to plunder foreign vessels in wartime), and "planters," were among the first English settlers to make their home in Newfoundland. Of course, to the Taverner brothers, as with most Poole merchants, "home" was a variable — it might be in England at Poole, in Bay de Verde at the head of Conception Bay in Newfoundland, or at Trinity, in Trinity Bay. Family ties became more enmeshed when Benjamin Lester married his cousin Susannah, a daughter of uncle Jacob Taverner.

At the time of his marriage, Benjamin was about twenty-six. He had spent thirteen years working his way up in his uncle's business and had recently established himself in Trinity. That thriving town, one of the first settled sites in Newfoundland, boasted a harbour with three welcoming arms (hence its name) whose beauty and romantic location had been extolled by many. One of the first to sing its praises was Sir Richard Whitbourne, who visited there in 1579 and called the harbour "the best and largest in all the Land," a site "well stored with grasse sufficient . . . to maintain great store of ordinary cattell, besides Hogs and Goats, if such beasts were carried thither."

Due to the migratory fishery, however, Trinity's growth was slow. A century later there were only five permanent planters. They were outnumbered by seven migratory fishermen with vessels at anchor in the harbour, including that of the fishing admiral in the southwest arm. By 1760, however, just ten years after Benjamin and Susannah Lester's marriage, Trinity was in its heyday. Two or three thousand people lived there for the summer months, ships crowded the harbour, and fish flakes stretched along the shores. (In winter the population again became migratory, as the well-to-do returned to England, fishermen turned to hunting and trapping, and other workers moved away from the frozen shores to locations inland.)

It is believed that Benjamin Lester soon started construction of a sizable two-storey frame house for Susannah and their family, a family that eventually included five daughters and a son. The house was a testimony to his growing success, although its construction suggested that the Lesters had ignored or forgotten the realities of Newfoundland winters, for its M-shaped roof created a valley where snow collected, melted, and dripped through the shingles to torment the family during the long winter months. But the house managed to withstand those winters for nearly two hundred years, until it was demolished in 1950. The foundations remain.

The John Bingley Garland house and the Garland store.

The Lesters' house was the focal point of what became Benjamin's thriving mercantile establishment, encompassing a huge expanse of property that included four wharves where two hundred people worked as shipbuilders, blacksmiths, sail makers, storekeepers, and farmers. There were factories for making cod-liver oil, a storage area for seal pelts and salt, and cellars for gunpowder and wine storage.

Lester became "the prince of merchants," and "the most influential of all Newfoundland entrepreneurs." No one outranked him. His empire stretched from northeastern Newfoundland to Labrador. He was Newfoundland's largest employer and its most prosperous merchant. Lester owned more land and more ships, conducted more trade, and exerted more influence than anyone on the island. By 1786 his firm and its competitors, Jeffrey and Street, were exporting an astounding hundred thousand quintals (about ten million pounds) of fish each year. Lester didn't ask anyone who worked for him to do anything that he had not done himself. He had sailed ships and drifted on the ice. He had done it all.

This giant was a complex man. He was thrifty, hard-working and parsimonious. He drank heavily, yet despised captains who drank too much. He demanded openness, yet fixed elections for his son and sons-in-law. When Trinity was captured by the French in 1762 during the Seven Years' War, he worked with the victors to prevent the town's destruction, but he was accused and convicted of turning over others' livestock and hiding his own. He was always on top of the business, travelling to all the fishing stations, and not averse to intimidating fisherman who were thinking of selling to others.

In 1776, Lester and his wife left to enjoy the rest of their lives in Poole's milder climate. Lester became mayor, as had his father, and a member of Parliament. At his death in 1802, half of his vast empire was left to his only

TRINITY: Joseph White, merchant of Trinity, died at Poole, England, 1771; he was then worth £130,000 sterling, all of which he made by fishing and trading at Trinity.

BANISHMENT: On Oct. 9, 1822, James Wade was sentenced to seven years transportation for stealing two sheep from J. B. Garland, Trinity; at the same time, James Lanigan, for stealing £20, 13 s 6d, from Slade and Kelson and £20 from Slade and Sons was sentenced to fourteen years banishment.

BANISHMENT: Mrs. Garland, who stabbed her husband with an awl and killed him, sentenced to twelve months imprisonment and then to leave the country, Dec. 11, 1869.

WEDDING RING: In 1871 a Trinity Bay fisherman found in a codfish a massive gold ring bearing the inscription: "God Above Continue Our Love." The ring was claimed by the relatives of Pauline Burnam, drowned in the wreck of the steamer *Anglo Saxon* at Chance Cove, in 1861; a reward of £35 was paid the discoverer.

son, who became Sir John Lester, the other half to his son-in-law, George Garland, husband of his youngest daughter, Amy. Three years later, Sir John, who had taken little interest in the business, died without a male heir, and thus Garland inherited the biggest firm in the cod fishery in England and Newfoundland.

George Garland was fifty-two at the time. Under his leadership the Lester empire expanded and he amassed a fortune, but he himself never set foot in Newfoundland. Amy had borne eleven children (eight boys and three girls) in the twenty years between 1779 and 1799, so there were sons aplenty to manage the Newfoundland concerns. Their eldest son, Benjamin Lester Garland, had been designated by his grandfather to follow his father in the business. The old pioneer had required, however, that young Benjamin change his surname to Lester in order to inherit, and so, in 1805, Benjamin Lester Garland made the lucrative but awkward change, becoming Benjamin Lester Lester. Much to his father's dismay, however, his interests lay more with politics and London's social life, and so it was his brothers (Amy and George Garland's sixth and seventh sons), John Bingley and George Jr., who took over the reins of the family business.

Around 1819, John Bingley Garland replaced Benjamin and Susannah Lester's old frame house, which had proved to be ill-designed, with a solid brick building. (Partially demolished in the 1960s, with only two gable walls remaining, the house is in the process of reconstruction.) But Garland lived there only briefly. In 1822 he married. He and his wife, Deborah Vallis, lived in St. John's for twelve years or so, then returned to spend the rest of their lives in England.

Early Anglican church, Trinity.

In Trinity, next to the foundations of the old Lester house, is the store built by the Garland brothers in 1819. It was the firm's prime mercantile building, and it is all that remains to tell of the vast Lester-Garland empire. Built of timber on a brick foundation, the store loomed over its neighbours, handsome and imposing. Stores and offices occupied the first floor, with storage above under its huge gambrel roof. It stands today, restored and furnished as in the 1820 period, a symbol of the Trinity fishery in its prime. The Lester-Garland store is open to the public in the summer months.

While English merchants and their agents settled in Newfoundland to exploit the fisheries, the Irish were arriving too. As early as the 1720s a few had come as servants, and by mid-century more than half the summer population was Irish, employed mostly by merchants and planters. Some were women who boarded ships from Poole that had stopped en route to pick up some female company for the summer months. Historian W. Gordon Handcock relates that the middle years of the eighteenth century brought violence to Trinity, for the society as a whole was dominated by "youthful males who often worked for crude and brutal masters." In Newfoundland, "this situation was further aggravated by an unregulated passenger traffic which saw excessive numbers of Irishmen landed. Unable to secure employment many were forced to subsist in the woods and to resort to mob violence." By 1775, when a jail

Holy Trinity, built for the town's Irish Catholics in 1833.

45

Trinity.

was built in Trinity, violence had somewhat receded, but "outbreaks of mariner rowdyism and drunken brawls remained a characteristic feature well into the nineteenth century."

In spite of the seemingly insurmountable difficulties caused by poverty, alcoholism, class distinctions and countless other societal ills, the churches were gaining a foothold and doing their best to provide enlightenment and solace to the long-suffering populace. Holy Trinity, the oldest church still standing in Newfoundland, was built for the town's Irish Catholics in 1833, when Trinity was at the height of its commercial importance. A simple, unadorned frame structure with restrained Gothic detailing, it is typical of the many churches of all denominations that were built throughout the Atlantic region at the time. Its tower was added in the late 1880s when a bell was acquired.

Right across the road stands the exquisite St. Paul's Anglican Church, the third church building to occupy the site. Proximity between these two contending faiths, however, did not, at least initially, bring the usual religious dissent that so often turned ugly. In fact, it is said that everyone in Trinity celebrated St. Patrick's Day and that the rum flowed like water on those occasions.

Not surprisingly, St. Paul's, like nearly everything else in Trinity, was associated with the Taverner and Lester families. The first church on the site, said to have been large enough to accommodate three hundred people, was built in 1734, almost exclusively at the expense of Jacob Taverner. He himself was a Presbyterian, but the church was used as the town's parochial church. The first church deteriorated and had to be replaced in 1820 by a new build-

TRINITY BAY: S.S. *Lion* lost in Baccalieu Tickle, Jan. 6, 1882. Rev. Hugh Foster and bride and fifty other passengers lost their lives. Only one body — that of Mrs. John Cross — was picked up.

TRINITY BAY DISASTER 1892: Twenty-four men perished on the ice while off from the land chasing seals.

ing, erected largely at the expense of John Bingley Garland, Jacob Taverner's grandson. While the church was under construction, services were held in the Garland living room, and upon its completion, John Bingley Garland preached the first sermon — aware no doubt that his grandfather, Benjamin Lester, had been vehemently opposed to lengthy sermons.

In 1892 the third St. Paul's was erected, a strikingly beautiful building with fine stained glass and elegant interior trim, with curved trusses supporting the roof. It is thought to have been built from the same plans as two identical churches in Nova Scotia — Trinity Church, Digby, and Christ Church, Windsor — built in the 1880s. They were the work of an American architect, Stephen C. Earle, who had designed at least forty New England churches. The design of St. Paul's was, in turn, replicated in churches around Trinity Bay.

St. Paul's is also remembered for John Clinch, a young Englishman who served as a preacher at the first Anglican church — a church that was never consecrated. And Clinch, when he started preaching there, had not been ordained. Consecration required the visit of a bishop, and it was many years before Charles Inglis, bishop of Nova Scotia, found his way to Trinity to con-

The third St. Paul's Anglican Church, Trinity.

secrate the second St. Paul's in 1827. The ordination required a lengthy and arduous trip to England, one that Clinch eventually made in 1785, a year after his marriage, although being a layman did not prevent him from performing marriages, funerals, services of worship, and baptisms. (It may have been Clinch who, in the year of his ordination, first baptized, then married, "in St. Paul's Church, an Eskimo Indian belonging to Mr. Stone, age about 30 years . . . Mr. Haklieanna." Three years later it was reported that "there died at Trinity, 'John August', the last male civilized Red Indian or Beothic [sic]. He was buried in the old Church yard, October 29, 1788."

Clinch had emigrated to Cape Bonavista in 1775, then moved eight years later to Trinity, where he was concerned about the "decay of true religion and the success of Popery." There, in 1784, he married Hannah Hart of English Harbour, and they produced seven sons and a daughter. Along with the delayed ordination, Clinch also received appointments as judge, magistrate, surveyor, and collector of customs.

But it is for his medical contributions that Clinch is remembered — in a professorship in the history of medicine at Memorial University of Newfoundland and in medical circles throughout North America — because it was he who administered the first vaccinations against smallpox in the New World. He had studied medicine in England, where a fellow student was

St. Paul's Anglican. Its graceful detailing and striking colours make it a Trinity landmark.

Edward Jenner, the man who later discovered the cowpox method of immunization. Outbreaks of smallpox were common in Newfoundland. According to Clinch's biographer, Frederick Jones, Jenner had sent threads of vaccine to Clinch, and when there was word of another outbreak, Clinch is said to have first vaccinated his wife's nephew in 1798. Then, he reported, in an 1802 letter to Jenner, "I began by inoculating my own children and went on with this salutary work till I had inoculated 700 persons of all ages." Clinch expanded his work to St. John's, and since it was seen "that the vaccine was saving hundreds of lives," he then dedicated most of his time to this work. But in whatever time he could spare he pursued another divergent interest. This remarkable man transcribed the first collection of over one hundred words of Beothuk, the language of Newfoundland's native people.

Like every outport, Trinity dealt with its share of shipping disasters. One of the most unusual is recorded in *When Was That? A Chronological Dictionary of Important Events in Newfoundland Down to and Including the Year 1922.* "The sail ferryboat between Trinity and the Northside was capsized by a squall of wind and sank, 1865. Hiscock, the ferryman, was drowned. Two women passengers, Miss Mary Hogarth and Mrs. Richard Fowlow, floated on the water, owing to the air under their hoop skirts, and were saved. Mrs. Fowlow held a baby fast asleep in her arms — Thomas Jenkins Fowlow."

Two Sealing Centres

CHAPTER 5

Newtown and Wesleyville

They were close neighbours at the northern tip of Bonavista Bay, the sealing centre of Newfoundland. Each was a separate fiefdom with its ruling family — in Wesleyville the Winsors, in Newtown the Barbours. These families were third-generation Newfoundlanders — members of the outport aristocracy.

Throughout Newfoundland, the name Barbour was synonymous with sealing. Family records and diaries list seventy-four skippers from Newtown and Pinchard's Islands. Of these, forty-seven bore the name of Barbour. The five Barbour brothers (sons of pioneer Benjamin Barbour) alone brought in more than one million seals.

Sealing was a hazardous way to earn a living. Newfoundland's shores are treacherous and its thick, grey fogs among the worst in the world. Men cast adrift on shifting ice died by the hundreds, either drowning or freezing to death. Yet in spite of the dangers, Newfoundland's young men became "kind o' restless in the spring." For them the seal fishery was enticing. Going to the ice offered good money — the only cash seen all year — and there was adventure and a certain rough glamour attached to it. Even young women were caught up in the excitement, as "The Sealers' Song" suggested:

> For at a dance no girls can prance,
> Nor dress in style more grander
> For an Irish reel, that takes the heel,
> To please a Newfoundlander.
> So here's to Susie Bess,
> And girls from all outharbours,
> For a kiss set in on a sealer's chin,
> Which never saw the barber.

FACING PAGE:
The home of Benjamin and Rebecca Barbour.

PREVIOUS PAGE:
The Blackwood house, Wesleyville.

Logs from some of the Barbours' ships, however, cast a different, if less appealing, light on the seal fishery:

> The first of this day, high wind from the N.E. and passing showers of snow. At 6 a.m. sent out the men to haul seals to the ship. At 8:00 a.m. was visited by many men from the shore and large crowds from different steamers seeking refreshments, some crippled, maimed and blind. . . . At 6 p.m. crews belonging to other ships completely crowding our ship, others with fires all around the starboard side in the shelter of bulwarks, others obliged to walk the deck, no place below, weather very stormy, impossible for men to stand. About 500 men onboard, not including our own men.
>
> Joseph Barbour, Master
> Samuel Barbour, Navigator, S.S. *Ranger*
> Pool's Island, Bonavista Bay
> March 19, 1886

The *Ranger* had left the ice for St. John's with 33,794 seals in her hold — and a total of seven hundred and forty men on board.

Next year, her log recorded another near disaster close to Pool's Island:

> The first of this day, fresh breeze from the S. by E. and much swell, ice passing hove the ship close to the shore. Ship in great danger, could do nothing to help her. At 5 a.m. the captain ordered all sails to be set, ship laying so close the men could put out their hands and touch the ice that was raftered on the rocks. As the ship passed the men threw pieces of ice between her and

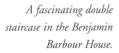

A fascinating double staircase in the Benjamin Barbour House.

the shore to act as fenders. She touched several times but did no real damage. At 5.30 a.m. got clear, going full speed all the time.

Log of the S.S. *Ranger*

Pool's Island, Bonavista Bay

23 March 1887

According to Carlson Barbour, a grandson of Benjamin, it was his uncle, Captain George Barbour (one of Benjamin Barbour's nine sons), who in 1898 on the S.S. *Greenland* had the most harrowing experience of any of the Barbour captains at the ice fields.

Forty-eight brave men lost their lives by frostbite and hunger in the raging blizzard that occured on Monday, March 21st, 1898, and lasted, I think, three days. . . . It was a beautiful morning. . . . Captain Barbour accordingly put out all his men, about 200 or more in four watches of 50 or more in each watch, with a master watch and a second master watch in each group, each watch taking different positions on the ice. However, by 6 p.m. a blinding snow-storm with high northerly winds came up, casting an awful gloom over the whole situation.

Captain Barbour immediately took onboard the men in the first watch, those nearest the ship, but, as the ice had become tighter the ship was unable to reach the remaining three watches, forty-eight of whom lost their lives. I have talked with some of the survivors who tell how terrible it was to watch the men dying; many of them became blind and would walk away from the pans where the men were huddled together trying to keep warm. They made fires by burning their gaff handles, flag poles and seals' fat. In their blindness some featured they could see the ship coming and would walk toward her, many of whom would fall through the ice and drown. Others fell asleep and never awakened.

After the storm the task of picking up the survivors began, as well as the gruesome task of picking up their frozen comrades; in some cases fathers finding their sons and brothers picking up brothers.

On March 27th the S.S. *Greenland* arrived at St. John's with the frozen corpses piled on her deck. Everything was done that could be done for the survivors and relations of the victims. It was said that the corpses had to be thawed out in water before they could be put in their caskets.

PLAGUE OF INSECTS: On August 30, 1855; swarms of insects destroyed all crops and even filled houses in settlements north of Cape Freels

The first Barbour to be born in Newfoundland was Benjamin Barbour, whose father, George, had left his native England to try his hand at the cod fishery. Benjamin, born in 1809, married Rebecca Green of Greenspond. The couple settled on lonely and desolate Pinchard's Island, Bonavista Bay, where their eldest son, Joseph, was born in 1842. Next year they moved to the equally remote Cobbler's Island, where ten more children were born to them, the

entire family supported by whatever Benjamin Barbour could harvest from the surrounding sea. Given their harsh surroundings, and living in an age of high infant mortality, it seems nothing less than miraculous that all eleven Barbour children survived and grew to adulthood.

Barbour ketch Seabird, *owned by E. & S. Barbour, Newtown.*

Benjamin and Rebecca Barbour had founded a Newfoundland dynasty — eleven children, seventy-three grandchildren, and two hundred and ten great-grandchildren — most of whom made their living from the cod and seal fisheries, in command of their own vessels. Sons Joseph, Thomas, William, George and James became sealing captains, while Benjamin, John, Edward and Samuel set their sights on the teeming shoals of cod along Newfoundland's shores. Edward and Samuel eventually formed their own company, E. and S. Barbour, and it became the largest business on the Bonavista north shore, in the coastal trade and the Labrador fisheries. The Barbour daughters were Mary and Keziah.

In 1873, Benjamin, then sixty-four, and Rebecca, fifty-three, decided to build themselves a fine house at Inner Islands (renamed Newtown in 1892), just north of Wesleyville. There the surroundings were somewhat less harsh, and the narrow tickles (a narrow difficult strait, as in an entrance to a harbour) between the islands offered shelter for the fishing schooners that were becoming increasingly important to the area's economy. The Barbours built a log cabin to provide immediate shelter, and began work on what became locally known as the "big house."

The entire family helped with its construction. Although Mr. Bridle, a mason, was hired to build the stone foundation, the Barbours themselves did most of the work. The older ones left by schooner for Gambo where pine trees were plentiful, and these they sawed into clapboard. The younger boys flattened nail heads, stuffed shavings between the uprights for insulation, then tacked birch rind on the outside sheathing before the clapboard siding was applied, using the same technique on the roof before it was shingled. When it was nearly done, a painter, Mr. O'Grady, was brought from St. John's to provide finishing touches to the interior — ornate scrollwork between the exposed

57

beams, and graining on the wood trim that was then varnished. The result was a handsome house, a "gentleman's house," simple but dignified — and sturdy enough to withstand the rigours of Newfoundland's forbidding winters.

The Barbours' new home was designed to house two families. A double staircase flanking the centre hall ensured that this could be done quite easily at any time. A partition dividing the house in equal halves would have allowed two families of this large clan to live together without stepping on each other's toes. And as the "big house" boasted thirty-two rooms, twelve of which were bedrooms, it might have seemed an inviting idea. But, for one reason or another, the wall was never built, perhaps because the Barbours were able to live together in harmony.

By 1875, when the house was finished and the Barbours were ready to move in, their eleven children ranged in age from thirty-three down to eight. In all, five of Newfoundland's greatest sealing captains lived in this house, as well as nine other Barbour men who captained ships for the cod fishery. Eventually Benjamin and Rebecca Barbour built homes for all their sons (the daughters had married and moved elsewhere), until each one had a house on Barbour's Tickle, between the two main islands at Newtown — sometimes called the Venice of Newfoundland because the small community is scattered between several islands and the adjacent mainland.

Benjamin Barbour, a venerable eighty-one, died in 1891, and Rebecca died fifteen years later. Edward Barbour (their eighth son) and his wife, Mary Jane Kean, were the next to move into the big house.

Mary Jane, a daughter of Captain John Kean, had been born into another prominent sealing family. She could rightfully claim that she had been on a sealing ship when only a few days old. Her father, twenty-eight, had contracted pneumonia at sea. When his ship came home he was too ill to be moved, so his newborn daughter was brought on board for him to see. He died a few days later.

Mary Jane was raised by her uncle, Captain Abram Kean of Flower's Island. With a cousin, Jennie, she worked as a cook on Abram's vessels when they sailed "down the Labrador." She was aboard the *E. Morine* in Rocky Harbour in 1885 during the "Seventh of June Gale" (the great gales often are remembered by their date) and recalled that "schooners were going in all directions, as those that had broken their chains were forced across others, causing them to break in pieces." Mary Jane and her cousin were rescued by Abram, who pulled his longboat up to the stern of the *E. Morine*, helped them in, and told them to crouch at the bottom of the boat. They and the crew barely escaped with their lives. The schooner was lost.

After her marriage to Captain Edward Barbour, however, Mary Jane's fortunes improved. Their son Carlson recalled one memorable purchase his father made.

FROM THE
JOURNALS OF
CARLSON BARBOUR
[1973]:
There have been fishing
skippers, sea captains,
school teachers, ministers,
merchants, engineers,
soldiers, sailors, one
lawyer and judge, one
doctor and one MHA
holding the name of
Barbour, but it has been
most renowned for its
many sealing and fishing
captains.

My father was standing on some wharf . . . in St. John's, when he saw the Ketch Seabird reaching across the Narrows. Eventually she found her way in the harbour and tied up to Steers' wharf. Father lost no time in arriving on the scene as he was very impressed with her and wanted to get a closer look. He was told that she had been sent here from England to be sold and that she had once been owned by Lord Dunraven, a yachting enthusiast. She had also been a member of the Royal Yacht Squadron in Queen Victoria's time. Lord Stanley spent his honeymoon onboard her, and it was said that Queen Victoria herself had also sailed in her. Father enquired as to what she was being sold for and, upon being told $4,000, he bought her there and then [with cash in his pocket it, is said]. . . . When she came to Newtown first, father would not allow anyone to go below before first removing their shoes, as she was done up so nicely [finished in mahogany, with ceramic stoves and wonderful brass fittings]. However it was not long before she was sent into the coasting trade and hard work. . . . She was a beautiful sight when under full sail. Many a time she sailed into and from St. John's with her deck level with water, and sometimes with the deck amidships under water. She could take it, as she was a good seaboat. Although she was a very poor sailor before the wind, on the wind she could not be beaten; she could sail right in the wind's eye, as the saying goes.

The *Seabird* was lost in a storm in 1951, having sailed for eighty-two years.

Joseph Barbour, eldest son of Benjamin and Rebecca, married Ann Parsons. He died at forty-eight, leaving seven children, the eldest of whom was a son, Alphaeus, who went on to earn a small fortune in the fishery. After he married, another impressive Barbour house soon rose to dominate the local landscape. It was bigger, more elaborate, and better sited than any house on the Bonavista north shore.

NEWTOWN B.B.: Mrs. T. Vincent and her child perished in a snowstorm Dec. 1902.

Built in 1904, the house of Captain Alphaeus Barbour exemplified the finest in Victorian furbelows. Officially the Victorian era may have ended after the queen's death in 1901, but the architectural style bearing her name was still much in favour. More to the point, Mrs. Alphaeus Barbour (née Adelaide Davis) had visited St. John's, where she took careful note of the many splendid houses arising from the ashes of the Great Fire of 1894, a fire that had destroyed most of the city. Mrs. Barbour sailed back to Newtown determined to build a house that would equal or surpass in every way the best that St. John's had to offer.

She certainly came close. The Barbours' new house told the world that they were an important part of Newfoundland's "outport aristocracy." They and their nine children enjoyed spacious rooms for entertaining, with ten-foot ceilings, ornate plasterwork, floral glass, and four marble fireplaces adding to its distinction. Anyone venturing north from St. John's to remote Newtown was duly impressed. The house, replete with tower and Victorian bric-a-brac,

was dazzling. It stood in regal splendour on a rocky point jutting into the ocean, symbolizing as much as anything could the Barbour family's success story, from humble beginnings on Pinchard's Island to Victorian magnificence in Newtown.

As did most families who earned a living from the sea, the Barbours encountered tragedy. Alphaeus Barbour's brother, Baxter, drowned at sea during the First World War. Their uncle, John Barbour, and two of his sons met a similar fate in 1918. (John was Benjamin and Rebecca Barbour's fourth son.) He had lived in a Newtown house that bore above its tall gateposts a sign warning "Prepare To Meet Thy God." No doubt he had. John and his sons drowned near Arichat, Nova Scotia. Another son had drowned as a boy. Yet to raise eleven children and lose only one of them and three grandchildren to the sea was a fate no worse than that met by most seafaring families — and better than many. For the generations of Newfoundlanders who lived by the rugged coast or on barren offshore islands, death was a constant companion.

While the Barbours of Newtown were connected with and supplied by Crosbies, the Winsors of Wesleyville had their merchant link with Bowrings. Samuel Winsor, the founder of this seafaring family, sailed from England's West Country with his wife, Mary Tiller, and established a fishery and supply business that he ran from their home on Swain's Island, just offshore from Wesleyville. Their son, William, born there in 1847, expanded the business, and settled with his wife, Emma Whiteway, in Wesleyville, a town that they and their descendants would one day virtually own. Emma's impressive family connections included Sir William Whiteway, three times the prime minister of Newfoundland.

The third generation of Winsors broadened the family's interests by entering Newfoundland's political arena, a forum not for the timorous.

William C. Winsor, known locally as "Captain Billy" and later, when he became minister of Marine and Fisheries in the Bond government, as "Honourable Captain Billy," began his life at sea when he was only nine and was taken "down the Labrador" with his father. At ten, old enough to "go to the ice" under his father's watchful eye, he joined the spring seal fishery and was soon bringing in record numbers of pelts.

In 1902, Captain Billy, then twenty-seven, married Josephine Blandford, from neighboring Greenspond. She was the daughter of another renowned sealing captain (and prominent local politician), Samuel Blandford, described by one contemporary as, "in his particular line, the most noteworthy of Newfoundland men today." Captain Billy was by then in command of his first ship, the Reid Newfoundland Company's *Virginia Lake*. That year he and his crew brought in from the ice 22,677 pelts — more than either his father or his father-in-law — ensuring his place in the annals of sealing.

With the backing of their two successful families, and profits from that year's highly successful seal harvest, it was not surprising that the newlyweds were able to begin building their first home. But it was not to be a modest honeymoon cottage. In fact, the house was so large and so ornate that it was five years before it was ready for the couple to move in. Perhaps they were keeping an eye on Alphaeus Barbour's new house, next door in Newtown (completed in 1904), and matching it, amenity for amenity. Both houses were handsome enough to impress any visiting dignitaries who might drop by, few of whom would expect to find such grandeur on this remote part of Bonavista Bay.

In 1913, only a few years after the Winsors had settled into their impressive home, the good people of Wesleyville watched with bemusement as a small building took shape on a hilltop. Here, in a Methodist town named for John Wesley, with a newly opened Methodist church financed largely by the Winsor family, Captain Billy was building an Anglican chapel for his wife. It was said that this was the fulfilment of a promise he had made to Josephine, a condition she had put to their marriage. She had no intention of travelling seven miles in an open boat to her Anglican church in Greenspond every Sunday for the rest of her life.

Annie Winsor Bishop, age eighteen or nineteen.

S.S. Imogene *arrived in St. John's on April 7, 1933, carrying 55,636 seal pelts.*

Captain and Mrs. A. Blackwood.

The little Chapel of St. John the Baptist was a pleasant wooden structure with a tall, graceful steeple, built in the same manner as that of the local Methodist church, with a ship's mast at its core. Both spires were visible for miles. When it was finished, the bishop of Newfoundland, the Right Reverend Llewellyn Jones, sailed up from St. John's to consecrate it. He noted that the "little church ready for consecration is situated on a hill, and is well seen when entering the harbour." Unfortunately the beautiful spires of both churches eventually succumbed to gale-force winds — that of the Methodist church was damaged, but the chapel's spire was completely removed. Nor did the chapel itself survive. Now all that remains is the stone foundation.

The Winsors' fine house eventually became the home of a woman who exemplified the resourcefulness of the Newfoundland outport matriarch. Canadian history books rarely mention the remarkable accomplishments of women in the years of the country's early growth, partly because their roles were undervalued, and, as well, because few of their accomplishments were recorded at the time. And yet the outports in Newfoundland were to a large extent matriarchal societies.

Her name tells her story. Annie Winsor Bishop Blackwood was the youngest child of Captain John Winsor and his first wife, Elizabeth. Her mother died, her father remarried a woman with her own large family, and Annie was raised by Captain Edward and Annie Bishop, her uncle and aunt, and took their name. She married Captain A. Blackwood, an eminently successful sealing captain who, it was said, had an instinct for the location of the main seal herd.

On the deck of the S.S. Imogene. *Governor David Murray Anderson pays a courtesy visit to Captain Blackwood. Left to right: Sir Edgar Bowring, owner of the* Imogene; *aide-de-camp to Governor Anderson; Governor Anderson; Captain Silas Gardner, navigator; Captain A. Blackwood, commander of the* Imogene.

Governor Sir Humphry Walwyn, visiting Wesleyville, 1937. Sealing captains form an honour guard on the steps of Captain W. C. Winsor's home.

Annie was in charge — not only of their four children but of the business end of the seal fishery. Outport merchants, unlike those in St. John's, had no office staff, and so Annie kept the books, paid the bills, and controlled the Bishop-Blackwood fortunes. As well, she was a commanding presence in Wesleyville. The local minister could not be hired without her approval. The church service never started until Annie had walked down the aisle, seated herself at the very front, and given a nod to the deferential parson. She was a businesswoman and not to be trifled with.

And Annie knew how she wanted the business run. On April 15, 1933, Captain Blackwood entered St. John's harbour on the *Imogene* (all of Bowring's vessels were named after Shakespearean characters) with the largest haul he had ever made — 55,636 seals. The men were hoping for a bonus from this incredible catch. Blackwood, anticipating a call from Sir Edgar Bowring to meet at his premises, waited for the summons.

Meanwhile, back in Wesleyville, Annie, who had received word of the prize catch, expected that her husband would demand a bonus for his men, and further, that if Sir Edgar Bowring refused, he would sever their connection. She disapproved. Feeling that she should be on the spot to say so, she summoned a Winsor relative, had a schooner quickly rigged and set out for St. John's, only to be forced back to Wesleyville in a storm. The scenario unfolded just as Annie had expected. Sir Edgar Bowring refused the bonus, asking Blackwood to tell his men that this was due to the Depression. Blackwood was adamant and broke off all ties with Bowrings — a decision that met with distinct disapproval at home. David Blackwood, eminent Canadian artist and descendant of Annie and the captain, sums it up succinctly: "There was frost in the air all that summer in the Blackwood home."

Barbour's Neptune II *being pulled through the ice, circa 1930s.*

Blown Off Course, Way Off Course

There are countless sagas of chilling adventures at sea, but few as gripping as that of Captain Job Barbour (of the long line of Barbour sea captains) and the crew of the *Neptune II*, and a voyage made shortly after the Barbours purchased the vessel in 1929. This record is compiled from Captain Barbour's book, *Forty-Eight Days Adrift* and from newspaper accounts of the remarkable voyage.

The *Neptune II* had delivered a load of cod and cod oil from Newtown to St. John's. Ready for the return trip, Captain Barbour recalled, "We loaded with a general cargo, and on the 27th [of November] we were ready to sail, but it was blowing up a storm. On the 29th, 10 ships got out of port. . . . I never intended to go out, but when I got back to the *Neptune* the last of the 10 was just going thru the Narrows, so I went up and got the tug and asked them if they'd tow me out, and he said well, Mr. Barbour, you'd better hurry up because its getting dark."

Two miles out from St. John's a strong wind came up. The *Neptune,* wrote Barbour, "spun along like a frightened tern churning the waves as she leaped upon them and leaving a foam wake behind." Soon the wind became a gale, then a hurricane; snow decreased visibility to nearly zero; and salt water penetrated and spoiled the casks of drinking water. By the next day, only thirty miles from home, the hurricane compelled them to run for open seas. The *Neptune* shipped water that took away the wheelhouse, booms, boats, bulwarks and sails.

They ran before the hurricane in huge seas. Ropes and sails were frozen, and the anchors were thick in ice. With this weight they could be easily swamped. Food was low, there was no fresh water. The crew took turns being lashed to the wheel for an hour — all any man could stand. They climbed the rigging to try to repair the sails and the wind "beat us in the face like huge birds of prey." There were 330 pounds of gunpowder in the wheel house, which could be blown if ignited by spontaneous combustion, plus twenty-five casks of inflammable oil in the hold.

A month out of Newfoundland, Barbour was still steering a course for home, but they were now some 250 miles out to sea and the western winds were continually battering them. "The sea would take 'er . . . and she'd go six feet under water . . . and all we could do was hang on for dear life." The crew realized that they had no control over their path and would be driven wherever the winds took them.

"We had come to regard ourselves now as playing a life-and-death game with the ocean, and with this was the thought that, as we had defeated it so often, it was only watching for the final chance to take us off our guard and in one fell swoop send us all to Davy Jones's locker."

On December 30, Captain Barbour decided that it was not possible get back to Newfoundland — they had little food and no water, and the ship couldn't take it — with the prevailing winds they had more chance of reaching dry land alive by heading for England. And they had a passenger near death. Mrs. Humphries, the wife of a crew member, the only female passenger, had been seasick and ill since the gale first hit them. Now she was very weak and near death. Barbour talked to her husband about a burial at sea. "Eef ya t'rows my wife's body h'overboard," Humphries said, "I'll 'ave to go wit'er, Cap'n Jobbie." (The hardy woman survived the ordeal.)

On January 14, they sighted land, but had no idea where that land lay — England, France? Finally they saw a lighthouse, then another, and were seen from land and towed in to safety. They were in Tobermory, Scotland, having been forty-eight days at sea on what was supposed to be a hundred-mile trip from St. John's to Newtown. Barbour sent a cablegram home. "Arrived safely Tobermory, Scotland. All well. Job K. Barbour." (The *Neptune II* was repaired, sailed home, and continued her life at sea.)

COAKER AND THE
FISHERMEN'S UNION

CHAPTER 6

Port Union and Sir William Coaker

Joey Smallwood was Canada's last Father of Confederation and the first premier of the Province of Newfoundland. He was a journalist, radio broadcaster, history buff, union organizer, an indefatigable politician, and a master in-fighter. And he was not one to stick to facts when a little judicious exaggeration would serve his purpose. Thus, when describing the legendary Sir William Ford Coaker, Smallwood called him the "greatest Newfoundlander since John Cabot!" Smallwood went on to describe the plight of the Newfoundlanders served by Coaker.

> For centuries, the fishermen had been in a state of political impotence, social servitude and economic dependence. Schools were few and far between, and illiteracy was prevalent. The fishermen, living in many hundreds of little harbours along the coast . . . were out of touch one settlement with another, even in sections approximately contiguous. There were the wide geographical and psychological differences between the Northern coasts and the Southern. Although they did the same kind of work and lived the same lives, it was as if they resided thousands of miles apart. . . . The strangest thing is that it should have been left until 1908 to start some kind of organization among the fishermen for the protection and advancement of their interests.

Coaker recognized and deplored a situation in which ninety percent of Newfoundland's population, the people who lived in the bays and coves along the island's six thousand miles of coastline, had no control over their livelihood. With no experience in the labour movement, and working with men who were independent by necessity, Coaker formed a union that became a model for such organizations in Canada and the United States. The story of Newfoundland's Fishermen's Protective Union is the story of William Coaker.

Coaker was born in St. John's in 1871. He spent his first five working years as an agent for a fish merchant, then turned to farming. But he was troubled by the terrible working conditions endured by the island's fishermen. In

FACING PAGE:
Sir William Coaker's "bungalow."

PREVIOUS PAGE:
Fisherman's shed, Wesleyville.

69

November 1908, after his crops were in and the summer fishery over, Coaker called a meeting in Herring Neck so that he and the men could talk. At that first meeting most of the talking was done by Coaker. He spoke for an hour.

Coaker was a dynamic orator. Smallwood recalled that he was "short, very thick-built, strong as an ox . . . dressed in the kind of clothes that would be worn by a farmer who had lived all but alone on an island for fifteen years." He talked the fishermen's language and electrified those who heard him. He told them that they were sheep, that Newfoundland was an empire built on fish, and that they were the last to benefit. He claimed that their humility was getting them nowhere, pointing out that they were captives of the merchants who set the price of fish as well as the price of supplies. They were the producers, and without them, the country would collapse. Nineteen men joined the union, and Coaker was elected president of its first local.

He spent the following winter travelling on foot, on snowshoes, and by dog-team, enlisting members, forming branches, and writing reports that were read and debated by the fishermen — men who had been largely illiterate and unaccustomed to voicing opinions in public. He became known as the fishermen's schoolteacher. Soon the men were writing letters to him; one year he personally answered 2,500 of them.

Within a year, two things had happened. First, Coaker had sold his farm, investing the proceeds in the Fishermen's Union Trading Company, providing people with an alternate source from which to buy supplies, usually at a price lower than that charged by the merchants. The men invested too. Second, news about Coaker had reached St. John's — and people there now knew that a fishermen's union was being organized in the north, with hundreds already signed up. The papers took note, first with derision, and then recognizing this as an event with significant ramifications. A convention was held, and more men enrolled. Coaker started a union newspaper, *The Fishermen's Advocate*, and was sued for libelling the merchants. The fishermen paid his fines.

By 1912, Coaker had decided that it was time for the union to have a voice where power lay and decisions were made — in the House of Assembly. The FPU party did well in the 1913 election, and Coaker entered the House in a working partnership with the Liberals, then the official opposition. When he spoke it was in a booming voice, his anger brimming over as he continually broke the rules of the Assembly. He was often reprimanded by the Speaker. Smallwood recalled that Coaker "denounced the Government with all the invective he could muster. . . . He talked fish until the Government members nearly screamed at the mention of the word. . . . It was hammer, hit, pound." In that first session, Coaker pushed through what became known as the "Sealers' and Loggers' Charter of Freedom," acts that changed for the better the deplorable conditions on sealing vessels and in the lumber camps.

By 1914, a short six years after its founding, the FPU had acquired an impressive 20,000 members. Coaker then accomplished two things that would

FISHERMEN'S PROTECTIVE UNION: In 1909 there was one Council of the FPU in Newfoundland, with a membership of 19; in 1922, Union statistics state the number of Councils as 200 with a total membership approximately 20,000; with total investments of one million dollars in the Union Trading Company and affiliated concerns; with a property worth $100,000 situated at Port Union, and with a large printing establishment doing a big general business and issuing a daily and a weekly newspaper at St. John's.

The Coaker house.

have seemed impossible a few years earlier. By agitating incessantly each fall for a price for fish that was a few cents per quintal more than the merchants were prepared to pay, he put more money into fishermen's pockets. And by selling flour through the union store, at a few cents lower than the merchants' price, he took less out of those same pockets. Coaker continued to write for the union paper, filibuster in the House, manage the union's trading company, and organize new locals. He established a light and power company, shipbuilding and shipping companies, and a cold-storage company. So that he could reach more people, the union bought him a yacht called the *F. P. Union*. Whenever he sailed into a harbour, crowds gathered, cheers went up, and everyone trailed into the local hall to hear him speak. He was revered in northern outports. (The Roman Catholic Church's hostility confined the union to the mainly Protestant northeast shore.) Some called him the Uncrowned King of the North.

Coaker decided that the union needed bigger and better premises than those in St. John's. He wanted to locate in the outports where the men were, and so he bought land in an uninhabited harbour in Trinity Bay. Soon trees were being felled and a town built. There were headquarters for the Union

Trading Company, warehouses, stores, piers, huge fish-storage buildings, offices for the newly formed Fishermen's Union Shipping Company, the Union Electric Company, houses, schools, recreational buildings, a church, town hall, woodworking factory, theatre, and the huge Congress Hall, a "handsome wooden structure," according to Smallwood, "fashioned after St. Paul's cathedral." Port Union was "built on the side of a hill that slopes gently back from the water's edge, and Congress Hall surmounts this hill, so that when lighted up at night with hundreds of electric lights, inside and out, it can be seen for miles out at sea."

Coaker habitually would "go about in an old suit, without collar or tie, and personally supervise the most minute detail of the endless ramifications of the different branches of the town's activities [while] boys from the telegraph office chase him around in a stream with messages from all parts of Newfoundland, as well as the various fish countries where the Union Trading Company ships fish." To no one's surprise, the town was called Port Union.

At the centre of Port Union the men built Coaker a house that became known locally as "Coaker's Bungalow." This simple building, although clad in aluminum some years ago, still retains its original interior detailing and furnishings.

In 1919, Sir Richard Squires, a former cabinet minister in the government of Sir Edward Morris and at the time a member of the Upper House, rallied support for the formation of his Liberal Reform Party. Coaker felt that his aims were compatible with those of Squires and so united with him in the Liberal Union Party. Coaker, as minister of Marine and Fisheries from 1919 to 1924, directed his attention to what he considered basic inequities in the way merchants conducted business — inequities that affected everyone in Newfoundland. When individual merchants arrived in foreign ports with a cargo of fish to sell, they had no agreed-upon price and each bargained individually with the buyers — and against each other. This rivalry between companies, Coaker felt, meant that they were setting themselves up to be beaten down to a low price. He wanted to see some kind of unified, efficient approach, and from his position in the House, pursued this end. The result was the Fishery Regulations Board, which was set up to control exports and ensure a unified marketing approach through permits and regulations. When put into place, these regulations brought about two years of continual volatile opposition. Eventually the merchants defied the regulations, selling fish in the old way, below regulation standards. The regulations were abolished, the price of fish fell, and many firms went bankrupt.

Coaker was knighted in 1923. Although exhausted by ongoing political battles, he set about bringing new enterprise to Newfoundland. With Squires, he sailed to England, where the two men promoted a pulp and paper mill for Corner Brook, a joint project with the British government. He died in Boston in 1938 and is buried in the town he founded, Port Union.

CONCEPTION BAY

CHAPTER 7

Harbour Grace

He was known as "an outstanding navigator, an able, brave, and bold seaman, an expert tactician, and highly competent in gun-laying." A British naval hero, perhaps? No, not exactly. Peter Easton was a pirate — probably, along with Captain Morgan and Captain Kidd, the most successful in the history of piracy. Easton, according to biographer E. Hunt, "controlled such seapower that no sovereign or state could afford to ignore him and he was never overtaken or captured by any fleet commissioned to hunt him down." The term swashbuckling might have been coined for this handsome, wealthy corsair who was, however, neither "a monster" nor a "cut-throat." One of the most colourful of the many characters who for a time have called Newfoundland home, Easton made his headquarters first in Harbour Grace and later in Ferryland.

Born into an established British family, Peter Easton began his Royal Navy career in a traditional manner, as commander of a convoy for the Newfoundland fishing fleet. But when James I disbanded the Royal Navy, Easton turned to privateering, and then to the more lucrative game of piracy, building up a fleet of forty ships, no doubt the largest such fleet in existence. It held sway and controlled traffic off the coast of Cornwall.

In 1612, Easton landed at Harbour Grace (named after Havre de grâce, the name used for Le Havre, France), a fishing community of Channel Islanders in northern Conception Bay. He was already rich from the avails of piracy. At Harbour Grace he built a fort, made repairs to his vessels, and added men to their crews. These men could volunteer or be commandeered, it mattered not — either way the pirate captain kept his ten ships manned and in top condition, furnished in a high style that befitted his reputation. He set sail from Harbour Grace and happily plundered coastal harbours all the way from Trinity Bay to Ferryland. Hunt records that "In addition to his depredations in the waters adjacent to Harbour Grace, where he took two ships, 100 men, and provisions from every ship, Easton plundered 30 English vessels in the harbour

FACING PAGE:
St. Paul's Anglican Church, built of stone after its two predecessors were destroyed by fire.

PREVIOUS PAGE:
Carbonear.

St. Paul's, interior.

of St. John's and raided French and Portuguese ships at Ferryland. The total damage inflicted by Easton on the fishing fleets was estimated at £20,400."

During these exploits, Easton kidnapped Richard Whitbourne, an established trader and colonizer, and kept him on board his ship for eleven weeks. In order to secure his release, Whitbourne promised to seek a pardon for Easton in England. In fact, the pardon had already been granted in February 1612, and was granted again later that year, but it never caught up with the peripatetic pirate, who ended his spectacular career in Villefranche, Savoy, a free port in what is now the principality of Monaco. There, thanks to his incredible wealth, he acquired a title, "Marquis of Savoy," bought a castle, and married a wealthy woman, all with the blessing of the Duke of Savoy, who was pleased to have Easton's two million pounds of gold in his domain. After 1620 nothing was heard of him again.

Harbour Grace, once Peter Easton had left the scene, did not settle down to become a placid, law-abiding backwater. The community teemed with activity during the summer months, although there was little permanent settlement of any kind until later in the century. When the French attacked in December of 1697, they found a village of one hundred men, fourteen houses, fifteen shallops (small open boats fitted with oars or sails, or both, used primarily in shallow waters), and an astonishing 381,000 kilograms of fish. Abbé Jean Beaudoin, a Recollect priest, wrote that "some of the merchants were men of £100,000 worth of property."

Gradually, during the early years of the eighteenth century, a thriving shipbuilding industry developed, and with it opportunities for winter employment. The merchants continued to reap the benefits of the abundant cod fishery, even though some years failed to meet their expectations. In 1749, George Garland, a justice of the peace in Conception Bay, wrote the governor, Sir George Rodney, on behalf of local merchants who, because they had suffered a bad fishing season, wanted permission to reduce their employees' wages. But the governor would have none of it. He replied: "I can by no means approve it, as both law and equity declare the labourer to be worthy of his hire. . . . I have only one question to ask, namely: had the season been good, in proportion as it has been bad, would the merchants or boat keepers have *raised* the men's wages?"

Immigration increased as the century wore on, and soon the Irish comprised almost fifty percent of the population. Unregulated passenger traffic meant that many arrived on the island unable to find work, often resorting to lawlessness and violence in what was still basically a harsh, frontier society. Governor Hugh Palliser, during his term of office (1764–68), noted with concern the number of single women who arrived on the island and became a "charge to the inhabitants, and likewise occasion much disorder and disturbance." Adding to the difficulties were recurring skirmishes with the French, religious riots, the loss of trade with New England during the American Revolution, and occasional and unexplained failures of the cod fishery. (There was a complete failure in 1790 after three bad fishing years.)

Throughout these two tumultuous centuries, order was maintained in Newfoundland first by the fishing admirals and later by magistrates appointed by the colony's naval governors. In Harbour Grace, two inadequate courthouses served Conception Bay during the eighteenth century. It wasn't until 1830 that the cornerstone was laid for a larger, much-needed courthouse.

Door, St. Paul's.

The courthouse, Harbour Grace, where justice has been dispensed since 1831. Its jail cells have only recently been retired from use.

Sealing Steamers in the Ice, Harbour Grace.

The town's merchants were elated. When the new courthouse was officially opened the following year, the "gentlemen of the town" were on hand to celebrate. As a correspondent for the *Newfoundlander* enthusiastically reported on July 21, 1831: "Upon Monday last, at half-past 6 o'clock, twenty-four gentlemen of this place sat down to a very excellent dinner at the Waterford Arms. . . . Few occasions have ever presented themselves in which so intense and harmonious feeling was so apparent and so general . . . the company spent the evening with much spirit and enjoyment — several excellent toasts were given — and many spirited addresses made."

Patrick Kough, the building's architect and contractor, was the honoured guest for the evening. Assembled dignitaries drank his health to "rapturous applause." The *Newfoundlander's* correspondent, rapturous as well, suggested that for Patrick Kough, the evening "must ever live among the proudest of his recollections."

The stone courthouse is still in use. It is a simple, straightforward, Georgian building with a few classical details — enough to offer a nod to its judicial purpose. A central round-topped window dominates the façade, while below it a single staircase leads up then branches in opposite directions, each flight leading to a recessed, pedimented door.

Sometimes, in those turbulent years, the justice offered inside the courthouse dispensed punishment that seemed not so much to fit the crime as to overwhelm it.

A case in point was the flogging of two Irish settlers, Philip Butler and James Lundrigan, in 1820, eleven years before the new stone courthouse was built. Their failure to appear on a summons before the surrogate court justices,

Captain David Buchan, a naval officer and Arctic explorer, and the Reverend John Leigh, a young Church of England missionary (recently arrived from Twillingate), resulted in the settlers being found in contempt of court. The sentence, thirty-six lashes for Lundrigan, was administered vigorously with a cat-o'-nine-tails on his bare back until he fainted. Butler received fewer strokes. This unduly harsh punishment caused an uproar and increased agitation for abolition of the Surrogate Courts. Justices Buchan and Leigh, on information later filed by Butler and Lundrigan, were charged with trespass for assault and false imprisonment, but both were acquitted.

(Apparently executions were not carried out at the Harbour Grace court-house. Three years after it opened, one Peter Downey was executed in St. John's for the murder in Harbour Grace of Robert Crocker Bray, his child, and a servant. Downey's body was sent to Harbour Grace, where it was exhibited for some time on Gibbet Hill.)

Many years before Captain Buchan and the Reverend Leigh were dispensing harsh justice on hapless settlers, another Harbour Grace clergyman had taken it upon himself to judge the behaviour of the town's residents, whose moral standards he usually found wanting. He was the Reverend Laurence Coughlan, a devoted and charismatic preacher who arrived in 1766 with his wife, and a daughter, Betsey. Coughlan was the first Church of England priest to serve Conception Bay and the small parish of St. Paul's. Yet his religious

The 1870 customs house, Water Street. On the site of pirate Peter Easton's fort.

affiliations were nothing if not complex. An Irishman, he was raised a Roman Catholic, converted to Wesleyan Methodism, ordained by a Greek Orthodox bishop, then again ordained as an Anglican missionary for the Society for the Propagation of the Gospel (SPG). Surprisingly, he is remembered today as the founder of Methodism in Newfoundland.

According to biographer Patrick O'Flaherty, Coughlan managed some-how to lead a "kind of double religious life" as he worked, under the auspices of the SPG, to comfort and convert the people of Harbour Grace. On occasion he would preach in Gaelic to Irish fishermen, to help them see the "Errors of Popery." And he fearlessly berated the town's leading merchants when their behaviour met with his disapproval.

Hugh Roberts was one such man — a man whom Coughlan publicly denounced for adultery. "You dirty low-liv'd scoundrel," roared Coughlan, "you rascal, you villain, you scum of the earth, are you not ashamed to be walking with another man's wife?" Warming to his subject in church, he advised his flock that they were looking at a "lump of iniquity" a sinner whom they should shun "as they would hell fire." On another occasion, Coughlan, never lacking courage, assaulted Roberts to prevent him from delivering a cask of bread to his workers on a Sunday, although those people had travelled twenty-four miles for it. Roberts, understandably, was not amused. As one of twelve "principal merchants of Harbour Grace," he petitioned Governor John Byron for Coughlan's dismissal, claiming that the clergyman was a "very unfitt Person, for a Justice of the Peace as well as a Missionary, being Ignorant of the Laws of his Country and a Person of no Education." The merchants also claimed that Coughlan, as a magistrate, was guilty of accepting bribes. Byron revoked his commission. Although a dispirited Coughlan continued to be warmly received by the less affluent people around Conception Bay, he returned to England in 1773 and died about eleven years later, "utterly broken in pieces."

After Coughlan's unhappy leave-taking, another Anglican priest, Reverend James Balfour, arrived in 1775 to minister to the small congregation at St. Paul's and spread the Word in Harbour Grace. He was optimistic. Things could not be worse for him in Harbour Grace, he thought, than they had been in Trinity, his first parish as an ordained minister for the SPG. About the only positive aspect of his stay there had been his marriage to Ann Emray, with whom he had four children. His Trinity parishioners, who numbered ten families, had built them a house. Such largess presumably promised peace and stability. But it was not to be. Balfour complained bitterly of the behaviour of his flock — of sexual excesses, dancing and work on the Sabbath, and confrontations between Irish and English. The good parson thought he might be making some progress, but concluded in general that Trinity was a "barbarous, lawless place," allowing that "These are Uncouth Regions here indeed, for a Man to spend his short Life in."

Balfour was transferred to Conception Bay and the parishes of Harbour Grace and Carbonear to succeed the irascible Lawrence Coughlan. But during his stay, Coughlan had influenced many inhabitants with his Methodist teachings, and thus Balfour found his hopes dashed, for he was not universally welcome. He found much to complain about — as did his parishioners, some of whom accused him of drunkenness. In 1792, Balfour, then about sixty-two,

HARBOR GRACE: Governor Dorrell [sic] wrote the Harbor Grace magistrates in 1755, ordering them to suppress Roman Catholic services and to exile priests of that Church.

CONCEPTION BAY: Devastated by dreadful storm in 1775, during which 300 persons were drowned; scene of many shipwrecks in great storm of Nov. 9–12, 1879.

HARBOR GRACE: Scene of election riots in 1836.

HARBOR GRACE: Election riots Nov. 2, 1860.

"MANUSSING": Capt. Lewis of the schooner *Mary*, returned from the ice fields, April 19, 1862, and summoned eleven of his crew to court for "manussing," i.e. refusing to work and forcing him to abandon the voyage; Magistrate Peters, of Harbour Grace, sentenced three of the accused to twenty-eight days' imprisonment and the other eight to fourteen days' imprisonment.

was dismissed by the SPG with a meagre pension. He died a bitter and unhappy man in 1809.

Balfour's successor was Reverend John Clinch, also formerly from Trinity, and famous for being the first in the New World to use the smallpox vaccine. Clinch was followed in 1798 by George Charles Jenner, a nephew of the doctor who had discovered the vaccine in England.

In the spring of 1803 a rector with the formidable name of Lewis Amadeus Anspach arrived at St. Paul's. Anspach had come to Newfoundland in 1799 at the invitation of the chief justice to establish a grammar school in St. John's. Personalities and financial disagreements prompted his resignation in 1802, and he requested permission to pursue his ministry elsewhere. He was invited to Conception Bay, where he became minister, justice of the peace and surrogate judge, and also established Sunday schools. In 1812 he returned to England but his interest in the colony continued. He wrote three books about Newfoundland, including *A History of the Island of Newfoundland: Containing a Description of the Island, the Banks, the Fisheries and Trade of Newfoundland and the Coast of Labrador* — a gift to the colony, as it was a ground-breaking project.

As parsons came and went, so did church buildings. The first small St. Paul's Church, built in 1764, was destroyed by fire in 1816. Arson was suspected — and with sectarian tensions always simmering, that may well have been the case. The next church was also burned in a disastrous 1832 fire in which ninety-six Harbour Grace buildings were destroyed. Wisely, when the splendid new St. Paul's arose from the ashes, it was built of stone. The cornerstone for the church was laid in 1835, the first service held in 1837, and it was consecrated on July 4, 1840. Today it is the oldest stone church in Newfoundland.

Whereas Britain welcomed Protestant churches to the colony, they extended no such courtesy to the island's Irish Roman Catholics, and for many years they were ruthlessly persecuted. This led to more than a century of sectarian violence throughout the island. In *A History of Newfoundland and Labrador*, Frederick W. Rowe writes that, given the history of English-Irish antagonism, conflict was understandable. "In Newfoundland [the Irish] were often tricked and cheated by the English shipowners, despised by the English establishment, encouraged in their alcoholic excesses, forbidden to attend mass, tried and sometimes given excessive fines and punishment, usually brutal whippings, in courts where frequently one of the presiding magistrates was a Protestant clergyman." The result was a belligerent populace, fired by religious intolerance (and often alcohol), and countless clashes.

Nowhere were these encounters more violent than in Harbour Grace. During the eighteenth century, authorities there fined practising Roman Catholics and destroyed their businesses and homes. Any building in which Mass had been said was destroyed. A riot in 1754 brought the instigator thirty-five lashes, other participants twelve. Tensions continued into the next century, and it wasn't until the 1850s that Catholics were able to build their own very impressive place of worship, an immense structure modelled after St. Peter's in Rome. It took years to build but, sadly, was destroyed by fire in 1889, only a few years after it was completed.

Throughout the century, sectarian riots occurred at election time, and many a wise voter stayed home. Henry Winton, a journalist and publisher, probably wished he too had stayed home. He became embroiled in religious and political disputes in the 1830s, and according to Peter Neary and Patrick O'Flaherty in *Part of the Main*, Winton described the residents of Harbour Grace and Carbonear as a "lawless mob." They proved him right. In 1835 he was attacked by thugs who cut one of his ears off altogether, while two pieces were cut from the other. Although a reward of £1,500 was offered by Governor Prescott, the perpetrators were never discovered.

The 1800s brought more people and more prosperity, and soon Harbour Grace was second only to St. John's in size. Activity in and near the harbour also reached a peak, with more than 2,000 men working on the sixty-two sealing vessels that crowded the harbour. In 1857 alone, 1,941 men killed 75,055 seals. Fishermen were bringing in 88,000 quintals of cod each year. And while fires and deaths continued to take their toll (fires in 1832 and 1858 left most of the town in ashes), the town's economic life was buoyant and what was destroyed was quickly rebuilt, as there were contractors readily available and money to finance the work. Seemingly a peak was reached in the late 1850s, to be followed by a valley — one of the declines that was tied so completely to the health of the fisheries. As the 1860s progressed, the cod and seal fisheries suddenly suffered a near collapse. Historian W. A. Munn recounted that "For some reason never explained the salt water around our Country became hostile to fish life. . . . [The situation] became acute in 1862 and got worse during the next five years." Nearly fifty merchants in Harbour Grace had to diversify to keep their businesses afloat.

Today, another of Harbour Grace's stone buildings still stands by the water to remind us of two ambitious men who, each in his own way, typified the commercial life of Harbour Grace. The building served as offices for one, and then the other. First on the scene was Thomas Ridley, a tough, no-nonsense merchant who, for half a century or so, succeeded in Harbour Grace in spite of arousing the antagonism of almost everyone in the community. Ridley was in his early twenties when he and his young wife arrived from England to work for his uncle, William Bennett. When Bennett was lost at sea a short time later, Ridley set up shop on the north side of Water Street, and before long was running a flourishing business. In 1832, when other merchants gave in to the demands of striking sealers and fishermen, Ridley refused to do so. In retaliation, his ship, the *Perseverance,* was boarded and nearly destroyed. Four years later, when he decided to enter the political arena, he was forced to withdraw due to local violence and intimidation. Then in 1840,

We are sorry that we cannot this week report more favorably of the codfishery. It has never been so bad as it is at present in this neighborhood. If there is not some change soon we fear it will be one of the worst seasons experienced for a number of years back.
The Standard and Conception Bay Advertiser. Harbor Grace July 8, 1863.

CAUTION
We beg to draw the attention of the Public to the following Section of an Act passed in the last Session of the Legislature: "Any person who shall be found at any season of the year, in any town or settlement in this Colony DRESSED AS A MUMMER Masked or otherwise disguised shall be deemed guilty of a Public Nuisance, and may be arrested by any Peace Officer with or without Warrant, and taken before any Justice of the Peace in the district or place where such person may be found and, on conviction in a summary manner, before such Justice, may be committed to Gaol for a period not exceeding seven days, unless he shall pay a fine not exceeding Twenty Shillings.
Police Office
Harbor Grace
The Standard. Harbor Grace January 14, 1863

Quite an amusing scene took place in the Magistrates Court on Thursday last, arising out of a mumming row which took place at Bareneed in the holidays. It appears that a number of persons disguised as Mummers made an attack on a party of men who were on the public road; they immediately resented the attack and pitched into the mummers, and a general fight took place for a short time, when the mummers had to fly. On Mr. Hennebury coming to see what was the matter he was struck by the party, and was obliged to take refuge in the house of a man by the name of Hall; the party then commenced breaking the windows of the said house. Hall brought some of them before the Magistrate for breaking his glass who were fined. Hennebury also brought some of them before the Magistrate for beating him, who were also fined. One of the party brought up then prosecuted the mummers, who were fined, whilst another informed against Hall for selling rum without license, and the Magistrates fined him also. Thus the Crown received some fifteen

while serving as magistrate and continuing to raise the ire of the populace, he was attacked and nearly killed. Perseverance, however, was something Ridley knew about, and finally in 1842 he was elected to represent Conception Bay in the Amalgamated Legislature. He went on to serve on the Executive Council from 1843 to 1845 while his company, by then called Ridley and Sons, continued to prosper.

Ridley's main competitor during these years was a man of a different stripe. He became even more successful than Ridley, and did so, it would seem, while gaining the respect and affection of the people of Harbour Grace and beyond. He was John Munn, an honourable, determined Scot, eight years Ridley's junior. After a few years working as a bookkeeper in St. John's, he arrived in Harbour Grace in 1833 and set up a mercantile business with William Punton, a master mariner from Greenoch. The firm expanded under Munn's steady hand and was soon the largest of its kind outside St. John's — and as it grew, so did Munn's reputation. He sat in the Amalgamated Legislature from 1842 (for some time with the irritable Ridley) until he resigned from politics in 1873. So influential was he that Harbour Grace was sometimes called "Munnsborough," since the candidates he backed usually won the election.

But in 1870, it all came unravelled. Although Ridley's firm and Munn's appeared to have weathered the collapse of the fisheries during the 1860s, such was not the case. Both were in difficulty. Thomas Ridley and Sons was declared insolvent. Munn's firm, however, survived and reorganized as John Munn and Sons, taking over many of Ridley's customers. Ridley himself retired to England, dying at age eighty in Upper Tooting, Surrey, in March 1879. John Munn died, also in England, about six months later. Munn's biographer, Elizabeth Wells, writes that when news of his death reached Harbour Grace, "much of Conception Bay put on mourning, with flags flying at half-mast, shops closed, and almost all work suspended for the day."

For some time, John Munn and Sons continued to expand. During the 1880s it was producing "boneless cod" for an eager American market, sending quantities of cod-liver oil to (possibly) less than eager consumers in Britain, and as a by-product, selling glue from fish skins to mend "everything but a broken heart." It all came to a tragic end in 1894 when the bank crash hit and the company closed. Robert S. Munn, John Munn's nephew and the only surviving partner, died within a week. The building that housed first Ridley's offices and then the Munn's, although in poor condition, still overlooks the harbour that brought such prosperity — and such turmoil — to nineteenth-century Harbour Grace.

Somehow it seems ironic that, almost two centuries after Peter Easton left Harbour Grace, a customs house arose on the site of his fort, overlooking the harbour where richly laden pirate vessels once lay at anchor. And it has its own story to tell, for it played a significant role in the commercial life of the town. Built in 1800, it was a wooden structure that by 1867 had reached such a state of disrepair that one writer to the Harbour Grace *Standard* called it an "old crumbling apology for a Customs House." It was replaced in 1870 by the present brick building, a trim Georgian structure with a three-bay façade, stone quoins and its original six-over-six sash windows. Today it serves as a museum. When open to the public in the summer, flags fly on adjacent standards. Among those of prominent local merchants can be seen the black flag of the debonair pirate, Peter Easton.

One of the many people who acted as surrogate customs officers at the "crumbling apology for a Customs House" was living in an elegant Georgian house directly across the road at 16 Water Street East. It is one of several substantial dwellings that once lined the street, defining by their very presence the importance of Harbour Grace in nineteenth-century Newfoundland. The customs man was E. E. Brown, and little is known of him other than that he was living in the house at mid-century. Even then, however, his home had stories to tell, for it had been standing there since about 1811. Much of the town's turbulent history had taken place at its front door.

The first owner is thought to have been a local lawyer, James Bayley, whose wife, Francis Maria Cawley, was a granddaughter of Joseph Webber, whose family had arrived from Boston in 1750 to start up a whaling industry in Conception Bay. The house was built on his land. Local legend has it that the house later served as a residence for British officers who, from time to time, were dispatched from St. John's to Harbour Grace to quell sporadic uprisings — perhaps the election riots that rocked the town in 1832 and 1840. The officers, it was said, could observe the parade grounds in front of the courthouse from the tall, twelve-foot window that lights the stairwell.

By 1855, however, the house had come into the hands of Joseph Godden, a local jeweller, magistrate, and a member of the House of Assembly. Like his friend, the estimable John Munn, Godden was a confederate. He resigned his seat in 1869 so that the better-known Munn might carry the day for the confederation forces. (Munn won that election, one of the few confederation supporters to do so.) Godden died at seventy-three after a brief illness, leaving his "universally liked and respected" family to mourn his loss. Their home remained in the family until 1992. Now called Garrison House, it has been restored to its original Georgian simplicity, looking much as it did nearly two hundred years ago when lawyer Bayley and his wife moved in.

In spite of the economic difficulties that Harbour Grace encountered during the 1860s, it was still a major centre when, in 1873, a judge and former speaker of the House of Assembly, Thomas R. Bennett, moved into town. Bennett, a Nova Scotian, had first settled in Fortune Bay on Newfoundland's south shore, and there set up a successful mercantile business, trading with the southern United States. When the Civil War put an end to that lucrative enterprise, the resourceful Bennett turned to politics. He eventually became Speaker in the government of Charles Fox Bennett (no relation). Thomas Bennett was

pounds by the transaction and each party left the Court highly delighted and satisfied with the whole proceedings. So much for mumming.
The Standard. Harbour Grace January 14, 1863

85

Aviator Mabel Bell and friends.

reelected in 1873, but in an unusual turn of events, the prime minister immediately appointed him to the Bench, to serve in the Northern District Court. So Bennett moved to Harbour Grace and built his new house, another in the row of splendid houses on Water Street East (many since demolished), near his neighbour and fellow legislator Joseph Godden. It was completed in 1879.

The Bennett house incorporated an older structure, perhaps the house in which he and his wife lived when they first arrived. The new addition stated emphatically that Bennett was a man of substance, for certainly the house was impressive and as up to date as anything in St. John's. Dominating the façade was a pair of five-sided projecting bays with matching dormers above, and a mansard roof, all in the Second Empire style — and the height of fashion in the 1870s. The tall windows offered a fine view of the sea from the promontory on which the house was sited. Bennett supplied the materials for the house and paid the contractor £85 for his work. In 1902, a year after Bennett's death, his widow sold the house to James Cron, a Harbour Grace merchant.

In the early years of the twentieth century, people began to arrive at Harbour Grace from far and near to watch the exciting events at the town's new airfield. British flyers Alcock and Brown's 1919 flight from St. John's to Clifden, Ireland (the first non-stop flight across the Atlantic), and Charles Lindbergh's flight from New York to Paris (the first solo flight across the Atlantic) in May 1927 had created enormous interest. Countless other adventurous souls were trying to equal or better these records. With a grant from the Newfoundland government, one hundred and twenty-five men removed scrub trees, undergrowth and rocks to prepare the hilltop site for a landing strip. On August 26, three months after Lindbergh's historic flight, two Americans, William Brock and Edward Schlee, flew in from Old Orchard, Maine, in the *Pride of Detroit*, on the first leg of a proposed round-the-world flight. They landed at the new Harbour Grace airfield to the cheers of a crowd that included Premier Sir John Bennett. Next day, they crossed to England; they continued to Tokyo, but had to abandon their flight there because their lack of navigational equipment meant that they were denied clearance at Midway Island. They returned to the United States by ship.

On September 7, 1927, less than a month after Brock and Schlee's departure, a single-engine aircraft flying from London, Ontario, to London, England, took off from Harbour Grace and disappeared. It was one of three aircraft in that one week to meet disaster while attempting to cross the Atlantic.

For the next ten years the residents of Harbour Grace saw dozens of the world's pioneer aviators fly out across the Atlantic (among them the noted Wiley Post in 1931). Many were never seen again. On May 20, 1932, Amelia Earhart, who at twenty-nine was already the first woman to fly the Atlantic (she had flown from Trepassey Bay, on Newfoundland's south shore, to Wales with a co-pilot in 1928) made the first solo transatlantic flight by a woman, crossing from Harbour Grace to Londonderry, Ireland, in fifteen hours and eighteen minutes.

A few years later, on September 15, 1936, First World War ace Eddie Rickenbacker landed at Harbour Grace, bringing with him mechanics and spare parts to repair one of his Eastern Airlines planes, the *Lady Peace*. That aircraft, on a return flight from London, had run out of fuel as it approached Newfoundland, and was forced to land near Musgrave Harbour on Bonavista Bay. (There were no casualties, and little damage to the plane — perhaps because it was reportedly carrying 40,000 ping-pong balls for buoyancy!)

The crowds of reporters that followed Rickenbacker (the Associated Press and *The New York Daily News* had each sent planes) brought the name of Harbour Grace to world attention once again. In 1997, as Newfoundland celebrates the 500th anniversary of John Cabot's landing, historic Harbour Grace can also acknowledge its own claim to fame. The year marks the 70th anniversary of the town's once-renowned airfield — and the 385th anniversary of the arrival of that charismatic pirate, Peter Easton.

CHAPTER 8

Carbonear

There were two intriguing Irish figures who came to the port of Carbonear and became part of the legend and history of that town: one was a princess, the other a talented young clerk with a vision. The story of the Irish princess resonates with the romance of the sea. That of the young clerk tells of its lucrative avails and its tragedies.

The princess, Sheila Na Geira of Connaught, was on a sailing vessel making for France when she was taken captive, first by a Dutch crew and later by the dashing Peter Easton, Newfoundland's pirate in residence, then living in Harbour Grace. Local legend holds that the princess fell in love with a member of the ship's crew, Lieutenant Gilbert Pike, and that on Easton's return to Newfoundland, they married and settled in Carbonear, on the western shore of Conception Bay, near Harbour Grace. Her grave is at the west end of town.

There is a much more substantial and visible history connected with the young man, John Rorke. His mercantile complex and his home still stand on historic Water Street.

Carbonear, one of the oldest settlements in Newfoundland, was the busiest commercial fishing station in Conception Bay. During the seventeenth and eighteenth centuries, merchants, many from Poole and others from elsewhere in England, Ireland or Wales, made fortunes in Carbonear. Among the first settlers were a number of Channel Islanders, and it may have been they who named the place Carbonear, a corruption of the word *charbonnier,* meaning, on Jersey Island, the location of a charcoal pit — and there were such pits on the shores of Conception Bay. The people of Carbonear built ships and successfully exploited the cod and seal fisheries. Carbonear's business statistics for the early 1800s tell the story: in 1822, a 100-ton vessel built there for the seal fishery; more than 100,000 seal pelts processed in 1824; by 1836, eighty ships and 2,000 men employed in the seal fishery. There was work for all in this and related industries, and this prosperity was reflected in Carbonear's fine houses.

FACING PAGE:
*The grave of Princess
Sheila Na Geira.*

John Rorke's imposing storehouses.

John Rorke was an Irishman, born in Cavan in 1807. As a lad of seventeen he immigrated to Carbonear where he had, like so many before him, family connections to help him get started. He worked first for the firm of Bennett and Ridley, the senior partner being his uncle. In 1830, Rorke married Mary Tocque, the daughter of a local merchant. He purchased the premises of Slade, Elson and Co. at Carbonear, and soon his firm had expanded to include a fleet of ships that traded in the West Indies and beyond, and fished in and supplied the lucrative Labrador market. Rorke was well respected as an honest merchant, and was elected to represent Carbonear in the House of Assembly, where he served for twenty years, including a term on the Executive Council.

In 1859 a fire swept through Carbonear, destroying the many frame buildings in its path, including the building that served as Rorke's shop, office and home. By the following year, a determined Rorke was busy rebuilding — this time with stone, the better to withstand anything the elements or fire could send his way. And he was right — the building, called the Stone Jug, still stands.

Across the road from the Stone Jug are Rorke's two storehouses, substantial frame buildings. That on the west side was built in the 1870s and known as the Molasses Store, as this is where (no surprise here) people brought molasses jugs to be filled. Both storehouses were built of massive timbers on a rubble-stone foundation, with clapboard siding, heavy plank floors and, like

90

the Stone Jug, a slate roof. The extent of Rorke's business is shown in the variety of products kept in these buildings — in one, cement, iron, lime and glass; and in the other, feed, paints, flour, and barrels of beef and pork. The two buildings were once connected by a bridge at the second-floor level with stairs leading from the ground up to the bridge. The two storehouses, together with the Stone Jug opposite, comprise the only complete merchant premises remaining in Carbonear, and one of the best-preserved examples in the province.

But though many of Rorke's ships, such as the *Callidora,* the *Thomas Ridley* and the *Lena,* had long lives and fine reputations, Rorke, his men and their families, like all who made their living from the sea, had to deal with the tragedies that accompanied that way of life. According to Frank Saunders in *Sailing Vessels and Crews of Carbonear,* in the summer of 1896, the year of Rorke's death, the *Clio,* built in England for Rorke, loaded cod at Labrador and sailed for Gibraltar. She unloaded salt at Valencia, headed back to Carbonear, and was never seen again. (Included in her crew was one G. W. Pike, perhaps a descendant of Gilbert Pike and his Irish princess.) Rorke's *Beatrice* was lost in the vicious winter of 1912 after it left the Azores. That winter, seven ships from Newfoundland were lost at sea with all hands. Over the years, five of Rorke's ships, the *Muriel, Snowbird, Clio, Beatrice* were lost with all hands, and *the Rose* with thirty-seven men — a total of at least sixty men.

John Rorke died at eighty-nine, but his firm and the Rorke Fish and Coal Company carried on, run by succeeding generations of Rorkes. When it ceased operation it had been in the same family for a hundred and forty years.

CARBONEAR: 124,417 sealskins manufactured there 1832.

CARBONEAR: Riots started by mummers on Old Christmas Day, 1862; Magistrate I. McNeill shot; military sent to the town from Harbor Grace and St. John's.

SNOWSTORM OF '68 was accompanied by terrible loss of life on the land. about thirty people lost their lives while travelling between Heart's Content and Harbor Grace; one man perished in Carbonear, and two in Harbor Grace; five people belonging to Upper Island Cove were found dead in the snow. there was a high wind, terrible drifts and intense frost.

PIKE, MRS. E: Died June 3, 1880, aged 98 years: was ancestress of a family of 13 children, 100 grandchildren, 128 great-grandchildren, and 2 great-great-grandchildren.

Laying the transatlantic cable, Heart's Content.

Interior of the 1866 cable station at Heart's Content, a terminal for the "greatest technological achievement of the age."

Newfoundland is the easternmost land mass on the continent of North America. Here the Conception and Trinity Bay areas reach out their arms into the Atlantic, closer to Ireland than to central Canada. The distance between Newfoundland and Ireland at this point is only about 1,880 miles, and because of this, the peninsula between Trinity and Conception Bays, and the remote communities of Heart's Content and Harbour Grace became household names around the world.

It was an American, the remarkably tenacious Cyrus W. Field, who persevered, in spite of several failed attempts, to successfully lay a transatlantic cable. In 1866 a galvanized cable 2,300 nautical miles long and weighing 5,000 tons was ready to be placed on the floor of the Atlantic Ocean. That July the 22,500-ton *Great Eastern*, five times larger than any ship afloat, attempted to complete the link, and to retrieve and splice cable that had previously been lost on the ocean floor. By September, the "greatest technological achievement of the age" had been successfully completed and the link made at Heart's Content on the east shore of Trinity Bay.

The event was celebrated around the world. Heart's Content achieved international fame, and East Coast newspapers could hardly contain their pride. The *Charlottetown Herald*, with lyrical enthusiasm, invoked the Bard of Avon to do justice to the day: "The dim vision of the immortal Shakespeare of putting a girdle round the earth is now an accomplished fact; and the farthest parts of the distant and fabled east are brought within speaking distance of the broad continent of America. It is stated that new cables, until six are in successful operation, will be sunk each year between Valencia, Ireland, and Heart's Content, Newfoundland, so that uninterrupted communication will always be ensured between the Old and New worlds."

The cable office in Heart's Content operated until 1965, when new methods of communication, including satellite, rendered it obsolete. The brick telegraph building still stands and is open to the public.

DAVIS, MISS MARGARET: Awarded $5,000 damages against James Duff of Carbonear in breach of promise suit, Feb. 13, 1904.

BELL ISLAND: Two little girls named Parsons, cousins aged 12, killed by falling over a cliff at Freshwater, June 10, 1915.

CHAPTER 9

Brigus

O n April 1, 1909, a Brigus native, Captain Robert Bartlett, reached his "Farthest North" — a spot closer to the North Pole than anyone had ever been. There he waited for the leader of his expedition to arrive, and their final push toward a goal that had captured the world's imagination and led many explorers to their death. Several weeks behind him, following the trail that Bartlett and two native assistants had marked out, came the man in charge, a man obsessed with winning the race to the pole, Robert E. Peary.

Bob Bartlett, circa 1900.

The two men had first sailed together in 1898 aboard Peary's *Windward,* commanded by Bartlett's uncle, Captain Samuel Bartlett. Bob Bartlett, then only twenty-three, was a master mariner and sealing captain, having commanded his first vessel six years earlier at his father's fishing station near Turnavik, Labrador. The young adventurer came from generations of sealing captains and Arctic explorers, and Peary, an American naval officer, felt sure that he had found just the man for his future polar explorations. He asked Bartlett to command his ship, the *Roosevelt,* on his next polar attempt. Bartlett accepted.

Bartlett took command of the *Roosevelt* in July 1905. Peary's biographer, Wally Herbert, writes that Peary had implicit faith in Bartlett, who "at thirty [was] already larger than life, and whose torrent of directions in times of stress was loud and profane enough to burst every bead of sweat on his neck." The ship reached Cape Sheridan, Ellesmere Island, that winter. Bartlett and others were to go ahead, marking a trail and leaving supplies at various caches along the route so that Peary could then proceed directly to the pole. After about four months on the ice, that attempt failed at the 87th parallel due to a shortage of provisions and the death of many of their dogs. The *Roosevelt* had also developed serious structural problems, and its supply of coal was almost gone. Peary, Bartlett and their crew headed for home. It was a perilous journey, with seventy-five days spent on the damaged ship, fighting their way through the ice floes to Etah on the Greenland coast, then south to Hopedale, Labrador, with Bartlett wondering daily "how it was possible for a wreck like ours not to sink." The *Roosevelt,* thanks to Bartlett's brilliant seamanship, arrived home in New York on Christmas Eve 1906.

Discouraged but more determined than ever, Peary mounted another expedition in 1908, with Bartlett again in command of the repaired and refurbished *Roosevelt.* Arriving at Cape Sheridan that September, Bartlett and his crew worked for months marking a trail on the ice ahead of Peary, and again setting up supply stations for the triumphant trek to the pole. Peary spent the winter in comfort aboard ship while his eager team "worked, trained, blazed the trails and prepared the way for their master." By February 21, 1909, a well-rested Peary was alone on board the ship.

It is impossible to know whether Bartlett expected to accompany Peary on his last lap to the pole, although he had certainly earned the right to do so. In any event, it was not to be. Peary was a driven man. He knew that this would be his last attempt — and he was not about to share the glory. He craved fame to the point of obsession, and when he arrived at Bartlett's last camp, insisted on going on to the pole with only the devoted Matt Henson, his longtime servant, and a few Inuit to accompany him. Bartlett, Peary's "last reliable witness," was dispatched back to the ship. Bartlett arrived at the *Roosevelt* on April 24, only three days ahead of a triumphant Peary, who, on his return, proclaimed that he had been to the pole and back.

Wally Herbert, himself an Arctic explorer, has conducted exhaustive research for his fascinating biography of Peary, *The Noose of Laurels.* He concludes that Peary never reached the pole (nor, Herbert claims, did his adversary for polar honours, Dr. Frederick Cook). "It is difficult to believe that Peary and his companions covered in a dead straight line the 296 nautical miles from Bartlett's camp to the Pole and back to Bartlett's camp in 7.8 days — an average of 37.9 nautical miles a day." (In land, or statute miles, 54.5.) "Across polar pack ice," claims Herbert, "this sort of average is nothing short of phenomenal."

Peary's claim was — and is still — widely disputed, but Bartlett stood by Peary. Both men, and the loyal Henson, were hailed as heroes.

Bartlett's most gruelling voyage, however, came four years later when a Canadian Arctic expedition set out in 1913 from Victoria, British Columbia, aboard a wooden barkentine, the *Karluk.* The leader of this venture was Vilhjalmur Stefansson, a capable man, but as difficult and as egotistical as Peary. With ten scientists, seven Inuit, one white passenger, and a crew of seventeen, they set sail on an expedition that was "ill-conceived, hastily assembled, and inadequately equipped." Eight of the men never returned.

Their destination was the Beaufort Sea, where the federal government planned to conduct scientific work and establish Canadian sovereignty over any newly discovered lands. Stefansson wanted to prove or disprove the existence of a mountainous area, Crocker Land, that Peary thought he had seen on a 1906 voyage. By mid-August the *Karluk* had become trapped in ice off the north coast of Alaska. It drifted for months, during which time Stefansson and five others left to hunt for caribou. Before they could return to the ship it had drifted farther away. It sank, finally crushed by the ice, in January 1914. Bartlett, who had carried the remaining supplies out onto the ice as he faced the inevitable destruction of his ship, set out to guide his remaining passengers to safety. A supply group of four headed for, and eventually reached, Herschel Island in the Beaufort Sea, but were stranded when ice broke up around its shores. They died there. Four others headed off on their own, after signing papers absolving Bartlett of any responsibility for their fate. They were never seen again. In March, Bartlett and his little group, their supplies nearly gone, reached the temporary safety of remote Wrangel Island, in the East Siberian Sea, farther north and west of Alaska. From there he left to find help, a seemingly impossible task. Accompanied by an Inuit and two dogs (that had to be eaten during their journey), Bartlett trudged an incredible 795 miles over the ice to Siberia, then southeastward to the Bering Strait. Arriving in Alaska on May 28, he acquired a ship and set out to find his colleagues. That ship had to turn back for lack of fuel. Finally, in September, he headed again for Wrangel Island. This time he met with another ship returning with the men, who had survived the six-month ordeal on that barren island — and more than a year in the frozen wastes of the Arctic.

Although he received an award from the Royal Geographic Society to honour his achievement, Bartlett was also forced to appear before a commission of enquiry, which, with the wisdom of hindsight, criticized him for taking the *Karluk* into such dangerous waters and for allowing the second group to leave the main party. This criticism may explain why he shortly thereafter acquired American citizenship and spent much of the rest of his life in New York. He later served in the two world wars, in the transport command, and in expeditions establishing supply bases for the U.S. military. He made numerous scientific voyages studying and collecting marine life for various institutions including the Smithsonian. Honours poured in from around the world to recognize his incredible achievements.

Whenever he returned to Brigus, Bob Bartlett lived in his summer home, Hawthorne Cottage, a building that, because of Bartlett's renown, has been named a National Historic Site. The house itself is a Regency cottage, a romantic architectural style that became fashionable during the 1820s and 1830s, particularly with the upper classes. It was a transitional style between the Georgian and Victorian, "dating roughly from the hopeless madness of George III to the trying sanity of Prince Albert," as architectural historian Marion Macrae has written. Usually square in plan (Hawthorne Cottage, however, is rectangular), Regency cottages were a storey-and-a-half high with a gently sloping roof and, almost always, a verandah that wrapped itself around three sides of the building. As a rule, French doors would open onto the verandah, so that the beauties of nature could be readily seen and enjoyed. Regency cottages required a romantic setting — either in a scenic glade by a stream, or on a hilltop with a

BRIGUS: Capt. John Bartlett anti-confederate candidate in the general election of 1869, introduced the public grindstone.

HUNTSMAN: Brig. commanded by Capt. R. Dawe of Bay Roberts, lost at the seal fishery with 44 of her crew, April 28, 1872.

PORTUGAL COVE: Theophilus Piccot and a companion attacked by an octopus, while off the Cove in a small boat, Oct. 27, 1873; cut off some of the tentacles with an axe and made their escape; estimated the body as 60 feet in length and 5 feet in girth; portion of one tentacle thrown overboard was six inches in diameter; portion brought in was 25 feet in length and three inches in diameter.

BAY ROBERTS: Town lost heavily when the *Tigress,* Capt. J. Bartlett, was destroyed at the seal fishery by an explosion of her boilers and 24 men killed, 1874.

COSTELLO: Five men by that name and a man named Whelen drowned Mar. 11, 1878, when a boat loaded with lumber and provisions, which they were taking from Brigus to Cat's Cove was swamped off Brigus Head.

PEARY AND HIS
ARCTIC CLAIMS
The promotion of Robert
E. Peary, the explorer, to a
captaincy in the signal
corps, served to recall his
double claim to Polar
achievement and admiral
rank. . . . Before going
abroad, Peary had sought
a rear-admiral's berth as a
mark of recognition from
Congress, but upon being
asked to show proof of
what he claimed to have
done to earn such
distinction, he explained
that a magazine contract
tied his hands for the time
being . . . As evidence that
the element of doubt,
instead of losing its
vitality, is gaining force in
important quarters, we
cite the view of the
astronomer royal of
Germany [who] . . .
asserts that Peary, by his
own account, could not
have been at the Pole, and
does not possess the
scientific knowledge to
locate the spot were he to
reach it.
The Daily News.
St. John's, November 3,
1910

view. Hawthorne Cottage met all these requirements — except, perhaps, the romantic site, and that it probably had in its original location.

Hawthorne Cottage was built in 1830 near Makinsons, a hamlet six miles southwest of Brigus. In its first four years this pretty house may well have overlooked the scenic South River, but for some reason its owners, the Leamons, soon decided to move it to Brigus, and there it has remained since 1834. The move inspired a lengthy ballad, "Squire Leamon's Housewarming," that recounted the perils of the mid-winter adventure as the house bumped along, drawn over rollers by horses — and the perils of the party they held to celebrate its arrival:

> The cloth was removed and down came the port
> Then Harris began with his glee and his sport
> For Harris, you know, is the funniest soul,
> That e'er passed round a bottle or fathomed a bowl.
> The jokes and the songs went round with each sinner
> Who would not be merry with wine after dinner?
> Each joined in his glass, each joke had its song
> Then the green-eyed Jealousy joined in the throng.

James Miner Harris, the schoolteacher in Brigus, proved to be the hero of the day when, wielding his crutch as a weapon, he prevented a duel between two jealous suitors — or so it is recorded in the ballad.

Hawthorne Cottage was inherited by the Leamons' daughter, Mary Leamon (she was Bob Bartlett's mother), when Bartlett was about eleven years old. He was the oldest of her eleven children. At his death in 1946 at age seventy-one, the house went to his two unmarried sisters, and when they died, to a nephew, Supreme Court Justice Rupert Bartlett, who, as a teenager, had

Bob Bartlett and parents aboard the Morrissey, *late 1920s or early 1930s.*

accompanied his uncle on five Arctic voyages. He donated it to the Canadian people in 1987. Of most interest is the first-floor parlour, now called the Arctic room, which houses the collection of Bartlett memorabilia — photographs, medals, and various awards that honoured this remarkable explorer and his life on Canada's last frontier.

Just a stone's throw from Hawthorne Cottage, behind a white picket fence that stretches along a quiet laneway, stands a pleasant frame structure that once housed two families, both of whom featured prominently in Newfoundland history. On one side lived William and Mary Bartlett, parents of the illustrious explorer. On the other were George Graham and Martha Crosbie, the progenitors of a family as articulate and feisty as were their Scottish ancestors, themselves descendants of Viking marauders and Robert the Bruce.

It was 1840 when Margaret Crosbie, a hardy, forty-nine-year-old woman who took adventure in her stride, set out from Dumfries, Scotland, with her sons, James, John and George. The boys ranged in age from thirteen to five. They were headed for the Miramichi in New Brunswick. Margaret's husband, Thomas, stayed behind, presumably preparing financially for the move and the purchase of a farm. It was three years before he finally joined them in Canada. In time, young James became a farmer, and the other two boys became plasterers. It was his skill in this trade that enabled George Crosbie to make a move to Newfoundland in 1858, establishing himself in a construction and mercantile business, first in Harbour Grace and then in Brigus.

Crosbie arrived in Brigus in buoyant times. The seal industry and the cod fishery seemed to promise limitless prosperity for all. He joined in the boom, supplying food, clothing and provisions from his dry goods store, in spite of what he called the "precarious nature of our fisheries." The Crosbie business grew and with it his family. George and his wife, Martha Ellen Chalker, daughter of an old Brigus family, produced eight children: Margaret, Thomas, Martha Ellen (called "Ellie"), Jennie, Walter, George Lamont, John Chalker and Robert.

By the 1880s, however, Crosbie recognized that the age of the wooden ship and the prosperity of the outports were coming to an end. He took a bold step and, in 1884, moved Martha and their young brood to St. John's, where he bought an old hotel, renamed it the Central, and refurbished it in the latest style. It soon became the most popular spot in town. But when the Great Fire of 1892 virtually destroyed the city, the Central too fell victim. Crosbie immediately started over again — undeterred even when his farmhouse, just outside the city, caught fire a few days later. He built a bigger and better hostelry, the Crosbie Hotel, which boasted such refinements as hot water, electricity and a bathroom on each floor. Three months after his new hotel opened, George Crosbie died at fifty-nine. He had made his mark in St. John's and was greatly admired for his honesty and determination. "He was a kind man," said

RYAN, MARY: Born in County Carlow, Ireland, in 1789, and came to Newfoundland in 1812; widow of Matthew Ryan; died at Spaniard's Bay Jan. 10, 1890, aged 100 years; she left 13 children, 96 grandchildren, 57 great-grandchildren, and 4 great-great grandchildren.

BRIGUS: John and Stephen Whalen drowned in Brigus Pond, January 19, 1908.

This double house was home to William and Mary Bartlett, parents of Captain Bob, and George and Martha Crosbie, who founded a Newfoundland dynasty.

his friend James Murray at Sunnyside, "and popular with all classes." *The Daily News* on March 11, 1895, also lamented the death of the "genial proprietor of the Central Hotel . . . [who had] passed from time to eternity after a short but painful illness."

Near the Crosbie-Bartlett house in Brigus a saltbox perches on the edge of a rock on an elevated site overlooking its neighbours. The house typifies Newfoundland vernacular architecture at its best, but its siting, its soaring two and a half storeys, and its distinctive round-roofed porch set it apart from any other house in town. The present owner points out that this detailing is found elsewhere in Brigus and in the Commissariat in St. John's.

Nothing is known of the builder, James Whalen, nor of the second owner, Dr. Duncan, but a later occupant of the house, J. B. Thompson, achieved notoriety of a sort and attracted the attention of Brigus and beyond when he presided at the trial of a noted American artist and writer, Rockwell Kent. Thompson probably moved into the house in 1895 when he was appointed stipendiary magistrate.

Kent appeared on the scene in 1912, painting and writing about Newfoundland and this village that so captivated him. He was then thirty-two. For much of his life he travelled to remote parts of the world. In 1920 he won fame for an illustrated book on his adventures in Alaska, after which he trav-

elled to the southernmost tip of South America, a journey that resulted in *Voyaging: Southward from the Strait of Magellan* (1924). He was an extraordinarily gifted artist, and his works are in the collections of the Metropolitan Museum of Art in New York City and the Art Institute of Chicago.

In Brigus, Kent bought a small house, Landfall, a Georgian style cottage that had been built for an old local family, the Pomeroys, on a site known as the "Battery," or "Freshwater." The former refers to gun emplacement, the latter to a water source for the sealing fleet. Perhaps it had been both. Kent called it his "sweet little house that rooted on the starved wind-free hillside." He was the first of three artists (the other two, A. E. Harris and Bradley Follensbee) to own the house. Landfall has been extensively renovated over the years.

Kent's stay in Brigus was periodically tempestuous. During his first summer he received a summons to appear in court, accused of assaulting a local justice of the peace, one James Hearn. The trial produced some high courtroom drama. During the proceedings Kent produced pencil and paper and sat sketching the plaintiff, on whom this had an exceedingly unsettling effect. Magistrate J. B. Thompson sternly informed Kent that he was accused of threatening Hearn, and asked him what he had said. Kent replied that he called Hearn "you low-down dirty, chicken-livered cur, you yellow dog, you sneaking crawling slithering reptile, you stinking scurvy skunk." Continuing

The Thompson house, a stately saltbox.

in this vein, and with similar epithets, he paused occasionally to spell the longer words for the judge, whom he described as an "old fool." Kent was fined five dollars.

Kent may have had little respect for Thompson or Hearn, but he had nothing but respect and love for Newfoundland, for what he called its "savage" weather, and its breathtaking beauty. In 1936 he wrote *N. by E.*, a moving account of his stay years before in Brigus when, on the last day of March, the Gale of 1914 brought tragedy to all of Newfoundland:

> Each day of March was like the first but maybe fairer. The sun dried the earth and brought out the green shoots of the grass in the wet lands. I left off my heavy hide boots and danced about light-shod. . . . My house stood out of the town and looked somewhat back upon it over the harbour. I could see the schooners still quiet at their moorings, where the bustle of preparation for the Labrador would soon begin. . . .

But the next day a neighbour looked at the moon and said, "That's a bad moon . . . we'll have weather, for you can hang a powder-horn on it." The storm hit with ferocious intensity, and for two and a half days it raged. "Look into it I could not," Kent wrote, "but glimpses I caught abroad . . . were of whole banks of snow in mid-air carried by the gale." He took refuge with neighbours, waiting out the storm as the terrible tension increased, and realizing then that "storm spells always death for some of the family of the followers of the sea." People crowded the cable office waiting to hear the worst.

But it wasn't until April 4, when the sealer *Bonaventure* entered St. John's harbour carrying scores of frozen bodies and thirty-seven blinded, frostbitten survivors, that the full extent of the disaster became known in Brigus. Kent recalled: "The horror of the news they told, my God! I shall never forget. Last night the entire crew of the steamer *Newfoundland,* one hundred and sixty men, had frozen to death on the ice."

That the actual total turned out to be seventy-seven dead in no way mitigated the terrible loss. People spoke of "tokens," or visions of dead ones, and as Kent wrote, "The drama written in the loss . . . is a world story. It includes all: mother-love, the tale of courtship, of youth, of marriage — it touches the whole gamut of emotion in ten thousand lives."

Avondale and the
Newfie Bullet

♦

CHAPTER 10

The Avondale Railroad Station and the Newfie Bullet

The first run of the *Newfie Bullet* took place in January 1882, across the eighty-four blustery miles between St. John's and Harbour Grace. The last run (when the rail line stretched west to Port aux Basques) was in September 1988. In the intervening hundred and six years there was conflict enough for governments to rise and fall over a project that, while highly desirable to most Newfoundlanders, faced daunting obstacles. That it was built at all was largely due to the efforts of one man who accomplished the near impossible.

The second half of the nineteenth century was the age of railroads. In North America, a Scottish engineer, Sir Robert Gillespie Reid, played a major role in their construction. Reid had already made his mark as a railroad builder, and was highly regarded in his field when, in 1890, he agreed to tackle Newfoundland's faltering railroad project.

By the time he took over, the most active part of Reid's life lay behind him. While still in his twenties he had prospected for gold and built viaducts in Australia, married in New Zealand, returned to Scotland, and then, in 1871, settled in Canada. Two years later he brought his wife, Harriet Duff, and their children to live in Galt (Cambridge), Ontario, while he worked on a host of railway and bridge-building projects. Reid's remarkable achievements included the International Bridge at Fort Erie, bridges along the Ottawa River, bridges for the transcontinental railways in the United States and for the Canadian Pacific line, bridges along Lake Superior, tunnels and bridges in the Canadian Rockies, and the bridge at Grand Narrows in Cape Breton. The first complete rail line he built was the line to Sault Ste. Marie. Reid was known as dependable, ethical and creative. He became famous — and rich — for his ability to surmount seemingly impossible geographical construction problems.

FACING PAGE:
Where the Newfie Bullet *once sped by, headed for Channel-Port aux Basques.*

PREVIOUS PAGE:
Avondale railroad station.

The construction of Newfoundland's railway had been lurching slowly along, ever since Sandford Fleming financed the first survey in 1868. In spite of general enthusiasm for the line, and the support of Newfoundland prime ministers Frederick Carter, William Whiteway and Robert Thorburn, the project was tremendously expensive and progress was minimal. By 1884, the firm that had initially undertaken the job had gone bankrupt.

But Newfoundlanders wanted to see the railroad completed so that their island and its scattered, isolated communities could be knit together. One writer of the time claimed it would be the panacea for all of Newfoundland's problems, including, in some mysterious way, its social and political inequities. "In time," he enthused, "it will kill out the old abuses of the out-harbours; the isolation, the outrageous prices — all will die away before the magic influence of the iron road . . . and in a few years [it will] change the moral, social and commercial conditions of the Colony." And if it could not erase all of society's problems, the railroad would certainly please the colony's merchants, miners, sportsmen, tourists, furriers and lumbermen.

By 1890, when Reid took over, only the stretch between St. John's and Harbour Grace had been completed. His company (Reid himself was then living in Montreal, with only occasional summer visits to Newfoundland) began the daunting task of continuing the line across the island's rocky, densely forested interior. For $15,600 per mile (payable in Newfoundland government bonds), Reid and his sons finished the job, despite all the problems that the terrain could pose and the elements could hurl at them. Perhaps the most challenging section was the entry to Trinity. Here was constructed the Trinity Loop. Like a modern highway overpass, the track went over a bridge, around a curve, and off in the other direction. Completed in 1898, it chugged along for more than 560 miles from St. John's to Channel-Port aux Basques, in something less than speedy style, hence the affectionate name, the *Newfie Bullet*.

On June 29, 1898, a group of excited passengers boarded the train in St. John's. They arrived twenty-eight hours later at Port aux Basques on the western tip of the island.

Politics, as ever, became part of the story. When the rail link to Port aux Basques was completed, Reid signed a contract to run the line for fifty years. His company would also take over operation of the coastal steamship service and run (and eventually purchase) the government telegraph line — giving it a virtual monopoly in transportation and communications. Controversy erupted when the conditions of the agreement became known — the government of James Winter and the receiver-general, A. B. Morine, had signed the contract while, at the same time, Morine was on retainer as Reid's lawyer. A classic conflict-of-interest brouhaha ensued. With a change of government and another look at the contract, the document was renegotiated in 1901.

Although much of the negotiations had been handled by Reid's sons (see Devon Place, page 150), and in particular the mercurial William, Reid's reputation in Newfoundland suffered in the aftermath of the controversy. His sons, in spite of his instructions, had become increasing embroiled in Newfoundland politics, and although removed from the scene himself, much of the antipathy rubbed off on him. Robert Reid was knighted in 1907, and made his last trip to the island that summer. He died in Montreal on June 3, the following year.

In spite of political machinations and an ever-increasing debt, the line continued to expand, but it needed continual government bailouts. In 1949, after Newfoundland became Canada's tenth province, the rail line became part of Canadian National Railways. After Confederation, highways were built in every direction (it was said that if you didn't watch where you were going, you might get paved over) and they proved to be the downfall of the railway. Trains were abandoned. Four years after the 1965 completion of the Trans-Canada Highway across Newfoundland, the *Newfie Bullet* made its last passenger run. It continued to carry freight until 1988 when it ceased operation.

At best the railway was a mixed blessing. It failed to open up the island as its backers had predicted, and there were other unforeseen, disastrous developments. David Macfarlane, in *The Danger Tree*, wrote, "From the time the trains began to run, the middle of the island was on fire." The locomotives' boilers, heated with fireboxes stoked with Welsh coal, spewed sparks all along its route, "tiny points of red, drifting heat . . . [that] floated like fireflies on the winds the trains made." Newfoundland, with sixteen thousand square miles of timber, watched forest fires that burned for months. "Sometimes it seemed as if the entire world was in flames." The railway was replaced by bus service in the late 1960s.

Happily, however, there is another chapter to the story, and new activity is occurring along the Bullet's old right-of-way. The line has been incorporated as the eastern, and perhaps most challenging, section of the Trans-Canada Trail. The opening is planned to coincide with the 500th anniversary of John Cabot's landing in Newfoundland.

When the Newfoundland railroad was being built, stations, of course, were needed and any suitable building, hotel, or private home was conscripted into service. In Avondale, a small town only thirty-six miles north of St. John's, one building was ideally suited for that purpose. It would serve the whole of Conception Bay north.

In the late 1800s, the Anglo Newfoundland Company had built a telegraph station at Avondale (named for Avondale in County Wicklow, Eire) to serve as a land-line to Heart's Content. It was the first known land-line telegraph station serving St. John's, and was in a key position on the line from St. John's to Clarenville.

Before standard station designs came into common use (many of them designed by Reid's friend, Sir Sandford Fleming), ingenuity produced some quite delightful elaborate structures, and where fancy was given free rein, the result could be quite startling. In Placentia, for instance, an elevated site was selected and the building adorned with a sizable turret, presenting a startling appearance on first glimpse, and giving passengers the impression that they were coming to a stop at the local castle. The Avondale station, on the other hand, was built in the Empire style, a two-storey frame building with a broad-eaved mansard roof and a small gable.

The Avondale building was taken over by Reid and the Newfoundland Railway around 1900. At Confederation in 1949 it became the property of the Canadian National Railways, serving until the line ceased operation. It was reopened in 1990 as the Avondale Railroad Station Museum. Avondale was the last of the many stations that welcomed the *Newfie Bullet* as it bumped its way across the province, the symbol of a dream that never quite lived up to expectations. Intended as a means of uniting Newfoundland, it ended up pulling it in opposite directions — the people on the eastern end of the line looking to Europe, and those at the western terminal to Canada and the United States.

St. John's

CHAPTER 11

St. John's: Soldiers and Clergy

In 1819, St. John's, with a population of more than 40,000, was coming into its own. The Napoleonic Wars were over, increasing numbers of merchants were setting up businesses in town, and since St. John's was the only community in Newfoundland with an educated and fairly wealthy middle class, some were leaving the outports to enjoy the relative comforts of town.

During the middle years of the century, the Commissariat, on the west side of King's Bridge Road, was at the centre of business and military activity in St. John's. Built in 1819, it is a dignified, unadorned Georgian building, thought to have been a near replica of the neighbouring home of Thomas Forth Winter, the assistant commissary general (1808–16), and his family. Construction of the building didn't begin, however, until after Winter's departure from the island, so it was a successor who was able to enjoy the amenities of the new building. With offices on the main floor and spacious living quarters above, the Commissariat, fittingly enough, looked east toward Fort William, and north to the home of the commanding officer of the Royal Engineers. At some point in the ensuing years, an enclosed two-storey portico was added to the façade in an attempt to provide protection from blasts of easterly winds off the ocean.

The assistant commissary general was one of the most important officials in the colony. The post was held by a civilian working with the forces stationed there, and he was responsible for supplying food and other goods to the garrison, for contracting, and for the military's pay. (One to occupy the post, from 1848 to 1853, was Oliver Goldsmith, a New Brunswick-born poet, the grandnephew and namesake of the renowned British poet.)

When the military withdrew in 1870, the Commissariat was taken over by the Newfoundland government. Two years later, suitable new occupants were found: it was leased to nearby St. Thomas' Church, a place of worship for the St. John's establishment. The Commissariat was to become a rectory.

St. Thomas' and the Commissariat had been linked since the church was opened in 1836 as the parish church of the British garrison, but while it was intended for use by the military, St. Thomas' was, from its beginning,

FACING PAGE:

The Commissariat, headquarters of St. John's military establishment.

PREVIOUS PAGE:

Methodist United Church, St. John's.

embroiled in Newfoundland's religious and political squabbles. A simple list of the clergymen who served at St. Thomas' gives no inkling of the animosities and intrigues that constituted the history of this and other churches in nineteenth-century Newfoundland. Life as a Newfoundland clergyman was not a profession for the faint-hearted.

The construction of St. Thomas' owed much to the labours of Edward Wix, a seemingly energetic and idealistic young priest who arrived in St. John's in 1830 and left, eight years later, "secretly and hurriedly, in a manner that both surprised and appalled the members of the church."

Born in Essex, England, in 1802, Wix earned a BA from Trinity College, Oxford, in 1824 and was ordained the following year. In 1826 he arrived in Halifax, but was back in England in less than two years to recover from a bout of typhus. There he married a Miss Brown and, that same year, the young couple returned to Nova Scotia. They were immediately transferred to Newfoundland, first to Bonavista, then to St. John's.

Wix worked diligently in St. John's. He helped organize temperance societies, was appointed to the town's board of education, and was active in the Society for Promoting Christian Knowledge. Most of all, he was an effective fund-raiser. A trip to England in 1833 resulted in enough money to build a garrison church in St. John's.

In 1835, a year before St. Thomas' was completed, Archdeacon Wix left on a six month foray to the outports, where he ministered to the needy. And from what Wix confided to his journal, the people of Newfoundland needed all the help he could offer. He was repeatedly shocked, he noted, by the material, moral and spiritual destitution he encountered everywhere. On the Isle of Valen, for example, he found "females dirty and almost naked." It was necessary therefore for baptisms to be held in homes, as the mothers lacked proper clothes to wear to church. On the French Shore, at Bay of Islands, a dissolute lifestyle, drunken orgies, and incest appeared to be the order of the day. "Profanity," wrote Wix, "is the dialect." And everywhere, anchored in the bay, were the "grog ships." On the positive side, he noted that the Catholics in Placentia were a friendly lot — compared, he said, to those in St. John's. Wix subscribed to the popular stereotype that the Irish were morally inferior, but his opinions may also have reflected his fund-raising interests — that is, the blacker the picture painted, the more money needed for missions.

It's anyone's guess what happened to the good archdeacon after his return to St. John's. Although St. Thomas' opened its doors the following September, within two years, in October 1838, Wix, by then in poor health, disappeared from the scene. According to a local historian, he left his wife and children behind. He was in debt to the tune of more than £1,000, and had been seen in the company of a prostitute.

Wix never returned to Newfoundland though, in spite of continuing ill health, he lived for another twenty-eight years. After "resting" in England until

St. Thomas' Church, Military Road.

GRAND JURY: First Grand Jury of Newfoundland sworn in April 12, 1826 . . found True Bill against [Capt.] Mark Rudkin, James Shachan and George F. Morrice for the murder of [Ensign] John Philpot in a duel which was fought on Robinson's Hill to the east of Rennie's Mill.

SISTERS OF MERCY: First arrived in Newfoundland, June 19, 1842; opened their first school in a wooden convents building adjoining the Cathedral, May 1, 1843; new stone convent built by Bishop Mullock and opened Sept. 29, 1857.

1843, he took a parish in Middlesex, then another, but resigned in 1850, again due to failing health. His next fourteen years, according to biographer Frederick Jones, were spent "nursing his health in Madeira, Italy, the Riviera, Algiers and Malta, while occasionally contributing to the *Gentleman's Magazine and the Church Review.*" Wix returned to England in 1866, and died at the age of sixty-four on the Isle of Wight, in his son's parish at Swanmore.

Few Newfoundlanders faced more daunting challenges than the man who built St. Thomas', now the oldest surviving church building in St. John's. He was Patrick Kough, an Irishman, said to have been the finest builder in the colony. The governor of the day, Thomas Cochrane, through whose auspices the land for St. Thomas' was acquired, described Kough as "one of the most respectable men in St. John's, an efficient member of the assembly, and the most trustworthy builder in town." Undoubtedly this was why the managing

FIRE AT ST. JOHN'S: Jan. 9, 1846 — property loss four million dollars.

CHRISTIAN BROTHERS: First came to Newfoundland in October, 1876; original band consisted of Rev. Bros. F. L. Holland, Prenderville and Mitchell. Mount St. Francis, home of Christian Brothers in Newfoundland, cornerstone laid Sept.9, 1877.

FIRE AT ST. JOHN'S: July 8, 1892 — 1,700 buildings destroyed, 11,000 homeless; property loss a million and a half dollars.

committee for the proposed St. Thomas' Church chose this particular Catholic as their builder.

Kough did not disappoint the committee. St. Thomas' was and is an aesthetic delight. Built of native spruce and pine, it contained two separate galleries, one for the troops and the other for the military élite and the parish's first families, including the governor. The church's dominating feature was its imposing tower, a landmark and the focal point of early paintings.

The building eventually attracted the attention of the British High Church *Ecclesiologist,* which, looking down its ecclesiastical nose twelve years later, gave St. Thomas' a backhanded compliment in noting that the marble altar and font that Wix had obtained from Italy were the "only attempts at ritual solemnity — nay decency — which the whole island, till a very recent period, possessed." It was a remark not atypical in colonial society, where those living in relative comfort at home frequently failed to understand the trials faced by their colleagues in the far-flung colonies

A native of County Wexford, Kough set sail from Ireland and landed in St. John's as a lad of eighteen, unskilled and with little formal education. He worked first as a carpenter, then as a contractor, and over the years supervised the construction of many of St. John's finest buildings. In 1830 he built the handsome stone courthouse and jail in Harbour Grace, work that landed him a contract to repair the roof of the newly built Government House and, two years later, one to build St. Thomas' Church. At about the same time, he erected for himself a substantial stone house (now a restaurant), some distance north of St. Thomas', at the foot of Kenna's Hill.

An early watercolour of St. Thomas' Church — the garrison church, built with the support of Governor Thomas Cochrane.

But though his professional life was successful, Kough was running into obstacles on political and theological fronts. His problems with Newfoundland's religious factions stemmed, not from differences with Protestants, but from his own Roman Catholic church and, in particular, with its bishop. In 1832, he ran for a seat in the Assembly representing St. John's and won, despite opposition from his bishop, Michael Fleming, who rejected his candidature and regarded him as an "Orange Catholic." Four years later, when Kough attempted reelection, the Catholic opposition had become so bitter that he was denied the right of attending church and the use of the sacraments. On election day, Kough resigned, claiming intimidation. He was by then fifty years old and the father of eight, so he may well have decided that political life was not worth the price he was paying — although he continued to serve on the Roman Catholic Board of Education. His outside interests turned to gentler pursuits as he developed a large farm called Ken Mount on the outskirts of St. John's. When he died at seventy-seven, an obituary in the *Newfoundlander* praised his "probity and consistency of conduct."

The pejorative label "Orange Catholic" may well have resulted from Kough's amicable relations with the St. John's establishment. Certainly the building management committee at Anglican St. Thomas' felt comfortable with their Roman Catholic builder — and those three gentlemen were decidedly among the city's élite. The committee comprised Edward Mortimer Archibald, attorney general (the likely builder of Retreat Cottage); distinguished merchant William Thomas (builder of the double house at King's Bridge and Forest Roads); and Hugh William Hoyles, lawyer, judge, politician and, during the middle years of the century, one of St. John's most influential men.

Interior, the Commissariat.

Front entrance, the Commissariat, King's Bridge Road.

Hoyles's family connections were impressive. Although born in St. John's, he was packed off to Nova Scotia's prestigious Pictou Academy for his education, then later took his legal training under Samuel George William Archibald, attorney general of Nova Scotia — and father of Hoyles's colleague, Edward Mortimer Archibald, who held the equivalent post in Newfoundland. (Local opinion suggests that Hoyles was a member of the first building committee at St. Thomas', though he was only twenty-two years old in 1836, the year that the church was completed. Biographer Frederick Jones suggests that Hoyles returned to St. John's "sometime before 1842.")

In any event, Hoyles was active in church concerns for most of his life, and involved in politics and education as well. He initially fought to establish denominational schools but in his later years came to see the "danger of religion in politics." (The subject still raises the hackles of Newfoundlanders today.) Hoyles became chief justice of Newfoundland in 1865, and was knighted by Queen Victoria three years later. When he died in 1888, the *Royal Gazette* eulogized, in the flowery language of the day: "His name had become a synonym for uprightness and integrity, and is respected, one might say revered, beyond that of any other native of the Colony."

With so many prominent local men active in the affairs of St. Thomas', it would not be surprising had the guest preacher at the official opening of the church believed that professional advancement might be near at hand. But it was not to be. The Reverend Charles Blackman had first come to Newfoundland in 1819 as a tutor to the son of Governor Charles Hamilton, but he continually encountered difficulties in obtaining the church postings he wanted. He was in Port de Grave when St. Thomas' invited him to preach at

The rear gardens, the Commissariat.

its opening service in 1836, but it was another two years before he was able to move to St. John's, where, in 1841, he was named principal of the Theological Institute. The next year he became perpetual curate to St. Thomas', but this did not satisfy Blackman's ambition. A devoted evangelical and charismatic speaker, Blackman's ambition was to become the bishop of Newfoundland.

Again his hopes were dashed. Edward Feild, appointed bishop in 1843, soon took a dislike to Blackman, declaring him to be incompetent and a liar — sentiments that, not surprisingly, antagonized the clergyman. Soon open conflict flared. Feild dismissed Blackman as principal of the Theological Institute, prompting Blackman to join forces with causes to which Feild was particularly opposed. Gradually, St. Thomas' became the place of worship for those who disagreed with Bishop Feild — they were the conservative merchants who, with the support of Roman Catholic clergy, campaigned for responsible government in the colony. Blackman died in 1853 a sorely disappointed man, embittered by what he deemed to be his own professional failure.

Door, St. Thomas'.

St. Thomas' survived the gales from without and within and grew over the years. Ten years after the church was opened, Newfoundland's weather had taken its toll. Wings had to be added to stabilize it after the Great Gale of 1846 moved the entire building six inches. To accommodate an increasing number of parishioners, the church was lengthened by thirty feet in 1874, enlarged again in 1883 and 1903 (at which point it could seat 1,300), and has been maintained in splendid condition to this day.

Interior, St. Thomas'.

CHAPTER 12

St. John's: The Governors

Governor Thomas Cochrane.

There was one other man without whose help St. Thomas' might not have been built — and he happened to be the most powerful man in the colony. Thomas John Cochrane was the first resident governor of Newfoundland. (Before this a succession of forty-one naval governors tried to cope with the instructions that came with the job — to maintain peace, protect fishing, oversee the judicial system, enforce laws and international treaties, and appoint officials, all of this during a brief summer's visit to the colony.)

It was through Governor Cochrane's influence that this lovely little church came to be built. He acquired the land on which it would stand, his only proviso being that it be reserved for use by the garrison. Somehow it does not seem coincidental that the church was named St. Thomas'.

Cochrane, however, was anything but saintly. Appointed to the post in 1825 at age thirty-six, he had already spent an astonishing twenty-nine years in the service of the Royal Navy. This lengthy "service" had more than a little to do with nepotism. When he was seven, his father, Sir Alexander Forrester Inglis Cochrane, had entered Thomas's name on the books of his ship *Thetis*, as a "volunteer." He kept his son under his command until 1805 when Thomas, by then sixteen, was promoted to lieutenant on the *Jason*. He was made its captain the following year.

Cochrane was to the manner born. His privileged background, along with his many years of command in the senior service, had instilled in him a taste for fine living. And when he found himself in a ragged, scruffy seaport at the far reaches of the empire, the situation did nothing to dampen his love of opulence and comfort. He simply brought his luxuries with him — enough furnishings, it was said, to equip a palace. All he needed was the palace in which to house them, and that was not long in coming.

The vice-regal residence that Cochrane built on Military Road (just west of where St. Thomas' rose a few years later) was a monument to his ambition and a dominating statement of the British presence. While the exterior of the

FACING PAGE:
Government House, Military Road. Estimated cost was £8,778; when completed in 1831, the final price was £36,000. Some things never change.

mansion resembles a relatively plain English country house writ large, its interior is indeed superb, with large, gracious rooms and a splendid freestanding stone staircase. It was large, it looked important, and it was, most certainly, expensive. Very expensive. Originally estimated to cost £8,778, Government House, when it was finished in 1831, cost an astounding £36,000 — more than four times what had been officially approved. And most of this increase was due to the frequent alterations demanded by the governor during its construction, and his champagne tastes.

The authorities were furious, and set up a court of inquiry. One can only imagine their reaction when, within a year or two of its completion, the roof of this expensive new building blew off in a windstorm. The dependable Patrick Kough, who had just finished building the courthouse in Harbour Grace, was retained to rectify the situation.

Cochrane was (his predilection for luxury and reckless spending aside) an able administrator, and during his tenure he brought about significant political and judicial advancements in the colony. His last two or three years in St. John's, however, brought him into constant conflict with squabbling legislators, and into the fray of the ongoing clash between religion and politics. He was eventually removed from office. It may have been with some relief that he left the colony in 1834. But in any event, his career was unimpaired. Home in England he became a Conservative MP. In 1841 he was promoted to rear admiral, then became admiral of the fleet in 1865. Historians saw him in a kinder light than did his contemporaries. Judge Daniel Woodley Prowse, in the latter part of the nineteenth century, wrote: "Cochrane is now universally admitted to have been the best Governor ever sent to Newfoundland."

Governor John Harvey.

The governors who followed Cochrane were a succession of men whose chief qualifications in many cases appeared to be wealth, a military background, a desire to put their own stamp on the colony, and a natural unsuitability for the job. These dignitaries sought, with limited success, to deal with Newfoundland's sectarian animosities and never-ending and bitter political disputes. More often than not, when the time came for them to depart for England or for a similar position in warmer climes, there were no tears shed on either side.

Henry Prescott, who occupied Government House after Cochrane, was the last of Newfoundland's nineteenth-century naval governors. His term of office lasted for seven turbulent years. Prescott, according to biographer Frederick F. Thompson, was defeated before he entered the fray, for "It was scarcely possible for the new governor to set a foot in the right place in a colony where Anglo-Irish quarrels were complicated by Catholic-Protestant enmity, and which was embittered by disagreements between merchants and fishermen and by West Country versus native rivalry for office." With some relief he resigned in 1842 and returned to naval life. He never looked back. By the end of his career he had been named Lord of the Admiralty. Still later he attained the rank of Admiral of the Blue, and finally received a knighthood.

After Prescott came the only colonial governor to serve in all four of the Atlantic colonies — first Prince Edward Island, then New Brunswick. Newfoundland came next and, finally, Nova Scotia. Sir John Harvey was an able and popular administrator, and a man who was readily noticed. One contemporary who recalled seeing him before he left for North America described him in snide terms as a "large, handsome man, but by far the most vulgar would-be-gentleman you ever beheld, extremely dressy withal, and my lord always remembered my asking 'Who was the gentleman with the embroidered stomach.'"

Governor John Le Marchant.

John Harvey, a highly principled man, found his years in Newfoundland to be fraught with difficulties, not the least of which was a continuing struggle to make financial ends meet. The governor was not born to wealth. His rise in the military had not been bought, but earned through hard work and courage in the field. But this lack of a private income presented problems in fulfilling the social obligations of his position. When he left Fredericton, Harvey was forced to sell much of his furniture to repay his debts (the sheriff there had seized his silver plate for a long-standing private debt in England). One can imagine the practical difficulties facing him when he and his family arrived in St. John's in September 1841, and moved into Government House, only to find that he was expected to purchase Prescott's furniture. To make matters worse, his salary was to be £1,000 a year less than the £3,000 yearly that he had been paid in New Brunswick.

It proved to be a very tough posting for the Harveys. Along with the unending sectarian conflicts, and the death early in 1846 of the youngest of their five sons (the eldest had died during the Harveys' New Brunswick years), the governor continued to be plagued with financial problems. And, according to his biographer, Phillip Buckner, Harvey found the frigid winters "nearly unbearable." Little wonder he jumped at the chance to leave Newfoundland, and did so that same year "with almost unseemly haste," when he was appointed lieutenant-governor of Nova Scotia.

Harvey's successor was the highly unpopular John Gaspard Le Marchant, who arrived in St. John's in April 1847, less than a year after the Great Fire of 1846 left 12,000 of the town's 19,000 people homeless. Le Marchant and, presumably, his wife, Margaret Anne, and their children moved into Government House, vacated the year before by the Harveys.

The new governor's first love was the army, and it is probable that he took the posting as governor solely to advance his military ambitions. He was not the administrator that his predecessor had been, nor did he possess Harvey's diplomatic skills. He let it be known that he had little use for local merchants who stayed in Newfoundland long enough to exploit its opportunities then scurried back to England with their profits. The merchants, needless to say, were not amused. Le Marchant was equally outspoken about

HOUSE OF ASSEMBLY:
First session ever held in
Newfoundland opened by
Governor Sir Thomas
Cochrane, Jan. 1, 1833,
comprised 15 members . . .
first session held at the
house situated on the
corner of Duckworth St.
and King's Road, of Mary
Travers, who later on
seized all the furniture
and fittings in payment of
rent due her.

EXECUTIONS IN
NEWFOUNDLAND:
Mrs. J. Snow of Port de
Grave was hanged from
the window of the old
courthouse which stood
on the site of the present
museum building, July
21, 1834; murdered
her husband; her two
accomplices Arthur Spring
and Tobias Manderville,
were executed January
1833.

CHOLERA EPIDEMIC:
Outbreak of cholera
occurred in St. John's in
October 1854 and the
disease was not wiped out
until the end of the year;
212 cases of cholera and
88 deaths during the three
months of the epidemic.

DIPHTHERIA
EPIDEMIC: Swept St.
John's in 1860; thousand
victims.

people on welfare who looked to government for handouts — an attitude that failed to endear him to people recovering from the devastating fire and coping with the second year of a potato blight similar to that in Ireland. These people, the governor stated firmly, should learn self-reliance.

Le Marchant himself was able to remain self-reliant, in part because of his own private income. Throughout his stay, he entertained lavishly at Government House. According to historian P. B. Waite, "Over and above his £3,000 income, [Le Marchant] spent some £4,000 to £5,000 outfitting himself for his North American missions and another £5,000 from his private purse for dinners and parties in the colonies."

The governor may have had his failings, but he was not without a sense of humour. Paul O'Neill writes, in *The Oldest City*, that shortly before Le Marchant left Newfoundland in the summer of 1852, an enraged crowd hanged him in effigy. When the procession reached the top of Cochrane Street where the effigy was to be burned, Le Marchant emerged from Government House to look carefully at the effigy and make sure that "his aquiline nose had been properly reproduced."

Le Marchant's career took him next to Nova Scotia, where he served as a lieutenant-governor, then to Malta and Madras, where he was commander-in-chief from 1865 to 1868. Knighted in 1865, he retired to England and died in London in 1874.

When Le Marchant left Newfoundland he was followed by another soldier and colonial administrator — and a governor who was undoubtedly the wrong man, in the wrong place, at the worst possible time. Newfoundlanders may well have looked back on Le Marchant's tenure with less animosity than before when the aristocratic Ker Baillie Hamilton moved into Government House with his wife, Emma Blair, and their daughters.

An evangelical Anglican who distrusted Roman Catholics, Baillie Hamilton was unprepared for the religious animosities that fuelled Newfoundland's politics, and so his arrival in 1852 as the Catholic-led Liberals campaigned for responsible government was, at best, ill-timed. Before long he was also feuding, not only with Catholics, but with the High Church Anglican establishment, siding with the evangelical element at St. Thomas' in their conflict with Bishop Feild. They quarrelled over several issues, among them the thorny question of who was to be Reverend Charles Blackman's successor. They also argued about the bishop's refusal of sacraments to those who failed to support the church financially, and the appointment of certain clergymen whom Feild refused to license. No doubt few tears were shed on either side when, three years after his arrival, Baillie Hamilton was dispatched to milder climes. He spent the next twelve years as governor of Antigua and the Leeward Islands, then retired to Tunbridge Wells and died there in 1889.

The next occupant of Government House was Charles Henry Darling, another colonial diplomat with a military background. Born in Annapolis

Royal, Nova Scotia, he was the only Canadian to serve as governor of Newfoundland. (Darling remains the only vice-regal representative in Newfoundland's history to be born in Canada, since to this date all were born before 1949, when Newfoundland became Canada's tenth province.)

Darling had been sent to effect damage control and to smooth the way for responsible government, a task made particularly difficult due to his predecessor's stiff-necked intransigence. Here was a man with ample diplomatic skills, and splendid military and social connections. He had served with his regiment in Australia, where an uncle, Ralph Darling, was governor of New South Wales. After further education at the Royal Military College in England, he was posted to Barbados and then to Jamaica. In 1841 he retired from the military, became agent general for immigration in Jamaica under Lord Elgin, served twice as governor of St. Lucia and then in 1854, briefly, as governor of Cape Colony (South Africa). That same year, Darling was named governor of Antigua, but before he could take over that post, he was asked to proceed to Newfoundland, where a man with his experience was needed immediately. He landed in St. John's in 1855.

Darling's private life had not gone as smoothly as had his professional career. By the time he moved into Government House, he was forty-six years old and had already been married three times. The first two wives had died. His third wife was Elizabeth Isabella Caroline Salter. She, presumably, accompanied him to St. John's, to enjoy the comforts and challenges offered to the residents of Government House.

Darling announced the inauguration of responsible government soon after his arrival in Newfoundland. All went relatively smoothly for a time, but within a year or so he was embroiled in the unending problems of the fishery on Newfoundland's west coast, where the French had claimed exclusive rights for the better part of a century. The flare-up in 1856 was more than Darling could deal with, and he left the colony in February of the following year to become governor of Jamaica. Darling's final appointment was as governor of Victoria, Australia. He was knighted in 1865, and died in England five years later.

The next couple to make their home in Government House were Sir Alexander and Lady Bannerman. They arrived in the summer of 1857 after honing their diplomatic skills for six years in Prince Edward Island, where Sir Alexander had been governor. Most historians agree that Margaret Gordon Bannerman was the more interesting and certainly the more intelligent of the pair, a woman remembered today due to her youthful involvement with Thomas Carlyle.

Born in 1798 on Prince Edward Island, where her grandfather, Walter Patterson, had served as the island's first lieutenant-governor, Margaret moved at a young age to Scotland. She met the young Carlyle in Kirkcaldy when she was nineteen, but rather than marry him, chose her distant cousin, "Sandy" Bannerman, a thirty-seven-year-old Scot described by Carlyle as a "rich

SNOW, JOHN: Resident of Harbor Grace, killed by blow delivered by Terrence Butt of Carbonear; verdict of "wilful murder" against Butt by Coroner's Jury, February 5, 1862; Butt, arrested at ship Harbor, Placentia Bay, was jailed at St. John's and afterwards acquitted of murder charge by St. John's jury.

JOURNEAUX, MISS:. Driven out of Jersey in open boat, without oars, April 18, 1886; was brought into Bay St. George, May 15, 1886 by French vessel, which picked her up in the Atlantic; arrived in St. John's on the S.S. *Curlew*, May 24, 1886; left for England June 2, 1886.

CHILDREN'S FESTIVAL: In connection with the Coronation of King George V and Queen Mary, held at Government House grounds under the patronage of H.E. Sir R. Williams, K.C.M.G., June 25, 1911, with 5,000 children present.

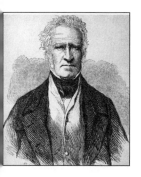

Governor Alexander Bannerman.

insignificant Aberdeen Mr. Somebody." Carlyle was heartbroken when Margaret married Bannerman, later writing of her in his autobiography: "The first love which is infinite can be followed by no second like unto it."

The Bannermans' 1825 marriage was a significant advantage to his career, which until then had been noted mainly for its failures. By the time they reached Newfoundland, Bannerman was in his late sixties, Margaret in her mid-fifties. In spite of his wife's bright mind (she had no real power, of course), Sir Alexander soon found himself in political hot water. He assumed that extensive power and responsibility went with his office, and so leapt right into the tussle of factional disputes. He was, however, no match for the tenacious, rancorous politicians struggling with the first years of responsible government, nor for the petition by some 8,000 Catholics indicting him for constitutional despotism. He retired at age seventy-six in 1864, and died in England later that same year. Lady Bannerman lived for another fourteen years, but in reduced circumstances, because her husband "had never been careful with his personal finances."

(Bannerman House, at 54 Circular Road, is one of the oldest houses in St. John's, but no one really knows where the name originated, for neither the governor nor his lady ever lived in the house. In all likelihood the name was derived from Bannerman Park, which abuts the house. The park was a gift to the city from the governor.)

After the Bannermans came Anthony Musgrave (later Sir Anthony), a governor described by one writer as a man with a "distinguished career in colonial service," and by another as someone with "no steady purpose in life save that of amusing himself." Paul O'Neill relates that Musgrave and his private secretary, Captain Mesham, were "exceedingly partial to the ladies." He quotes Alex A. Parsons as saying that Musgrave was a "man without scruples, without a due sense of moral rectitude, without principles . . . he was an evil element in our society." No such flaws are included in Musgrave's profile in the *Dictionary of Canadian Biography*, in which Kent M. Haworth describes him as a man with "great administrative abilities" who saw the solution to the colony's economic, social, and political problems in a confederation with the British North American colonies. The truth likely lies somewhere between the two extremes.

Musgrave was a widower when he came to govern Newfoundland. (His wife, Christiana Elizabeth Byam, had died five years earlier.) It is possible, therefore, that "ladies" were indeed entertained at Government House. Perhaps it would be surprising if this were not the case. Tragedy struck again in the early summer of 1868 when his son (one of two children born to Christiana), died, leaving Musgrave disconsolate. The following year he left to become governor of British Columbia with the mandate to unite this colony with Canada. He married again in 1870. His bride this time was Jeanie Lucinda Field, and presumably she accompanied him to later postings as governor of Natal, South Australia, Jamaica, and Queensland. His administrative abilities would appear to have been exceptional. As for his personal life, we shall never know.

Musgrave's successor, Stephen John Hill, landed in the summer of 1869, after a military and diplomatic career that had taken him to India, Africa and the Caribbean. A man of "embarrassing energy," he found himself in the midst of a heated political uproar about confederation with Canada, a proposition that the new governor decidedly favoured. What he did not favour, nor really understand, was the concept of responsible government. And his opinion of the electorate did little to change his mind on that subject. "The mass of voters in this Colony," he wrote, "are an ignorant, lawless prejudiced body, the Majority of whom living as they do in Outports in almost a primitive state of existence are unfit subjects for educated and intellectual men to attempt to reason with on the advantages of Confederation."

Hill was, however, above all a pragmatist, and he learned to accept Newfoundland's political realities. By the time he reached the end of his term in 1876 and retired to England, Sir Stephen (he was knighted in 1874) had come to be known as a genial companion, liked and trusted by politicians and merchants alike. It was no mean accomplishment.

Newfoundland's next governor was Sir John Hawley Glover, a capable diplomat with a successful career as a naval officer and colonial administrator behind him. At the time of his marriage to Elizabeth Rosetta Scott in November 1876, he was forty-seven years old and had been governor of Newfoundland for only a few months. His new wife happily settled into her role as first lady. The two of them travelled frequently across the island, visiting remote outports, meeting the inhabitants, and generally getting acquainted with the people he was governing. In 1878, accompanied by geologist Alexander Murray and historian Moses Harvey, he took a two-month trip across the island, a jaunt recorded by the prolific Harvey the following year in *Across Newfoundland with the Governor*. By the end of his term in 1881, he knew more about the colony than many of its ministers.

Glover's successor, Sir Henry Berkeley Fitz-Hardinge Maxse, arrived in the autumn of 1881, but died in Government House in 1883. Glover was recalled by Premier Carter to deal with the colony's pressing political and religious tensions. His arrival was greeted with enthusiasm, for he was one governor who had truly enjoyed the respect of Newfoundland's people. As historian Daniel Woodley Prowse remarked, "No more honourable, generous, kind-hearted, or active ruler ever presided over our government." Glover died in London, England, in 1885, and a monument to his memory was erected in St. Paul's Cathedral, London. A replica of that monument was placed in the Anglican Cathedral of St. John the Baptist in St. John's (the cathedral was completed during his second term).

The next governor to find himself in the midst of Newfoundland's continuing religious squabbles was, as it happened, an atheist — and a man with a mind of his own. Sir George William des Voeux sailed into St. John's in 1886,

Governor Anthony Musgrave.

BLAND & TOBIN
100 Barrels prime Irish
PORK, per
Blandford from Cork
And of former
Importations
40 Puncheons RUM
40 Ditto MOLASSES
30 Hhds. Muscovado
SUGAR
100 Frikins Prime
Cumberland BUTTER
The Newfoundlander,
February 23, 1837

in the midst of the uproar resulting from Sir Ambrose Shea's aborted tenure as governor. Shea's dismissal had outraged the colony's Catholic majority, so it was unlikely that the appointment of any outsider would have mollified them. Des Voeux, of Huguenot descent, believed that "all religions were more or less mistaken." Consequently, he took an even-handed but surprising approach to his new post, and attended a different church every Sunday. This did not, initially at least, endear him to the fractious Newfoundlanders, but he eventually won their grudging respect, thanks to his support of Newfoundland's position in its fishery dispute with France.

Des Voeux and his wife, Marion Denison Pender, were parents of seven children, four of whom survived childhood. Presumably some if not all of them lived with their parents in Government House, but their stay was a short one. In the spring of 1887, just a year or so after their arrival, Des Voeux was offered the governorship of Hong Kong, and so one of Newfoundland's better governors left the colony after too short a term.

Des Voeux was followed by Sir Henry Arthur Blake, who remained there for such a short time that his tenure left barely a mark on the face of the island's politics. He and his wife arrived from the Bahamas in 1887, to be replaced there by an outraged Sir Ambrose Shea, after the latter's near appointment as governor of Newfoundland. It was hoped that the switch of these governors would calm the troubled political waters in St. John's — an exercise in wishful thinking, it would seem, on the part of the Colonial Office.

The next governor found on his arrival in 1889 that Newfoundland's political waters were, if anything, as turbulent as ever. He was Sir John Terence Nicholls O'Brien, a man of integrity, but rigid, undiplomatic — and quite unsuited for the job.

Like so many of his predecessors, O'Brien had seen military service in the farthest reaches of the British Empire — in his case India and Ceylon, followed by seven years in Heligoland (Germany). But he was ill prepared for the complexity of Newfoundland's politics, and for the next six years he and the colony endured a mutual antipathy. The governor saw Newfoundland's politicians as "uniquely corrupt, devious, venal, and incompetent," with no desire to follow the "proper" course. "I'd like to shake them up," said O'Brien, "and put a little public spirit instead of codfish into them." His interference in local politics in 1894 played a significant part in causing the instability that precipitated the bank crash. When Sir Terence and Lady O'Brien left for England in 1895, they and the people of Newfoundland were happy to bid one another farewell.

But the next governor proved to be even more difficult. A lonely, rather bitter man with no colonial experience, Sir Herbert Harley Murray listened to O'Brien's opinions on events in Newfoundland when he arrived in mid-March 1895, some months before Sir Terence departed. Murray had financial skills that proved helpful in the aftermath of the bank crash, but his political and diplomatic skills were virtually non-existent. A widower, Murray spent his four years in St. John's a solitary and unhappy man, mainly because of his constant feuding with anyone who declined to sanction his every idea. He died in England in 1904, five years after his departure from Newfoundland — another governor to whom the populace said a grateful goodbye.

The last of the nineteenth-century governors was Sir Henry McCallum. A graduate of Royal Military College, Woolwich, McCallum and his wife, Maud Creighton, arrived in Newfoundland in 1900. Succeeding the controversial Governor Murray, the new governor created controversy of his own by refusing Prime Minister Robert Bond's request for a dissolution of the House of Assembly so that a general election could take place. Having started in discord, he continued in the same, and was recalled after a year in office, a period which must have seemed much longer to all involved. MacCallum was later posted as governor of Natal and Ceylon. He was replaced by Sir Cavendish Boyle, the governor remembered today as the composer of "Ode to Newfoundland," a paean to the island colony that readily acknowledged — and celebrated — its often harsh climate and geography.

> When sun-rays crown thy pine-clad hills,
> And summer spreads her hand,
> When silvern voices tune thy rills,
> We love thee, smiling land
> We love thee, we love thee, we love thee smiling land.

But the governor, who had experienced less than one full winter in Newfoundland when he penned his ode in January 1892, was already aware of Newfoundland's climatic realities, as the following verses made evident:

> When blinding storm gusts fret thy shore,
> And wild waves lash thy strand,
> Thro' spindrift swirl and tempest roar
> We love thee wind-swept land . . .
> When spread thy cloak of shimm'ring white,
> At Winter's stern command,
> Thro' shortened day and starlit night,
> We love thee, frozen land. . . .

Sir Cavendish's final verse suggested that additional help from above would never go amiss:

> As loved our fathers, so we love,
> Where once they stood we stand,
> Their prayer we raise to heav'n above,
> God guard thee, Newfoundland.

Nine governors succeeded Sir Cavendish Boyle before Newfoundland became part of Canada in 1949, after which the royal representative was a lieutenant-governor. The eighth of these governors was Humphrey T. Walwyn, a man who served in that post for ten years (1936–46), the longest term of any governor, naval or resident, since the first naval governor was appointed in 1729. Walwyn served under three monarchs, George V, Edward VIII and George VI. Lady Walwyn, Eileen Mary van Straubenzee, left a record of those years in unpublished journals.

In them she recorded notable events and her delight in their posting — the people, their travels through the breathtakingly beautiful island and through Labrador, her work as chief commissioner of the Newfoundland Girl Guides, entertaining at Government House, and her greatest delight — trips where she could test her skill with a fishing rod in her hand.

THE JOURNALS OF LADY EILEEN WALWYN

1936
Newfoundland

We landed at St. John's up to time on January 16th. There were great preparations to welcome us. As the ship entered the harbour all steam ships in port sounded their whistles while the mercantile premises were decked in bunting. . . . There were arches at the entrance of the Shipyard and again at the gate of Government House. I think they had "Farewell" to the former governor and "Welcome" to us on either sides of the arches which was quite a good idea.

My first impression (and indeed a lasting one for me) was that Government House was a homely friendly building which seemed, in its turn, to welcome us on arrival. . . . Our bedrooms were comfortable, and the house seemed warm to us. I soon realized that it did not come up to the standard that most Newfoundlanders were accustomed to. I well remember that some of the ladies who attended my meetings not only sat in their coats, but even did not part from their snow boots. There was a glorious staircase, and on the ground floor a succession of spacious living rooms, Humphrey's office, a ballroom, drawing room, dining and billiard room. The kitchens were below stairs. The strange thing is I have no recollection whatever of the kitchen which all goes to show how seldom I penetrated therein.

Cabot's Matthew, *in stained glass.*

The Barbour store, Newtown (since demolished).

Bay de Verde — one of the last "real" outports.

St. Paul's Church, Trinity.

Doorway, St. John's.

Chimney pots, St. John's.

In Newfoundland the gate only, and not the whole fence, is painted.

Cape Spear lighthouse.

The Barbour house, Newtown.

St. John's.

*   *   *

Within their first three months in Newfoundland, Sir Humphrey, accompanied by Lady Walwyn most of the time, made forty-two official visits. In March they had their first experience of the *Newfie Bullet,* on a trip to various outports.

> This we thoroughly enjoyed, travelling in our special coach named the "Terra Nova." This coach had been built in the 80s but was most comfortable. There was only a single line of track and we averaged about 20 miles an hour. Only two trains ran a week, so when we felt like a stand easy we pulled the communication cord and stopped the train for as long as we liked. We did this frequently later on in the season when we saw a likely lake which might hold some trout, which was always the case. We had an excellent cook on board, and it was all the greatest fun. . . . It was sad indeed the realize what real poverty existed in those "outports" and they were called. I had some really heartbreaking letters not only asking for clothes and food, but imploring me to find them work. I did all I could to help them. On woman wrote begging me to find her husband work which I was able to do. I hear from her still.

 *   *

> It was easy to realize how much the date November 11th meant to the Newfoundlanders, for their record in the war of 1914–1918 was second to none. . . . Every year a huge crowd gathered at the war memorial when wreaths were laid, and this year in particular we had an added ceremony planting trees, when Humphrey, James, and I did our share and were presented with silver spades which I have to this day.

*   *   *

1939
King George and Queen Elizabeth visit Newfoundland.

> It was hard to realize that we were entertaining the King and Queen, they were both so easy and friendly. . . . The King was most easy to talk to, mostly about the Navy. He amused me by his references to some Admirals, one of whom in particular he had no use for, and showed no hesitation in expressing his opinion, which I was glad to be able to

truthfully share. The sun shone in the afternoon for a garden party of over 1000, and one of the highlights of the afternoon was the Investiture when H.M. invested Sir John Puddester as Knight Batchelor [sic], a Ceremony new to Newfoundlanders, and the first time in 500 years that such a ceremony was held in the open.

*   *   *

War is declared.

1941

The American troops arrived in the S.S. *Edmund B. Alexander* to "defend us" under the 99 years base treaty. We went on board to welcome them, and threw one of our mammouth [sic] dinner parties for them, and later we had tea-dances for them which were very popular.

Later in August we had a most thrilling experience going by the "Terra Nova" to Placentia which was the nearest railway point to Argentia, now the American Naval Base. Dorothy Outerbridge was with me in the train and Leonard had gone by road with Humphrey. They both went on board the Prince of Wales to meet Winston Churchill, who had come to sign the Atlantic Charter with President Roosevelt. Humphrey had quite an amusing experience. On arrival on board Winston emerged on deck to meet him and started to talk to him, when he realized that the National Anthem was being played in honour of Humphrey, whereupon Winston was heard to say "of course, I forgot."

We went to Ottawa to stay with the Athlones which we thoroughly enjoyed. We had a very interesting dinner with the Prime Minister, Mackenzie King, who showed us his treasures. This included a Bible Box in which he told me he had kept all the correspondence connected with the Abdication of King Edward VIII as not a soul was to share that secret with him and he thought they would never think of looking for it in the Bible Box.

1943

There was a continuous arrival of survivors from torpedoed ships, and I was on call to meet them at the Caribou Hut where we handed each one an entire supply of clothes and all they needed for their comfort. We each were in charge of one garment, and I found I had been put at the end of the line handing out bath towels. When I asked why I had been pushed to the end of the line they said because I was so sympathetic I held up proceedings. It really was a pathetic sight to see these men. One I remember particularly. He said "This is the third time you have had to do this for me this year."

1946

We left Government House on January 17th preceded by mounted police, to join the dear old Terra Nova. Hundreds were at the station to bid us farewell. We stood on the rear platform of the train, the band playing "Ode to Newfoundland," and "Auld Lang Syne," so this was farewell to Newfoundland, and Island where we had been in close touch with a loveable loyal people who had responded with such genuine readiness at all times to our efforts on their behalf.

ST. JOHN'S OVER A CENTURY AGO: Sporting people found pleasure in cock fights which were held at Brine's farm . . . where, as one notice in *The Gazette* says, "A main of cocks will be fought on Tuesday next, the 23rd inst., at three o'clock in the afternoon for five guineas a battle and fifty guineas the main or odd battle. . . ."

St. John's was in 1807 a bright and interesting place to live and much gayer on the social side than it is now [1923]. About 700 troops, engineers, artillery and infantry were in garrisons here . . . we should judge that the girls of that day had a very good time indeed. Balls, picnics dinners and theatricals, amateur and professional were the order of the day, and though deep drinking was the fashion and every man was supposed to absorb at least a bottle of port at supper or dinner. . . .

The quantity of spirits that was consumed in St. John's at this time was simply amazing, almost incredible. The imports of rum alone for a population of about 20,000 were about 220,000 gallons, or about 11 gallons per head for everyone in Newfoundland, besides brandy and gin, wine, beer and cider . . . the consumption was about five or six gallons per head.

To a stranger visiting St. John's in 1807, we think the general impression must have been one of abounding dirt and untidiness. manure and wood chips and fish offal were thrown on the streets, and multitudes of dogs and pigs added to the filth

I'SE THE B'Y

I'se the b'y that builds the boat,
And I's the b'y that sails her!
I'se the b'y that catches the fish
And takes 'em home to Lizer.

Chorus
Hip your partner, Sally Tibbo'!
Hip your partner, Sally Brown!
Fogo, Twillingate, Mor'ton's Harbour,
All around the circle!

Sods and rinds to cover your flake,
Cake and tea for supper,
Codfish in the spring o' the year
Fried in maggoty butter.

I don't want your maggoty fish,
That's no good for winter;
I could buy as good as that
Down in Bonavista.

THE RYANS AND THE PITTMANS

(known in Newfoundland as "Rant and Roar")

Chorus
We'll rant and we'll roar like true
Newfoundlanders,
We'll rant and we'll roar on deck and
below
Until we see bottom inside the two
sunkers,
When straight through the channel to
Toslow we'll go.

I'm a son of a sea-cook, and a cook in a
trader;
I can dance, I can sing, I can reef the
mainboom,
I can handle a jigger, and cuts a big figure
Whenever I gets in a boat's standing room.

If the voyage is good, then this fall I will
do it;
I wants two pound ten for a ring and the
priest,
A couple o' dollars for clane shirt and
collars,
And a handful o' coppers to make up a
feast.

. . .
Farewell and adieu to ye girls of St.
Kyran's,
Of Paradise and Presque, Big and Little
Bona,
I'm bound unto Toslow to marry sweet
Biddy,
And if I don't do so, I'm afraid of her da.

. . .
I went to a dance one night at Fox
Harbour;
There were plenty of girls, so nice as you'd
wish,
There was one pretty maiden a-chawing of
frankgum,
Just like a young kitten a-gnawing fresh
fish.

Then here is a health to the girls of Fox
Harbour,
Of Oderin and Presque, Crabbes Hole and
Bruley.
Now let ye be jolly, don't be melancholy,
I can't marry all, or in chokey I'd be.

SOUTHERN CROSS: Sealing steamer lost on her way from the Gulf to St. John's on or about March 31, 1914; 173 men lost.

S.S. *STEPHANO:* 2,144 tons nett [sic], built in 1911 for the New York, Newfoundland and Halifax S.S. Company, operating the Red Cross Line. Torpedoed by a German submarine October 8, 1916, off Nantucket, U.S.A. Four other steamers torpedoed by this submarine at the same time and place. *Stephano* engaged in the seal fishery several springs and brought in over 73,000 seals.

CHAPTER 13

St. John's: Merchants and Politicians

The road to success in St. John's was a well-travelled path, albeit rough in spots and with precipitous edges. It led steeply upward as a diligent immigrant developed into a successful merchant, became smoother with the social respectability of a good marriage, acquired potholes as he tackled the torrid trail of Newfoundland politics; then reached the peak, an appointment to the Bench or, as a final flourish, a coveted knighthood.

The area encompassing Rennie's Mill Road, Circular Road and Empire Avenue is an example of this success made visible. The nineteenth-century occupants of its houses, and others that grace the nearby residential streets, include, among others, a governor, a prime minister, a Father of Confederation, numerous merchants, and two men embroiled in the saga of the legendary *Newfie Bullet.*

A house known as Winterton was one of the most interesting of these historic buildings. Unfortunately it fell victim to a fire in 1996 and thus was destroyed a symbol of two of St. John's most distinguished families.

When Winterton was built, it must have seemed to the people of St. John's the epitome of architectural splendour, and certainly it was, at least when seen in the midst of the motley hovels and hurriedly built shops and cottages that made up that town at the turn of the eighteenth century. The builder was, in all probability, George Winter, the deputy ordnance storekeeper of the day, and a member of one of the town's leading merchant families. It stood on land granted to Winter's father, James, in 1774, but that gentleman, lured in later life by England's amenities and less rigorous climate, had repaired to that country many years before his death. Legend suggests that the house served as a wayside tavern for a time, a stopping place for travellers who made their way along the primitive road that led from St. John's to Portugal Cove.

The house appears on an 1816 map as part of George Winter's extensive holdings. He was the father of eleven children, and it seems that he divided his estate evenly among them. Several of his offspring, following in their grandfa-

FACING PAGE:

Winterton, 8 Winter Avenue. Destroyed by fire in 1996.

Sir James Spearman Winter.

ther James's footsteps, chose to leave Newfoundland for England's gentle shores. But not George's grandson James. James, later Sir James Spearman Winter, became a moving force in the colony's social, religious and political life. He was a Grand Master of the Orange Order, and a leader of the Protestant forces in Newfoundland's often bitter religious feuds. He served as attorney general during the late 1880s and then as a Supreme Court judge from 1893 until he left the Bench to lead the Tory forces to victory in an 1897 election. But Winter's term as prime minister was short-lived, for he went down to defeat in the election of 1900. He died in Toronto in 1911.

Earlier that year, Sir James's nephew, Charles George Preston, had sold Winterton (the house was included in his one-eleventh share of his grandfather's estate) to Martin Williams Furlong, a teacher turned lawyer and Liberal politician.

Politics in Newfoundland was a particularly risky profession, and seldom did anyone retain power for long. Furlong was no exception. He began his political life in 1889 but was defeated in his bid for election in Ferryland. A few months later he was named solicitor for the House of Assembly — even before being called to the Newfoundland bar. (He was admitted to the bar the following year.) He kept that position until 1893, when he won an election as a Liberal candidate for St. John's West, a seat he held until his defeat the next year. Once again, in 1897, he contested Ferryland, but lost when James Winter and his Tory government swept to power. His political ambitions thus dampened, Furlong became the legislative law clerk, handling the government's legal negotiations with the Reid Newfoundland Company, whose railway was finally completed in 1898 — seventeen troublesome years after it began.

The island's contract with Robert Reid, who took over construction of the railway in 1890, was so beneficial to Reid that no one could believe the government would sign such a deal. Reid, a no-nonsense Scottish engineer and veteran of the building of the Canadian Pacific, demanded — and got — one million acres of land on either side of the track, plus a fifty-year operating monopoly on coastal shipping, postal and telegraph service, and passenger operations — all tax exempt. Nor was that all. Generous government grants and a $75,000-a-year steamship subsidy were part of the package, on top of $15,600-per-mile construction costs. David Macfarlane writes in *The Danger Tree* that the Reid contract was "in many ways a model for future private investment in Newfoundland. To pay for its nationalism, the island could only give itself away, limb by limb."

Furlong, as solicitor of the House from 1890 to 1893, would have been involved in the original negotiations with Robert Reid. Certainly he had ongoing connections with the Reid Newfoundland Company after 1897, by which time it was being run by Reid's sons. Furlong became the company's solicitor in 1907, and a director in 1911. That same year he purchased Winterton.

We'll never know why Martin Furlong didn't change the name of his house, once it was his. Given the animosities that fuelled the politics of the day, one wonders how he could have happily settled into a house named for the family of his arch rival, Sir James Spearman Winter. In any event, Furlong lived there until his death five years later.

Furlong's son, Robert Stafford Furlong, grew up in Winterton and lived there for most of his life. Among his treasured possessions was his father's collection of first edition and rare Newfoundland books, a collection the son continued to expand until it became one of the largest of its kind extant. A lawyer, as was his father, Robert Furlong became chief justice of Newfoundland's Court of Appeal. He died in 1996. Winterton survived for nearly two hundred years, and many of Newfoundland's notables knew it well.

Sir Marmaduke George Winter was a son of James Winter, of Her Majesty's Customs, and Harriet Pitman. He was born in Lamaline, on the Burin Peninsula southwest of St. John's. Although his elder brothers, James (later Sir James Spearman Winter, the tenth prime minister of Newfoundland) and Thomas, had received their schooling in St. John's, the family decided to send young Marmaduke to Canada for his education, and off he went to Toronto and Upper Canada College. Later, after a few years of business experience in Montreal and then in New York, Marmaduke returned home to Newfoundland and, with Thomas, started T. and M. Winter Ltd., a wholesale provision agency. Before long it was supplying ships to the seal fishery, exporting cod, and dealing in fire insurance. Marmaduke himself was overseeing a host of other manufacturing concerns. Somehow, through skill, prudence and a certain amount of luck, he managed to avoid the financial collapse that ruined many of St. John's citizens after a catastrophic bank crash in 1894.

Winter and his family lived in Bannerman House on Circular Road until, in 1905, he decided to build a newer and more impressive home nearby. He called it Winterholme. This massive, sixty-room mansion soon became the grand dame of the entire neighbourhood. Winter, his wife, Alice Augusta Lilly, and their family moved into Winterholme in 1907. However, he retained ownership of Bannerman House (then occupied by his son, Robert Gordon Winter), held it until 1927, and then sold it to William Angus Reid, secretary of the Reid Newfoundland Company, and the man responsible for much of the conflict surrounding construction of the Newfoundland Railway.

For the Winters' showplace there could be no other design than the then-popular Queen Anne, a style described by Witold Rybczynski in *Home: A Short History of an Idea* as a "not very historic appellation . . . and a not very historically accurate style," and by others as "Bloated Gothic." Queen Anne was on the throne from 1702 to 1714, so the style, interpreted two centuries later in Newfoundland, lent itself to the vagaries of individual architects. But historian Gordon Handcock depicts Winterholme as "one of the best examples of Queen Anne Revival Style anywhere in Canada." Its double bay windows

Bannerman House, built circa 1849, home of butcher John Mitchell and his wife, Ann March, one of Newfoundland's many successful business women.

EXECUTIONS IN NEWFOUNDLAND: Five men found guilty of inciting the troops of the garrison of St. John's to mutiny, hanged on Gibbet Hill, Signal Hill 1800.

POLARIS: Arctic exploration steamer; crew of 19 men brought to St. John's in S.S. *Tigress* May 12, 1873; the rescued men had been 197 days on the ice; drifting southward after the wreck of their craft in the Arctic regions.

CAHILL, R. found guilty of manslaughter, June 2, 1874, and sentenced to two years' imprisonment; he killed his wife.

Winterholme, 79 Rennie's Mill Road, the splendid residence of Sir Marmaduke George Winter and his family.

and decorative shingling were typical of the style that people of the day found so appealing.

Winter spared no expense. The final cost, $115,000, was an astonishing amount for the day — and about $30,000 over budget. (It's unlikely, however, that the Winters had to worry too much about the cost overrun.) The house was surely the talk of the town, with lavish detailing, imported wood trim, and spacious rooms for entertaining — everything that Marmaduke, Alice Augusta, their two sons and two daughters could wish for.

In 1910, Winter took the next step along the path to success, and ran for public office. He was elected a member of the Executive Council. In 1919, because of his patriotic efforts during the war, he was named a commander of the Order of the British Empire, and in 1923 achieved his highest honour, a knighthood. After Alice's death, he married again in later life, this time to Florence Hayward. Sir Marmaduke died in 1936.

Three years later, at the outbreak of the Second World War, Winterholme was leased to the Canadian Army. It was to be used as an officers' mess, on the understanding that the elaborate decorative details and plaster ornamentation were to be left intact, and the house returned, unchanged, to the family at war's end. The Winters' son, R. Gordon Winter, took it over after the war and lived there until 1960. His son, Gordon A.

Winter, a lieutenant-governor of Newfoundland, also grew up in the house, and was a signatory of the 1948 Terms of Union between Newfoundland and Canada. Later, its days of glory over, Winterholme, by then an old dowager, was converted into seven apartments. Now, the seven apartments removed and the house restored, it serves as a very successful Heritage Inn. It has recently been recognized as a National Historic Site.

In 1846, many years before Winterholme was built, John O'Mara, from Waterford, Ireland, bought Crown land at what is now 70 Circular Road. O'Mara founded a prosperous mercantile firm with offices on Water Street. He dealt in general merchandise, became a shipowner with interests chiefly in the seal fishery, served as a justice of the peace, and worked on behalf of the poor of the town through the Benevolent Irish Society. O'Mara married first Mary Allen, then Margaret Nowlan. He built a frame cottage that remained in the family for twenty-six years. After O'Mara's death, the land was bought by James Murray, then owner of Rennie's Mill, who named the house Sunnyside and, over the years, undertook a series of additions around the original O'Mara cottage, which remained to form Sunnyside's central section.

When Murray purchased Sunnyside he had, at forty, overcome some major hurdles. His father, also James, had been a Scottish immigrant from Murrayshill, Perthshire, who ran a milling and baking business on the banks

Sunnyside, the O'Mara-Murray house, at 70 Circular Road.

139

TELEPHONE SYSTEM: first telephone in St. John's operated between the houses of John Delaney, postmaster-general, and that of John Higgins, March 20, 1878. . . . Two telephones were installed in 1884, at Archibald's Furniture Factory, situated where T. & M. Winters' premises are now, and at his residence in Devon Row.

ADVANCE: Brigt. visited St. John's, June 16, 1883, en route to Arctic to search for Sir John Franklin.

of the Rennie River. According to Paul O'Neill's *A Seaport Legacy*, the "hard-tack" produced by the senior Murray was "so hard that a hammer was packed with each barrel sold" — suggesting that he had, if nothing else, a knack for creative marketing. James Murray Sr. died intestate in 1854, leaving his son James, then twenty-two, to support his mother and nine younger siblings.

Young James farmed his extensive lands and took over his father's business concerns, built a thriving mercantile enterprise, and became the owner of the mill on Rennie's River. His 1873 marriage to Jean Ritchie took place in Edinburgh. When the newlyweds returned to St. John's, Murray was able to offer his bride a choice between two homes, the Circular Road property, or a substantial double house facing both King's Bridge Road and Forest Road. Murray, then at the peak of his career, had purchased both properties the previous year. Jean chose the modest one-and-a-half-storey house at 70 Circular Road. The Murrays soon built an addition to the east, and then, twenty years or so later, another. Two sons, Andrew and David, were born to them (and a daughter, who died young), and both were sent to Scotland for their education. The brothers eventually started a mercantile business of their own.

In 1892, Murray was on a visit to Scotland (perhaps to see his young sons) when a telegram informed him that a devastating fire, one of many but by far the worst, had destroyed much of St. John's: "Everything east of Beck's Cove in ashes. Sunnyside safe."

Murray returned promptly to St. John's. The fire had started when a drayman, working in a stable at Freshwater and Pennywell Roads, dropped his pipe in the hay. The flames spread quickly and could not be doused — the city's water supply had been turned off for the laying of new mains. Two peo-

Murray premises in Beck's Cove, built after the Great Fire of 1846.

ple died in that fire, which raged all night, and two-thirds of the town was destroyed. Nineteen hundred families were left homeless.

The Great Fire of 1892 spelled financial ruin for Murray and scores of others. While the Murray premises on Beck's Cove (built after the Great Fire of 1846, and still standing) had been spared, his newly built mercantile premises on Water Street had been consumed by the flames. Two years later, the crash of the Bank of Newfoundland brought the final blow. Murray's political career, however, continued successfully. A stirring and humorous orator, he had been elected a member of the House of Assembly for the District of Burgeo in 1889, and won again in 1893.

For the rest of his life Murray amused himself and entertained the people of St. John's by writing magazine articles and letters to the local newspapers. He was fifty-seven when he died in 1900. His obituary, noting that he had "passed over to the great majority," described him as a man who "wrote with surprising fluency and intelligence on public affairs. A volume of his writing, well worthy of being collected, might easily be compiled from his contributions to the Newfoundland daily and weekly newspapers." Murray was not "without faults or prejudices," the obituary went on to say, "but he was generous and liberal-minded. . . . He rose early, read or wrote for an hour every morning, went downtown before breakfast and opened his place of business

Family — if not architectural — harmony exemplified in the adjoining homes of two Rennie sisters. Circular Road and Rennie's Mill Road.

Sutherland Place on Kings Bridge Road, begun in 1883 by William Pitts, who died the following year. His son, James, lived in the north side of the house until 1918. Sir Leonard Outerbridge, later a lieutenant-governor of Newfoundland, lived in the south side for many years and watched the Great Fire of 1894 from a third-floor window.

for the day, and returned to his residence on Circular Road, long before most people in town were stirring. . . . When a young man, none ever struggled against heavy odds in the battle of life more bravely than he did, and few if any left a more enduring impression on the trade business and literature of his country."

The Bond house,
2 Circular Road, built
by Sir Robert Bond for
his mother, Elizabeth.

Murray's wife, Jean, lived on at Sunnyside. Remembered by a grand-daughter as a "very quiet but very determined person and very Scottish . . . a real scholar," Jean Murray insisted that her grandchildren learn the Greek or Latin derivation and the proper pronunciation of any word they looked up in the dictionary. She died in 1932, by which time a son and his family were living in the house.

Today, more than half a century later, Sunnyside is still in the Murray family. The drawing room, remarkably, remains furnished as it was in the 1870s, when James and Jean Murray first lived there. In fact, it looks as though they had just stepped out for a while and might reappear at any moment. Architecturally, the house has changed very little. The stable and the pretty little neo-Gothic style lodge with latticed windows and fanciful bargeboard (both built for the Murrays in 1890) are added adornments. All are cared for by James and Jean Murray's granddaughters, Ramsay and Jean, who have spent a lifetime cherishing and protecting their unparalleled legacy.

The manager of James Murray's many business concerns was the enterprising Edward Rothwell, an English bookkeeper who sailed to Newfoundland in 1863 in search of his fortune, or at least in hopes of a better life. He began working for Murray in the mid-1870s. In 1887 he and John Bowring founded the fishery supply firm of Rothwell and Bowring. Two years later Rothwell — what else? — entered the political arena and he was elected MHA for Burin. And somewhere along the line he married the daughter of William Frederick Rennie of Rennie's Mill, a man whose position in the community was elevated by his service as Usher of the Black Rod in Newfoundland's House of Assembly.

Elizabeth Bond.

Sir Robert Bond.

Another Rennie daughter, Emma Hoyles Rennie, had married John W. Withers, Queen's Printer of Newfoundland, an office to which he was appointed in 1889. (He succeeded his father, John Collier Withers, who had held that position for the previous sixty years.) Educated at Cambridge, Withers was firmly entrenched in the St. John's establishment, active in Anglican Church affairs and education matters. He was, according to one biography, "Politically . . . Confederate, so far as Canada; and Federal, so far as the Empire is concerned." After his death in 1921, Emma continued to publish the *Royal Gazette and Newfoundland Advertiser*, the semi-official government publication that her husband had edited.

On Circular Road, just east of Sunnyside, the father of these Rennie women built adjoining houses for them. The houses were splendid. No modest semi-detached dwellings these, but solid, dignified mansions — their potential impact somewhat diminished, however, by the decision to employ completely different architectural styles for each house. Whereas other double houses in St. John's were designed with unifying architectural details (see the neo-Gothic Sutherland Place on King's Bridge Road, or Devon Place, between Forest and King's Bridge Roads), no such restriction impeded the architect retained by Mr. Rennie. The challenge facing the architect was the client himself. More than likely, it was his daughters.

Each Rennie daughter, it seems, had a mind of her own. Thus, one house followed the neo-Gothic mode, with late Victorian bric-a-brac aplenty, while the other featured the more dignified Second Empire style, its mansard roof bearing no relationship whatsoever to the elaborate gables and nooks that decorated her sister's house. A connecting door allowed for easy communication between each half of the building. Both houses were of wood construction, but it is anyone's guess as to what colour each was painted after the builder wrote *finis* to the project. Certainly it would be difficult to imagine the sisters agreeing on any one particular colour, much less its shade. Today, the houses are each painted a defiantly different colour, an honest acknowledgment of the diverse beginnings of this interesting building.

Farther east on Circular Road, where it meets King's Bridge Road and Empire Avenue (names that remind one of the many years that St. John's served as an outpost of the British Empire), stands a home built by yet another Newfoundland knight, Sir Robert Bond. Descended from an old Devonshire family, Bond was born in St. John's in 1857, sent to England for his education, then to Scotland to study the law. Before being admitted to the bar, however, he decided to enter the political fray at home in Newfoundland. Politics remained the guiding force for most of his life.

Bond remained a bachelor all his life. In 1886 he built a Victorian neo-Gothic house at 2 Circular Road for his mother, Elizabeth. Designed by the popular architects J. and J. T. Southcott, the house appears squeezed uncomfortably into its tiny triangular lot, partially hidden by the converging roads,

*Retreat Cottage,
14 Kenna's Hill, built
about 1834, and home to
several prominent St.
John's citizens.*

which are built well above grade. These roads loom above the house. Passers-by peer over a rail fence and down to the entrance level. There is an answer to the puzzle of building's siting. When the house was built it lay on a large tract of land in the valley of the Rennie's River. Then the railway came through, and part of the back portion was lost. And while there was always a gentle slope down to the house, the slope became repeatedly steeper as the city fathers saw fit to build layer upon layer over the original adjacent roads. What was once a dignified townhouse, suitable for the mother of the equally dignified Robert Bond, has lost some of that dignity in its much altered siting.

When Bond resigned from politics in 1914, exhausted after a lifetime in the forefront of the Liberal ranks, he retired to his own home, the Grange, in Whitbourne. Four years later, when asked to resume his leadership of the party, he declined, writing bitterly to his colleague George Shea, "I have had a surfeit of Newfoundland politics lately, and I turn from the dirty business with contempt and loathing."

Small wonder. Bond had entered the Assembly in 1882, when he was twenty-five. Two years later he was elected Speaker of the House, then the youngest MHA to attain that honour. By 1889 he was serving as colonial secretary in Sir William Whiteway's Liberal cabinet. But when the Liberals were reelected four years later, a political brouhaha erupted when seventeen of the twenty-six successful candidates were charged with election bribery and corruption. Prime Minister Whiteway and his cabinet resigned in April and the Conservatives took over. By the end of 1894, fifteen Liberal members had been unseated by the court, Bond and Whiteway included. Then, in December of that year, the banks crashed. As historian Frederick W. Rowe remarked, "St. John's firms one by one collapsed and the banks closed their doors. For all practical purposes, Newfoundland was bankrupt."

It was Robert Bond who saved the day. The Tory government had resigned immediately after the bank crash, to be replaced by the Liberals under Daniel J. Greene, whose government promptly passed an act allowing "those politicians disqualified earlier in the year eligible for reelection." Within weeks Greene resigned to make way for Whiteway, who, on February 8, 1895, formed a new Liberal government, with Robert Bond once again colonial secretary. During the following stressful months, Bond solicited funds from Canada and Britain, liberally using "his own personal credit on the Colony's behalf. . . . His generosity, the universal respect for his integrity, and the skilled leadership he displayed . . . made him Newfoundland's all-time political hero." He became Liberal leader himself in 1897, and prime minister three years later, a position he held for almost nine years. After the defeat of his government in 1909, he moved to the opposition benches until he resigned from political life five years later.

A staunch nationalist, Bond served his country well. Knighted in 1901, he received countless other honours along the way. It seems, however, that they were not enough to allay his disillusionment with the political shenanigans and intrigues that continually disrupted the political scene in his beloved Newfoundland.

North of the Bond house, at 14 Kenna's Hill, stands Retreat Cottage. A fascinating house, it was built in 1834, and was home to several individuals who figured prominently in the colony's development. Like the colony, the house grew and changed shape in fits and starts, altering in varying degrees every time a new owner took over. Fortunately nothing destroyed its original integrity, and every alteration simply added to its charm. In 1970, by great good fortune, it came into the hands of an architectural historian who has encouraged public awareness of Newfoundland's architectural heritage. The fate of Retreat Cottage seems safely assured for the foreseeable future.

In 1820, John Murch Brine paid £230 to Thomas Pitts of the Royal Newfoundland Regiment for the land on which Retreat Cottage stands.

Not long after Brine's death, the property (and perhaps a building) was purchased by young Edward Mortimer Archibald, one of the colony's leading legal lights and a man who would later be at the centre of the tumultuous advent of representative government in Newfoundland. The house was likely built by Archibald or extended from an original saltbox — a structure with a low rear extension (known locally as a linhay), the shape of the whole resembling a saltbox — shortly after he acquired the property. Archibald, twenty-four at the time of the purchase, was already an acting assistant judge. He had married in September of that year, and may have planned to move to Retreat Cottage with his bride, Catherine Richardson. For some reason, the couple chose other quarters, and instead rented the cottage to Christopher Ayre, Governor Cochrane's secretary. Ayre lived there until his wife died three years later.

By 1847 Retreat Cottage was in the hands of another St. John's merchant, William Thomas. He too leased the house to a number of people, one of whom was Edward Dalton Shea (later Sir Edward), proprietor of the *Newfoundlander*. Another of Thomas's tenants was Thomas Beck, who as sergeant-at-arms for the Assembly had become embroiled in one of the more bizarre events in Newfoundland politics. When George Lilly, acting as an assistant judge, denied a warrant issued by the Speaker of the Assembly, Beck, acting for the Speaker, entered the judge's chambers, arrested Lilly, and dragged him out by the collar — assisted by other eager participants who happily pushed from behind, and held Lilly, first in the Speaker's room and then in Beck's home (not Retreat Cottage, but an earlier dwelling). Lilly was not released until two days later when the Assembly was adjourned.

In 1868 Retreat Cottage acquired a new owner. He was John Hayward, a lawyer and politician from Harbour Grace. Hayward and his wife, Flora Currie, enjoyed a tragically brief marriage. Their wedding took place in July of 1843, but on August 6 of the following year, her death was announced. She was nineteen. A year later Hayward married again. His bride this time was Laura Wilhelmina Pack of Carbonear.

Hayward moved into Retreat Cottage at about the time he was appointed assistant judge of the Newfoundland Supreme Court. Hayward, the first owner to actually occupy the cottage since Brine's time, was forty-eight, and ready to "retreat" from the continual discord and squabbling that marked so much of political life in nineteenth-century Newfoundland. In 1865 he was appointed Newfoundland's solicitor general. During his years as a politician he actively campaigned against confederation. When the frenzied debates surrounding that question were settled in the election of 1869, Hayward no doubt found the relative tranquillity of the Bench inviting. He lived in Retreat Cottage until his death in 1885.

William Thomas, who owned and leased Retreat Cottage during the middle of the eighteenth century, made his own home in a stately mansion at 3 Forest Road. This building in fact comprised two houses, with William's half facing Forest Road, while his brother Henry's, at the rear, overlooked King's Bridge Road. (This was not the first house shared by the brothers. They had lived previously on Devon Row in a house known as Brookfield, a building long gone, probably destroyed in the Great Fire of 1846. We can only assume that, since they lived in such proximity to each other, their wives were equally happy with this arrangement.)

Charlotte Bowring.

Devon Place, Forest and King's Bridge Road. Built prior to 1849 and home, at one time or another, to Bowrings, Reids, Crosbies and other distinguished Newfoundland families.

The Forest Road and King's Bridge Road houses were built around 1844 (coinciding, possibly, with William's marriage in 1847 to Elizabeth Job) on property that he had purchased in 1843 from Edward M. Archibald, then owner of Retreat Cottage. The Thomas brothers' father, William Bevil Thomas, born in St. John's in 1757, had married Elizabeth Way, of Dartmouth, Nova Scotia, and conducted mercantile businesses in Dartmouth and St. John's. Of their two sons, it was William Jr. who became the most prominent. He had a reputation for integrity and compassion and worked tirelessly to help the poor and disadvantaged. In the often bitter sectarian squabbling that plagued Newfoundland, William Thomas emerged with his reputation unsullied. He is remembered today as an honourable man.

The Thomas brothers' homes were similar in style but not identical. Each had individual architectural detailing. In later years, probably when architect James Southcott held sway as St. John's favourite house-builder, projecting bays were added to the Forest Road house, adding a Victorian touch to the otherwise Classical Revival exterior.

In 1872 both Thomas houses were bought by James Murray, who was at the time a tenant in the northern (King's Bridge Road) house. That same year he also acquired Sunnyside, on Circular Road, which, after their wedding the following year, his bride chose as her home, and the Murrays moved there.

So the Forest Road and King's Bridge Road houses were leased — the former to Charles Bowring, the latter to the Honourable Nicholas Stabb, both of whom were among St. John's mercantile élite. Stabb died four years later. His widow, Rachel Chancey, lived another eighteen years. According to O'Neill's *A Seaport Legacy*, she died "at the age of eighty-nine, after dictating telegrams on her death bed to her two absent sons, Thomas and Nicholas, saying that she was dying, and sending them her love."

The Bowring name is now recognized worldwide. It initially gained prominence in Newfoundland soon after an enterprising English watchmaker, Benjamin Bowring, first sailed into St. John's harbour in 1811. That raw and rowdy frontier port offered boundless opportunities for a man with drive and determination — and Bowring had plenty of both. During the next four years he made several trips back and forth between England and Newfoundland in order to assess the business possibilities in the colony. Finally, in 1815, he decided to settle. His wife, Charlotte, and their children joined him a year later.

Bowring set up his watchmaking shop but grew discouraged after a series of fires, all within five years, destroyed the premises. In the meantime, Charlotte, by then the mother of three or four (a daughter's name and birth date are missing from the family tree), had set up a small dry-goods shop adjacent to her husband's watchmaking store and her store was prospering. So Bowring, never a man to miss an opportunity, changed directions. Thus began the Bowrings' business empire, its impetus coming from another of the many Newfoundland women with merchandising and administrative ability.

The Bowrings were admirable citizens of St. John's. They were Unitarians, staunch supporters of the antislavery movement, active in charitable societies, and instrumental in establishing a public library in the town. By 1834, the business had become so successful that the Bowrings and three of their children (by then numbering three sons and a daughter) were able to return to England, leaving their thriving retailing firm in the hands of son Charles Tricks Bowring. (A fifth child had drowned in 1828.) In time, Charles's brothers returned to St. John's, and joined him in the firm that in 1839 became known as Bowring Brothers. The company had expanded from the modest dry-goods store in St. John's to a firm that supplied the outports with produce. It eventually branched out into the cod and seal fisheries. Father Benjamin turned over the Liverpool end of the business to Charles, and renamed it C. T. Bowring and Company. It soon became a major international shipping and insurance company.

Seven years after Benjamin returned to England, Charles followed suit and moved his young family to Liverpool. There his son, Charles R. Bowring, grew up and in due course joined the family firm for his business training. By 1864 young Charles, then twenty-four years old, was judged sufficiently prepared and ready to find his niche in the business, and off he went to learn the ropes in the St. John's branch. Within five years he was named manager and senior partner in Newfoundland, and this he remained for the rest of his life. The family's faith had not been misplaced. By 1876, when it was awarded the postal contract to deliver mail to Newfoundland's coastal communities, the company's fleet numbered fifty-seven ships.

Not surprisingly, Charles Bowring was soon bitten by the political bug. He was elected to the House of Assembly for Bonavista Bay in 1873, by which time he had married Laura Warren, and they had produced their first child, a son, Charles Warren Bowring. They lived in the house on Forest Road. Four years later, when Robert J. Pinsent bought both it and the rear house on King's Bridge Road, the Bowrings stayed on as tenants. And someone, probably Pinsent, decided to name the houses Devon Place.

Devon Place was a suitably distinguished home for Charles Bowring, a man who was by this time among the most powerful men in St. John's. His political career eventually foundered, but Bowring's business acumen, along with his considerable political and social connections, stood him in good stead. In 1886 his friend, Prime Minister Robert Thorburn, appointed Bowring to the Legislative Council, where he replaced his father-in-law, John Henry Warren.

Thorburn, as it happened, was also the Bowrings' neighbour in Devon Place. He had purchased the King's Bridge Road side of the building from Pinsent in 1884. The year following his appointment to the Legislative Council, Bowring, whose family by then included six sons and a daughter, bought his (Forest Road) side of the house from Pinsent. Bowring lived there until his death, at fifty, in 1890. Laura Bowring, presumably, stayed on in the house for some time. In 1906, the Bowring family purchased the north side of the house, thereby turning Devon Place into one spacious and very impressive home. Ten years later, Sir Edgar Rennie Bowring (Charles's cousin, the son of his uncle John) sold the entire property, and once again it became a double house.

As for the north (King's Bridge Road) half of Devon Place, it too housed a series of prominent Newfoundlanders — in fact much of the colony's history was shaped by the influential men who throughout the years lived on one side or the other of this truly historic building.

Take Robert John Pinsent, a lawyer (said to be the finest in Newfoundland) and a politician (but not a very successful one). When he bought both houses from James Murray in 1877, Pinsent had been fighting the anti-confederation forces for some years — with the exception of one brief flip-flop to the other side — and his political career was foundering. His home life at Devon Place involved the six children from his first marriage, and three born to his second wife, the wonderfully named Emily Hettie Sabine Homfray, whom he had married about four years before the move to Devon Place. Pinsent was appointed to the Supreme Court in 1879, and knighted in 1890. Three years later he died suddenly in England, where he had gone seeking medical help.

Pinsent had sold the King's Bridge Road side of Devon Place to the Honourable Robert Thorburn, a political opponent, back in 1884. At the time, the house was occupied for a brief period by Ambrose Shea, one of Pinsent's political allies. Two years later, Shea was knighted and promised an appointment as governor of Newfoundland, but in no time that honour was withdrawn due to vigorous anti-confederate and anti-Catholic objections. Shea became instead governor of the Bahamas, an appointment he considered something of a consolation prize. A bitter Sir Ambrose and his second wife, Louisa Bouchette, left St. John's in October 1887.

Devon Place remained in Thorburn's hands. He became prime minister of Newfoundland in 1885. Knighted in 1887, he then went down to ignominious political defeat two years later, in 1889. Four years after that, he switched briefly to the Liberal side of the political fence, but after losing an election that year, devoted himself to his equally demanding business affairs. Sir Robert Thorburn died in St. John's at the age of seventy. He was a "decent man," wrote his biographer, J. K. Hiller, "with a strong sense of public duty who as a result found himself used by others."

(Politics makes strange bedfellows, but seldom more often than in Newfoundland. Sir Robert Thorburn, for example, a Protestant, led the Conservative party. His tenant in Devon Place, Sir Ambrose Shea, a Roman Catholic, led the Liberals and, for a time, the Conservatives. Both men were delegates to the first Colonial Conference early in 1887, just before Shea's Bahamas appointment. Presumably they were, if not friends, at least respectful adversaries.)

When Sir Edgar Bowring sold both sides of Devon Place in 1916, the south half went to Henry (Harry) Duff Reid, who one year later became president of the Reid Newfoundland Company, founded by his father, Sir Robert Gillespie Reid. In 1918, two years after the move to Devon Place, Harry's wife, Jessie (Paterson), died. He later married Marcelle Robert of Montreal.

In 1920, Devon Place was sold to the wife of Sir John Chalker Crosbie, and events within the walls of this historic house continued in as lively a fashion as before. The first generation of native Newfoundland Crosbies (the sons and daughters of George and Martha Ellen Crosbie, originally of Brigus) were by this time making their mark. They pursued life in high gear while, with a combination of enterprise, native talent, and good marriages, they founded an ever-expanding business empire and an ever-expanding clan. They were a down-to-earth, aggressive family, and their explosive lifestyle occasionally provided the residents of St. John's with plenty to talk about.

John Chalker Crosbie was all this and more. When his father died in 1895 he was only eighteen or so. He took over the Crosbie Hotel for a while but found that too confining. Later that year he became manager of a fish by-product exporting firm; within five years of his father's death he had founded a fish exporting business, Crosbie and Company Ltd. Five years later he had

Codfish drying at mercantile premises, possibly Crosbies'.

branched out into the insurance business. Success built on success, and eventually the family was running a produce company, a fish exporting firm (the biggest exporter to Brazil of salt cod), and shipping and mercantile enterprises. Somehow it does not seem surprising that, while still in his early thirties (and this being Newfoundland), John Crosbie launched a successful political career. He was knighted in 1919. The Crosbies' power emanated from St. John's and encompassed all of Newfoundland. Sir John Chalker Crosbie was a rough diamond, brazen, ambitious, and adventurous — all qualities that ensured survival in the cutthroat atmosphere of St. John's Water Street. It was an atmosphere so vicious that within five hours of his death in 1932, while his sons were arranging his funeral, five of his competitors in the fish business were soliciting the firm's clients.

On Sir John's death his son, Chesley, "Skipper Ches," took over and further expanded and diversified the empire, until it included everything from a herring plant to whaling, sealing, deep-sea trawling, an airline, and a construction business. When he died, command of what became the Crosbie Group of Companies went to his younger son, Andrew, and Ches's brother Percy. Ches's older son, John Carnell, a brilliant scholar, entered Newfoundland and then Canadian politics, holding a number of cabinet posts, serving as minister of Finance, and of Justice.

While the men of the family were highly visible on the local scene, the indomitable Crosbie women managed their men and their boisterous families with aplomb. Martha Ellen (or Ellie, as she was called), Sir John's sister, was every bit as strong as her brothers. When her husband, Captain Harry Bartlett, died at sea, she raised their two daughters, remarried, had two sons, and, on her father's death, took over management of the Crosbie Hotel. She was a formidable businesswoman and a tower of strength within the family. Her sister-in-law, Sir John's wife, Mitchie Anne Manuel, was the mother of thirteen children, two of whom died young. Mitchie was stern and iron-willed, never more so than when her husband needed a firm hand to keep him in line. She was acknowledged, according to Michael Harris in *Rare Ambition*, to be the "power behind the throne," and was credited with the "making of Sir John." Harris quoted family members who never remembered her "losing her temper or even raising her voice, possibly because her husband did enough bawling for any two adults." Her daughter Vera (Perlin) established a school for the mentally handicapped in St. John's, purchased a house so the school could provide proper facilities, then hired staff and managed the school.

CHAPTER 14

St. John's: The Great Fire of 1892

Military Road marks the northern boundary of the Great Fire of 1892. Almost every building south of that road was destroyed in the last of three great fires that wiped out much of nineteenth-century St. John's. Government House and St. Thomas' Church, on the north side, likely owe their survival to the Roman Catholic prelate of the day, Bishop Michael Howley, who, as the flames threatened to leap across Military Road, instructed firefighters to tear down the home of a Mrs. Kelligrews. Her Cochrane Street house was already on fire and threatening its next-door neighbour, the handsome, mansard-roofed frame home of George Thomas Rendell. Had the Rendell house caught fire, the flames might well have skipped to the other side of Military Road to consume the buildings there.

The house (82 Cochrane Street) was built in 1878 on leased land — and its owner, Rendell, had to wait another twenty-seven years before he could call the property his own, finally obtaining title for £350 from Mary Stripling. The house was probably designed by the firm of J. and J. T. Southcott, for it bears all the earmarks of their distinctive style — good proportions, simplicity of line, a mansard roof, and projecting bay windows. It is one of the few St. John's buildings south of Military Road to survive the fire.

George Rendell was a Devonshire man. He was a lad of seventeen when, in 1843, he set sail for Newfoundland, no doubt to join other family members there. He became a successful merchant and, for more than half a century, was a partner in the firm of W. and G. Rendell. In 1888 he was appointed to the Legislative Council. His daughter, Margaret Rendell, was the first Newfoundlander to become a professional nurse, after graduating from Johns Hopkins Hospital, Baltimore, in 1897.

Margaret was about thirty-four years old when she graduated. Three years later she married into one of Newfoundland's foremost political families. Her husband was George Shea, son of newspaper editor Edward D'Alton Shea, and a nephew of Sir Ambrose Shea. George too had political ambitions and,

FACING PAGE:

The Rendell-Shea house,
82 Cochrane Street,
spared when its neighbour
burned to the ground.

Laying of the cornerstone,
Cabot Tower,
June 24, 1897.

in 1902, ran successfully for mayor, serving a four-year term. Margaret's father died in 1909, but her mother lived on in the house. Twenty years later, George Shea purchased Margaret's family home at auction, and when he died it reverted to Margaret, who, in 1935, assigned it to their son, Captain Ambrose Shea.

Devon Row, five adjoining houses on Duckworth Street, may also have been designed by Southcott, although no one knows for sure. If so, these houses, four dignified storeys high, were the only brick houses built by that firm, except for one on Rennie's Mill Road. Because Devon Row was built of brick, it survived the Great Fire of 1892 — although that escape was somewhat miraculous.

St. John's after the Great
Fire of 1892.

Devon Row, Numbers 1 to 4 Duckworth Street, grandeur in redbrick.

Row houses such as those that made up Devon Row were not for hoi polloi, since few ordinary working people could afford such quarters. Devon Row was built for successful merchants or middle-class professionals who could afford its tempting amenities. These included French doors on the lowest level, which at the time opened onto small gardens, and on the second floor, wrought-iron balconies that offered a magnificent view of the harbour. Elaborately plastered ceilings graced the principal rooms, and each of the five floors, from basement to the fourth, boasted a fireplace: stone in the basement; Italian white marble on the first floor; plain grey marble on the second; wood on the third; and iron on the top floor, where small round-topped dormer windows looked out over the city and the harbour.

Devon Row was built in the early 1870s by James and Hannah Martin, who, like so many other Newfoundlanders, had come to escape the dismal economic prospects in Devon. In time they became relatively affluent, enough so that it is possible they were able to retain James J. Southcott, a fellow Devon expatriate, to design their five impressive (and expensive) houses. (As there is no list of houses built by Southcott, Devon Row cannot be attributed to him with certainty.) Today, sadly, only four houses remain — the fifth was destroyed in recent years to make way for a bank.

The Martins themselves never lived at Devon Row, perhaps because the rental income from the five units was such that it made economic sense for them to retain their living quarters above Hannah Martin's china shop on Water Street. Eventually they sold the houses and returned to England.

Among those who did live there was one of the colony's most distinguished citizens, a man who brought honour to Newfoundland, not from political or commercial success, but because of his brilliant, inquiring mind.

157

He was Moses Harvey, a Presbyterian minister, prodigious essayist, lecturer, historian, and enthusiastic naturalist. He and his wife, Sarah Anne Brown (called Jessie), lived at 3 Devon Row.

Born in Belfast, Harvey was ordained there and served in England for a few years before accepting a posting to St. Andrew's Free Church in St. John's. It was 1852, and Moses was then in his early thirties. He and Jessie settled contentedly into St. John's life, and became the parents of three sons. Harvey served his church well for more than a quarter of a century, then resigned and went on to pursue his other diverse interests. One of these was writing — he wrote an astonishing nine hundred articles for the *Montreal Gazette*, and in his later years remarked with self-deprecating humour, "It makes one shudder to think of having produced such a quantity of printed matter."

Perhaps Harvey's greatest love was Newfoundland's natural history. He wrote and lectured extensively on the subject. Thus, when a giant squid was dragged out of Conception Bay in October 1873, Harvey was presented with a severed tentacle, since, in the words of a local clergyman, he was known to be "crazy after all kinds of strange beasts and fishes." Next month an intact squid was discovered in Logy Bay, and this enabled him to offer proof of their existence to British and American zoologists who, until then, had doubted that such creatures existed. They were named *Architeuthis harveyi* in his honour.

Harvey's biographer, F. A. Aldrich, writes that Harvey, more than a century ago, worried about the excessive use of Newfoundland's waters by foreign fishing fleets — a subject that still enrages fishermen and politicians, and results in occasional altercations in Newfoundland waters today. The Grand Banks, wrote Harvey, "are most esteemed for their codfish and are in consequence the general fishing grounds of all European nations." Plus ça change . . .

The seal fishery also troubled Harvey, for while he approved of the fishery itself, he disliked the methods used in the kill, lamenting that the "crystal ramparts" of ice that were once happy nurseries of the mothering seals had become a slaughterhouse.

In 1886, Harvey was made a fellow of the Royal Geographical Society. The following year, due to his growing prestige and, in large part, to his warnings of problems facing the cod and seal fisheries, the governor in council set up a fisheries commission with Harvey as secretary. Then, in 1891, more honours: he was named a fellow of the Royal Society of Canada and awarded an LL.D. *in absentia* by McGill University.

The Great Fire of 1892 came terrifyingly close to destroying the brick houses that made up Devon Row. Harvey wrote in vivid detail of that day, July 8, 1892:

> I began to think of my home in Devon Row, and for the first time I realized that in all probability it would be included in the general destruction. Through a suffocating atmosphere, laden with burning sparks and blinding

smoke, I wended my way homeward, and found that all the inhabitants of Devon Row were packing their goods and preparing to remove them to places of safety, as it was believed to be impossible to save the Row. I followed the general example, and we continued to work for two hours and a half, and were successful in carrying to a place of safety all that was portable — thanks to the aid of numerous kind friends. Meantime the torrent was bearing straight down on us. Devon Row consists of six brick houses, four stories in height, with a tarred asphalt roof . . . and a wooden balcony behind, so that it presented many vulnerable points. The inmates were all doing their best to fight the fire, and a strong force assembled at number 5, the house next to the fire. The roof was kept wet — wet blankets placed at the end of the balcony, brooms in active service to sweep off sparks as they fell in myriads. Still, we had little hope of escaping, as far stronger buildings and better protected perished. The torrent approached; the house next the Row blazed up, and the blood red tongues of fire shot out, licking the gable-end and mounting towards the roof. We stood looking on, expecting every moment to see the roof or windows on fire. We held our breath, waiting for the final catastrophe; but the fiery bombardment did not take effect; the sparks flew off without a lodgement; the flames from the burning house next it began to collapse after the roof fell in, and with a sigh of relief we realized that Devon Row was saved. Had it gone, all the houses below it, with the railway station, would have been destroyed.

(Harvey's mention of six houses in Devon Row is puzzling, since he mentions that number 5 was the house next to the fire. An insurance map of 1914 shows only five units, suggesting that the six came from a slip of the pen.)

In 1893, Canada's Department of Marine and Fisheries set up a floating station in the Gulf of St. Lawrence, due in large part to Harvey's efforts and the encouragement of the Royal Society of Canada. This in time led to the establishment of what would become the Fisheries Research Board of Canada. These were exceptional achievements that owed much to this one remarkable scholar in nineteenth-century Newfoundland.

In 1900, Jessie Harvey died, and with her loss Moses Harvey sank into depression. The following year, early in the morning of September 3, he was found dead in the back garden of his Devon Row home. He had jumped from a window.

One building that did not survive the Great Fire of 1892 was St. George's Hospital, a stone structure that began its life in 1842 as one of two barracks on Signal Hill. Both were converted into hospitals when the garrison left Newfoundland in 1870. After the 1892 fire, the stone from St. George's was stockpiled and later used by a skilled stonemason, Samuel Garrett, to build four compact row houses on Temperance Street, houses built as wedding presents for his four daughters.

Temperance Street row houses built for Samuel Garrett's daughters.

Garrett was so proficient in his profession that he was retained to build the Cabot Tower, a dramatic landmark that rose on Signal Hill between 1898 and 1900, built to commemorate (somewhat after the fact) the quarter centenary of Cabot's landing in 1497, and Queen Victoria's Diamond Jubilee in 1900. Local legend has it that on Cabot Day, June 24, that year, Sir Edgar Bowring and Judge Prowse had arranged for the USS *Massachusetts* to sail into St. John's harbour as part of the celebrations surrounding the opening of the tower. But the government of the day had been slow in paying its share of the construction costs, and so Garrett (who, no doubt, had dealt with governmental delays before) wisely refused to turn over the keys to the tower until he was paid.

Garrett's four stone houses march in steps down Temperance Street. The epitome of solidity, they are constructed of two-foot-thick dressed stone that extends for three stories and a basement, with eight feet of those thick stone walls beneath the present sidewalk. But inside, personal taste came into play. Fireplaces, one in each of the major rooms, had decorative mantels each distinct from any of the others, and each house had interior trim differing from its neighbour's. Obviously each daughter had a say in how her house would be finished.

Of the four houses, all built between 1894 and 1896, the first to be occupied was 35 Temperance Street. Lauretta Garrett Mcfarlane moved in soon after her 1901 marriage. Her sister, Emily, moved next door five years later, after her wedding to Joseph Dewling — a wedding that took place in St. Thomas' at 6:30 in the morning! "The bride was tastefully gowned in cream amazon cloth," reported the *Evening Telegram*, "with trimmings of white moire, and silk and embroidery, and carried a beautiful bouquet of white sweet peas." This account did not suggest that there was anything at all unusual

Eugene Delacroix, The Massacre of Scio (Scenes des Massacres de Scio).

about a wedding held at the crack of dawn, but mentioned that, after the service, the "wedding party drove to the residence of the bride's parents, where a sumptuous breakfast was provided." Among the "pretty, valuable and useful" presents that the bridal couple received was a "stone dwelling house, with lot, on Temperance Street, from her father." After the wedding, when Emily and Lauretta were living side by side, they were to share their every whim by ambling next door through a tunnel that connected the two basements.

Samuel Garrett's other two daughters never lived in the houses built for them. One, Mary, died at twenty-four. The fourth daughter, Eliza, lived at home and, presumably, never married. The houses they would have occupied were rented until Lauretta's children took up residence there.

When Samuel Garrett died at seventy in 1914, local papers mourned the loss of "another of its best and most trusted citizens," recalling that he had "helped many a poorer neighbour over a tight place" so that the "fragrance of his name will not soon fade from many a household." A loyal supporter of "Britain and British institutions," he was, claimed *The Daily News*, "prominently identified with the volunteer movement, having taken part in the riots in the 60s." Nor, with the optimism so prevalent at the time, did he ever doubt the "final triumph of British arms" in the war that began in the year of his death, and eventually claimed the lives of thousands of Newfoundland's finest young men.

Nineteen fourteen was the year when another Newfoundland tragedy left the colony in mourning. Seventy-seven sealers perished after being trapped on the ice in a howling blizzard. They had been inadvertently abandoned by their ship. Ten thousand people lined the docks to greet the *Bonaventure* when it arrived in St. John's harbour carrying the crew of the *Newfoundland*, "piled like cord wood under a tarpaulin on her fore hatch." David Macfarlane wrote in *The Danger Tree* that one man "died on his knees, with his sixteen-year-old son in his arms. He was trying to shield the boy from the storm. It was difficult to pry the bodies apart."

The man blamed for the *Newfoundland* tragedy was the legendary Abram Kean, the greatest sealer of his day — and perhaps the only sealer whose proficiency earned him an OBE. That honour was awarded in recognition of his one millionth pelt. This milestone was reached twenty years after that terrible error in judgment, the worst he would ever make, sent seventy-seven sealers to their death. So sure was Kean that the men could manage the five miles across the ice to their ship, the *Newfoundland* (captained by his son, Wes) that he sent them over the side of his ship, the *Stephano,* after providing them with tea and biscuits. Shifting ice and a blinding snowstorm compounded the error, and the *Newfoundland*'s crew never found their ship. Their bodies were discovered two and a half days later.

Abram Kean lived in the west end of St. John's at 10 Waterford Bridge. Nearby, on the banks of the Waterford River, stood Vail's Bakery, a thriving operation owned by Gilbert Browning, an entrepreneurial Scot with a finger in many pies, and not just those produced at Vail's. By the time he entered the bakery business in 1869, he was already the owner of a sawmill, a cod-liver oil factory, a boot factory and a biscuit factory.

Browning had departed his home in Ayreshire for Newfoundland after the Great Fire of 1846 created a demand in St. John's for skilled artisans. He was then in his mid-twenties, an ambitious and energetic young builder. Within two years of his arrival he had attracted the eye of Kenneth McLea, a local merchant who retained Browning to design and build a splendid house at the foot of Shaw Street, a house he named Richmond Hill. Browning knew his craft and practised it well — so well that he had the confidence, thirty years later, to buy Richmond Hill for himself.

Richmond Hill was a handsome, well-proportioned house, suggesting that Browning and McLea both had either a good eye for scale and design, or access to the latest pattern book. On the façade, a central inset door topped by a Classical Revival pediment was balanced by French doors on either side. Above, three five-sided "Scottish" dormers provided light to the second floor. The kitchen was in the basement, as was the custom of the day. (It was felt that the kitchen should always be located as far as possible from the main part of the house, in order to avoid cooking smells. Convenience for the household staff was not an issue.) A circular well between the ground floor and the second floor, surrounded by a wrought-iron railing, was a delightful architectural feature that also helped the circulation of warm air during Newfoundland's frigid winters.

In 1861, not long after Kenneth McLea settled in at his newly built Richmond Hill, he decided to run for public office as the Conservative candidate for St. John's West. He was then in his early sixties. Catholic-Protestant animosity was at its height, and the election that year spawned riots, one of which resulted in the deaths of three men. McLea withdrew from the election when a mob smashed his business premises. He was appointed to the Legislative Council early the following year, but he didn't live to enjoy this position, dying in June 1862 on a visit to Richmond Hill, England. Richmond Hill, the house, stayed in the family until 1875, when his descendants sold it to the Reverend George Bond, who, in turn, sold it four years later to the man who had built it, Gilbert Browning.

Browning and his wife, Elizabeth (née Blair), had four accomplished sons, Thomas, John, Donald and James, two of whom became lawyers after graduating from university in Glasgow. All were prominent in the professional and commercial life of St. John's. Gilbert Browning died on a visit to Glasgow in 1892. Daughters Mary and Elizabeth eventually inherited Richmond Hill, and it remained in the family until 1930.

Not too far from Richmond Hill is a pleasant frame house at 16 Topsail Road, agreeably situated on a spacious two and a half acres. It was built in 1896 when hundreds of other St. John's houses were rising phoenix-like from the ashes of the 1892 fire. It was called Brightside by its builder, Alexander (Sandy) Macdougal, and his wife, Polly (née Ayre). Brightside boasts no identifiable architectural style, although it may have borrowed a few stylistic idioms from what was known as the Shingle Style along the eastern seaboard of the United States. Asymmetrical, with plenty of gables, bay windows and porches, the style allowed for flexibility and thus appealed to builders of both modest and more grandiose homes.

In time, Brightside came into the hands of Frank Bennett, son of Sir John Robert Bennett, a prominent local businessman and politician, and president of the nearby Bennett Breweries. Most of the city's more substantial homes were in the east side of St. John's. Brightside, on the west, was an exception. Its proximity to the brewery is the likely explanation.

Beside a quiet road on the northern outskirts of St. John's stands a cottage with a name recalling a bloody battle that took place on Khios, an island in the Aegean Sea, off the coast of Turkey. There, in the 1820s, Greek Christians were massacred by Turks during Greece's war of independence.

The cottage is called Mount Scio, its name taken from a magnificent painting by Eugene Delacroix, *The Massacre of Scio (Scenes des Massacres de Scio)*. It depicts an incident during those wars of Greek independence in which Byron fought and died. In 1821 the Greeks had risen against the Turks, and in January 1822 they declared their independence. For the next five years they fought Turkish efforts to regain control of the country. Delacroix's paintings, typical of the Romantic movement then becoming popular, portrayed scenes of violent physical action, with lots of dramatic emotional content and psychological impact. They brought contemporary events vividly to life.

Brightside, 16 Topsail Road, the home of Frank Bennett and his family.

TELEGRAPH: Line from St. John's round Conception Bay to Harbor Grace completed November 24, 1851; first message sent from Brigus to St. John's by F. N. Gisborne, March 6, 1852; concern was known as the St. John's & Carbonear Electric Telegraph Co.

MARCONI: At Signal Hill, St. John's, succeeded in establishing wireless telegraph communications across the Atlantic Ocean with Poldhu, Cornwall, December 12, 1901.

BENNETT'S BREWERY: John Grant and Thomas Walker lost their lives in the fermenting vat, Oct. 28, 1845; gutted by fire, March 18, 1907.

C. F. BENNETT'S mill and factory destroyed by fire, supposedly of incendiary origin, Oct. 22, 1856.

BENNETT'S FOUNDRY: Opened at the Riverhead, St. John's, August 31, 1847; destroyed by fire, November 1, 1856.

But how, why, and when did a Greek place name associated with such violence come to be part of a pastoral Newfoundland scene? The answer lies, in all probability, with Edward Kielley, a St. John's surgeon who had travelled as a young naval officer to Russia and Greece. Years later, in 1837, Kielley, then middle-aged, bought the property from Thomas Ambrose, who held the Crown grant, as a summer retreat. This was some twenty years after the Scio massacre, but by then he might well have seen copies of the famous painting — and recognized that the view from his cottage was astonishingly similar to that depicted by Delacroix.

Kielley's biographer, Patrick O'Flaherty, writes that "Kielley's cosmopolitan experience and military loyalty . . . held him apart from other Roman Catholics in St. John's, most of whom were Irish immigrants, and led him to identify and associate with the ruling Protestant establishment in the colony." He became a friend of Governor Thomas Cochrane and Chief Justice Henry John Boulton, one of his patients, and so became known as a "Tory of the first water." His career (he was district surgeon for a while and then head of the St. John's Hospital) was marked with continual conflict and controversy, partly because it was well-nigh impossible for a man as passionate and committed as Kielley to keep an arms-length distance from the political storms of the day, and partly because he was Irish — self-described as a "plain man who spoke the feelings of his heart."

It was usually his tongue that got Kielley into trouble. In 1837, after two other physicians had apparently mutilated a woman in labour while "assisting" in the birth of her baby, Kielley railed, "They have butchered the woman, and deserve to be hanged!" The physicians in question claimed damage to their

The Keilley/Carter house, Mount Scio, its name inspired by a Delacroix painting.

CANTWELL, MICHAEL: Injured by explosion at Cabot Tower, December 3, and died December 5, 1918.

ALCOCK and BROWNE [sic]: Capt. Alcock and Lieut. Browne left St. John's in a Vickers-Vimy aeroplane June 14, 1919, and reached Clifden, Ireland, within 16 hours, June 15, 1919; both knighted for feat by King George V, June 20, 1919; Sir John Alcock killed in aviation accident at Rouen, France, Dec. 19, 1919.

reputations, but the resulting trial ended in a non suit. Next year, the outspoken Kielley was again in hot water, this time for calling John Kent, an Irish-born, hot-tempered politician, a "lying Puppy." Although Kent was thirty years his junior, Kielley threatened to beat him up. Kent, an MHA, complained to the House that his privileges as a member had been violated, and in the resulting uproar, Kielley was arrested, jailed, released, went into hiding, then sued for assault and false imprisonment, as well as damages of £3,000. He was eventually vindicated, and his litigation expenses were paid by the government.

For the most part, Kielley was known as a compassionate and dedicated physician and "decidedly first among the civilian medical practitioners," in St. John's. Fortunately, he was often able to retreat from the demands of his medical practice and the ceaseless squabbling in St. John's to the silence and serenity of Mount Scio. There, with his wife, Amelia Jackson, their two sons and a daughter, he spent some of his happiest days. He died at about the age of sixty-five, on March 8, 1855, in St. John's.

During the next thirty years or so, Mount Scio changed hands several times. One of the owners was John Bowring, one of Benjamin's sons. He and his wife, Mary Rennie, moved in not long after their wedding in 1856. They became parents of nine children, one of whom was the illustrious Sir Edgar Rennie Bowring. It was here in 1858 that Edgar was born. He joined the family firm at seventeen, and by the age of thirty-two was named senior resident partner. One of Newfoundland's leading businessmen and benefactors, he was knighted in 1815, and twice served as Newfoundland's high commissioner to Great Britain.

Sir Edgar is remembered today for his generosity to the people of St. John's, Bowring Park being one example. In the park is a replica of Sir George Frampton's celebrated statue of Peter Pan, inscribed "Presented to the children of Newfoundland by Sir Edgar R. Bowring, in memory of a dear little girl who loved the Park." Betty Munn, the little girl in question, drowned with her father, John S. Munn, when the steamship *Florizel* was wrecked off Cappahaydon, Newfoundland, in 1918. (Another statue is dedicated to the Fighting Newfoundlander, and the "undying memory of the Royal Newfoundland Regiment," founded in 1793, and nearly annihilated on the bloody battlefields of the First World War. Of the 5,482 men who fought there, two thirds were killed or wounded — sent to fight for the Empire by a country with a population of only 250,000.)

A later owner of Mount Scio was Walter Baine Grieve, another hot-headed politician, who in 1909 (long after he had sold Mount Scio) was arrested on charges of criminal libel because of allegations of impropriety aimed at Sir Edward P. Morris, a man described by historian Frederick Rowe as an "Irish demagogue, witty, cunning, kowtowing to the masses and . . . unscrupulous." It was Grieve who, in 1887, sold Mount Scio to Viola Carter, a member of one of Newfoundland's most distinguished families. It has remained in the Carter family to this day.

The Carter family, originally from Devon, had since the end of the eighteenth century been well established as merchants, and were part of the colony's small ruling élite in both Ferryland and St. John's. They were renowned in Newfoundland. In fact, Robert Carter, who emigrated in the early 1740s, his wife, Ann Wylley, and their son, William, born in Ferryland, were all credited with nothing less than saving the colony from the French.

Carter's moment in the sun came in 1762, when French forces had taken St. John's and Bay Bulls. Commandeering a fleet of shallops, arming and provisioning them at his own expense, he set out with his "shallop navy" and sent French vessels into retreat. Meanwhile, Ann was "manning" a cannon, scoring a hit on the mainmast of a French ship, staying on the firing line, and joining in the chase on her husband's shallop. British forces followed up the attack and St. John's was retaken. William Carter, their eldest son, made his mark when the French once again (in 1796) took Bay Bulls. Risking his life, he alerted officials at St. John's and prevented an invasion there. William Carter was made a judge of the vice-admiralty court, the second position in the colony, and one that in practice meant governing for the winter, when the naval governor returned to England.

It was William's grandson, George John Carter, who married Elizabeth Viola Goodridge (Viola), a young woman who also came from one of Newfoundland's prominent families. Her brother was Augustus Frederick Goodridge, who for a short period was prime minister of Newfoundland.

(George Carter was a cousin of Sir Frederick Bowker Terrington Carter, prime minister, chief justice, and a Father of Confederation.)

Viola and her four young children (perhaps she was by then a widow) made the move to Mount Scio in 1887 to escape an epidemic of diphtheria that was then ravaging St. John's. A family opposite her had been wiped out in a week, and so Viola did what all prudent Victorians would do — she took to the country, away from the "foul air" of the city. Urbanization and overcrowding caused many epidemics in the days when sanitation was poor, so her decision was understandable and probably wise. Epidemics of diphtheria were sweeping through western Europe and North America during the late nineteenth century, the bacteria spread from one person to another by coughing and sneezing, and often harboured by carriers who were unaware that they were spreading the disease.

Viola's grandson recalls that she would enjoy the outdoors but always sat under a tent in order to avoid tanning. This was done by ladies of the day, not because of undue concern about holes in the ozone, but because pallor for women was then fashionable. (Her grandson recalls that another grandmother took daily doses of arsenic to achieve the same results — alternating between one and two drops per day.)

Mount Scio began life as a small Regency cottage, a style popular in the early years of the nineteenth century, and brought to this side of the Atlantic by British officers on half pay who had seen service in various exotic locations. The Regency was a transitional style built by and for gentlemen — men of refinement and taste. It was usually a building of one and a half storeys, and square in plan, with large windows and an encircling verandah.

Today Mount Scio looks much as it did a century and a half ago — at least on the ground floor. The treillage, French windows and shutters are all original, as are the interior folding doors. The second storey, however, is newer — added by the Bowrings as their family grew. Its gable roof allowed for more spacious rooms, and the large, hooded windows provided additional light for bedrooms. A 1917 fire caused considerable damage to the house, but the necessary repairs were done without destroying the original integrity of the house. Nestled into the rural landscape, it overlooks forty gently rolling acres dotted with fruit trees, a trout pond, and fields of savoury, a herb that grows particularly well in this soil. And the view? Just look at the Delacroix painting.

CHAPTER 15

St. John's: Quidi Vidi

REGATTA: Available records show that the Regatta has been held at Quidi Vidi Lake, St. John's, for the past century [i.e. circa 1823] for the first fifty years the races were rather intermittent, but for the half century of the immediate past they have been maintained regularly, except 1892, the year of the Big Fire, and 1915–1918[sic], the period of the Great World War. . . .

In 1856 there was a Women's Race, won by the following Quidi Vidi crew: Ellen Walsh, stroke; Jennie King, Mary Brace, Lizzie Hauton, Crissie Squires, Jessie Needham; Robert Hennebury, coxswain.

In 1884, as the Amateurs were rowing her to the home stakes, the *Terra Nova*, on the Lake for the first time, filled with water and sank. S. Gosse, J. Martin and M. Power, all of Torbay, drowned. The *Terra Nova* was renamed the *Myrtle* next year.

Quidi Vidi. Even on this island known for colourful, unusual place names, the hamlet of Quidi Vidi stands apart. No one knows where the name originated, but historically it was pronounced "Kiddy Viddy," "Kittavitty," or "Kitty Witty." And the name certainly goes back a long way in Newfoundland's history.

As early as 1697, Quidi Vidi was raided and razed by the French under Pierre le Moyne d'Iberville, who had busily destroyed most of the settlements on the east coast of the island since claiming it for France in the 1660s. The village is noted on a 1751 map showing houses there in "Kitty Vitty Harbour." Located as it was away from the town centre, it escaped the raging fires that destroyed so many early buildings in St. John's. In 1762, during the Seven Years' War, when the French had reclaimed many settlements on the island, Quidi Vidi was again the scene of a battle, when nearby St. John's was recaptured by British forces under Thomas Graves and William Amherst.

The flood of Catholic Irish settlers started about this time. It was the beginning of the Irish influence in Newfoundland, an influence still heard in the charming, unmistakable lilt of Newfoundlanders' speech. The Irish (who settled mainly along the Avalon Peninsula and the south shore), though badly treated, changed the face of the island through persistence and sheer force of numbers.

Among the earliest Irish immigrants were two Mallard brothers who settled in Quidi Vidi. The Mallard name first appears in 1803, where a Registry of Deeds shows a transaction of chattels between William Mallard of Kittavitty and Cunningham, Bell & Co., St. John's. In later years the name popped up now and then, as a brief item in local newspapers. The Mallards' triumphs and tragedies echoed those of many, if not most, families who eked out a living in nineteenth-century Newfoundland outports, as various newspaper reports indicate:

1842   John Mallard and his son drowned while crossing the lake on the ice, January 11.

FACING PAGE:
Mallard Cottage, one of Newfoundland's oldest buildings.

1851   Mallard, James of Quidi Vidi, married Mrs. E. Hay of St. John's at St. Thomas' by Rev. Wood. Sept. 18.

1852   Mallard, Ann. Inquest: Went to visit her brother-in-law Mr. Morrisey in the forest, returned home, hung up her hat and dropped dead, at Quidi Vidi. February 19.

1869   Mallard, John. Native of Newfoundland. Died of fever aboard the brig *William Nash the 13th*, on passage to Boston from St. Domingo. 6 July.

BULL BAITING: Took place near Quidi Vidi Lake, August 14, 1831; repetition of exhibition forbidden by official notice, published in *The Royal Gazette* under date of August 15, 1831, and signed "A. Hoggsett, Clerk of the Peace."

Mallard Cottage, probably built by the brothers after their arrival in 1803, still stands. According to a report by Mary Cullen, architectural analyst, while Mallard Cottage shows evidence of the English influence found in Cape Cod cottages so prevalent in New England and Nova Scotia, it also shows distinct Irish connections. "The one and a half storey, hipped roof form and central chimney, two-room floor plan are associated with Irish building in Newfoundland." The five-bay, central-door façade may have been added in an effort to copy grander and larger merchant and government buildings. The house appears to be almost a miniature, "due in part to its lack of foundation and the half size windows tucked up under the eaves to light the attic storey."

Mallard Cottage, located at a safe distance from the fires that ravaged the main sections of St. John's, is part of Newfoundland's visible history today. It remained in the Mallard family until 1985, at which time its new owner inherited a hundred and eighty years of history and twenty-eight layers of wallpaper.

FACING PAGE, TOP:
Window residents, Mallard Cottage.

FACING PAGE, BOTTOM:
Preparing for the Race at Quidi Vidi.

CHAPTER 16

St. John's: Cape Spear

Only a year or two before Mount Scio was built, amid pastoral surroundings north of St. John's, another solid, square wooden structure had risen high on a rock promontory southeast of the city. Its occupants enjoyed a view even more dramatic, and far more forbidding than anything seen from the gentle slopes along Mount Scio Road. From their aerie on a cliff four hundred feet above the pounding Atlantic, the lighthouse keepers at Cape Spear might be justified in imagining that on a clear day they could almost see Ireland, nearly 3,000 kilometres to the east.

Construction began in 1835, and by the following year the Cape Spear beacon was announcing to approaching ships that they had finally sighted the coast of North America. One fisherman said that the Cape Spear light was "like the rays of heaven suddenly showing through the fog." It was a welcome message but a forbidding one too, for it warned that treacherous waters lay ahead — the island's steep granite cliffs were often blanketed with thick, grey, unending fog, and at the foot of the cliffs, hidden beneath high seas, lurked shoals and sandbars. (Countless lives had been lost before authorities in Britain could be convinced that lighthouses should be a priority. British records from early in the eighteenth century show that one in eight ships that left England for the New World failed to reach its destination.)

The first lightkeeper at Cape Spear was Emanuel Warr. He was there for ten years, but after his death in April, 1846, an Irishman, James Cantwell, took over. There have been Cantwells there ever since. (A sixth-generation descendant is still employed at the lighthouse.) James Cantwell obtained the position after coming to the attention of Prince Hendrick of the Netherlands, whose ship, the frigate *De Ryn* (Rhine) became lost in a heavy fog off St. John's in the summer of 1845. Cantwell, after searching for hours, found the ship and safely piloted it into the harbour. Two weeks later, as he was leaving, the prince wrote a letter of recommendation:

> The undersigned, Commander of His Majesty's *De Ryn* declares that pilot James Cantwell of St. John's piloted the above mentioned ship from the sea

FACING PAGE:

The Cape Spear light, where six generations of Cantwells kept watch.

Marconi and his assistants with Mr. Cantwell outside the Cabot Tower, circa 1901.

to the harbour of St. John's on the 9th August, 1845, and again piloted the ship to sea on August 26th; giving all evidence of being competent and fit for his work and is deserving of all recommendation.

> On board HMS *De Ryn*
> August 26th, 1845
> The Commander
> Hendrick, Prince of the Netherlands.

It is doubtful that Cantwell found lightkeeping an easier task than piloting, although it may have offered slightly more security for a man with a family. But it was a poorly paid, lonely and dangerous business, "less like a job than a form of slavery," according to Harry Bruce in his article "Sentinels of the Shore" (*Imperial Oil Review*, spring 1991). "Some keepers had to contend with untreated injuries, shortages of fresh water, shipments of rotten meat . . . windows so encrusted with salt they couldn't see through them, storms so fierce the windows bulged inwards and no one dared step outside, and living quarters so damp they suffered pneumonia, tuberculosis or arthritis."

The Cantwells, however, carried on, and kept the Cape Spear light burning for five succeeding generations — every hour of every day, for more than one hundred and fifty years. By the time the present keeper, Gerry Cantwell (the sixth generation), and his five siblings were growing up in the lighthouse, conditions had improved immensely. There were then twenty-seven rooms in the lighthouse, not all of them large, but it meant that the Cantwells never felt cramped. Also living there, in their own quarters, were an assistant, his wife, and their three children. Gerry's mother, Margaret, had moved to Cape Spear after her 1941 marriage to Frank Cantwell. Margaret and Frank were the last to occupy the old lighthouse. "When I was living there," says Gerry, "it had

174

Cape Spear lighthouse interior, showing rack of signal flags.

grown to thirty-plus rooms. . . . They just kept adding on and adding on as families grew. There were six of us kids, and the assistant, who also lived in a section of the house, had three kids. So there were thirteen of us, including adults, all living in one house."

Margaret Cantwell taught all nine children until they were ready for high school. In a 1990 interview she recalled with nostalgia her years at Cape Spear. As Gerry put it, "Mom can talk fifty years back." And indeed she could, with a pleasure that suggests that, although conditions were spartan, "shabby treatment" was not the way they would describe their lives: "My husband [Frank Cantwell] was the keeper. He had an assistant. . . . If [Frank] had to be down in the fog alarm he'd be back at eight A.M.; he had to wind the light every one and a half hours — wind it up like you'd wind up a clock. The two men would take turns every other night — if it was foggy, one of them had to go to the fog alarm. I would do it sometimes if Frank was busy. . . . We didn't mind the storms — even if we did lose the lights we had lots of coal. It was comfortable. . . . The children didn't feel isolated."

Gerry Cantwell is likely to be the last of his line to man the Cape Spear light. Today, in the age of automation, navigation is done by computer and communication satellite — less romantic perhaps, but efficient and economically sound. Since 1955 the light at Cape Spear has operated from a new concrete tower, and the lighthouse itself, home to so many generations of Cantwells, has been restored to the original 1835 design. It is now the centrepiece of Cape Spear National Historic Park — a reminder of those stoic Newfoundlanders who, for more than a century and a half, ensured that their "swift-winged arrows of light" shone brightly to warn the wary sailor from their shores.

Notice to Mariners.

LIGHT-HOUSE ON
Cape Spear,
NEWFOUNDLAND.

NOTICE IS HEREBY GIVEN.

THAT a Light will be exhibited in the Light House which has been erected on *Cape Spear*, on the evening of THURSDAY the 1st of *September* next and thenceforth continued every nigh from Sun set to Sun-rise, for the benefit of Navigation.

The character of this Light—which will burn at an elevation of 275 feet above the level of the sea—will be that of a POWERFUL REVOLVING LIGHT, showing a brilliant Flash at regulated intervals of ONE MINUTE.

The STATIONARY LIGHT on Fort Amherst, at the entrance of this Harbour, will be continued as heretofore.

THOMAS BENNETT
HENRY P. THOMAS
JAMES M'BRIDE
B. BONIFANT
JOHN SINCLAIR

Commissioners.

St. John's Newfoundland,
August 25, 1836.

THE AVALON AND BURIN
PENINSULAS

CHAPTER 17

Ferryland

I came to builde, and sett, and sowe, but I am falne to fighting with ffrench-men," complained a discouraged Sir George Calvert, first Baron Baltimore, in 1628. It was a complaint that might have been made by almost any Newfoundland settler during the centuries of French-English conflict on the island, as the two countries fought for dominance over the fishing grounds.

More than a century after Peter Easton and his pirates discovered its potential, Lord Baltimore started a short-lived colony of English Catholics at Ferryland, on the shores of a picturesque harbour on the Avalon Peninsula, about thirty-seven miles south of St. John's. Baltimore, a recent convert to Catholicism, had resigned as England's secretary of state, and in order to keep an eye on his tiny Newfoundland settlement and his two managing agents there, he left for Ferryland in 1627. His stay was brief but he returned the following year, planning to settle permanently. With him came his second wife, Jane, all but the eldest of his eleven children, and two Catholic priests. The family moved into the relative comfort of a large stone house, but within months Jane departed for Virginia, presumably taking some or all of her stepchildren with her. Perhaps she had been warned about Newfoundland winters (they last from October to May, claimed Baltimore) but he remained. After enduring an exceptionally severe winter, escalating objections to his policy of religious toleration, and the ongoing attacks of French privateers all along the Avalon Peninsula, he too decided he had had enough. "In this part of the worlde," wrote Baltimore, "miseryes is my portion." He left for Virginia in 1629. Even there, his miseries were far from over. Rudely received because he was a Roman Catholic, he was deported to England. His wife and children followed him in another ship that was lost at sea with all hands.

Baltimore's departure from Newfoundland did not, however, spell the end of Ferryland. In 1638, Sir David Kirke, an adventurer and trader, arrived on the scene accompanied by his wife, their children, and a hundred colonists. He took possession of Baltimore's mansion and other Ferryland property, and

FACING PAGE:
Abandoned Ferryland light.

PREVIOUS PAGE:
Ferryland.

proceeded to turn Ferryland into his personal fiefdom. He became the first governor of Newfoundland. Backed by his Company of Adventurers to Newfoundland (its coat of arms is that of the Province of Newfoundland today), he attempted to wrest control from the West Country merchants on behalf of London interests. Accused by the merchants of disrupting the fishing industry by establishing taverns along the coast, he returned to England in 1651 to face charges of tax evasion and oppression, charges that were never substantiated. His wife was allowed to return to Ferryland to take care of his business interests there. Sad to say, Kirke died in jail three years later while imprisoned on a suit by Lord Baltimore's heir for the seizure of Ferryland in 1639.

Kirke's wife and her family remained in Ferryland, despite claims by Baltimore's heirs. Some Kirke descendants were there until the 1700s, having survived political upheavals, continuing struggles between competing English merchants and between the English and the French, and attacks by the Dutch in 1673 and the French in 1694. It was captured by the French two years later when all resident planters were deported to England.

During the 1700s, Ferryland received a great influx of Irish settlers, and by the next century it had become a major fishing and supply centre. Given all this activity over so many years, it seems surprising that it wasn't until 1871 that a lighthouse was built. Although the light became automated many years ago, the tower and the weathered house beside it still stand at Ferryland harbour. Unlike other Newfoundland lighthouses, with fabricated steel towers manufactured elsewhere and hauled to the site, the tower at Ferryland was built of brick then coated with steel to protect it from fire and the unforgiving weather. The simple frame house, built at the same time, was a double house with room for the families of both the lightkeeper and his assistant. Some winters the ice storms were so fierce that the house developed a coating of ice, which in effect sealed it from the winds that ravaged Ferryland Head.

The story was much the same for other lighthouses along the rugged coastline of the Avalon Peninsula, a peninsula that reaches out into the rich fishing grounds of the North Atlantic. It was named by the idealistic Lord Baltimore after the legendary site where Christianity was introduced to England. With its four major bays — Trinity, Conception, St. Mary's and Placentia — the Avalon Peninsula was among the first areas to be fished and soon became Newfoundland's most populous region. Yet there were no lighthouses there — nor anywhere else on the island — until 1813, when authorities decided that the entrance to St. John's harbour at Fort Amherst warranted a light. Even then that light had to be maintained by voluntary contributions, since there was as yet no colonial legislature to provide financing. It was another twenty years before the next lighthouse was built, after Governor Cochrane gave the idea his backing. Gradually more lighthouses appeared; by the early 1880s, a system of thirty-three lights marked the coast from Twillingate south in a clockwise direction to Port aux Basques.

The light at Cape Race was the first light seen by most ocean-going ships bound for Canada and the Newfoundland fishing fleets. Far below in the roiling surf, rocks, considered to be the "greatest hazard on a generally perilous shoreline," awaited the unwary. Dudley Witney, in *The Lighthouse*, writes:

> It was at Cape Race that Newfoundlanders wishing to go to England in a hurry would wait to catch the swift mailboats. Children, women, and even pet animals had to suffer the tedious and rough journey from St. John's, only to find themselves on top of a cliff, a hundred feet above the uninviting rocks of the shore, facing a single iron ladder down to the pilot ship. Local lore had it that if they survived the trip down the ladder and out to the mail boat, they would enjoy the journey, whatever the weather.
>
> To the west, at Cape Pine, high above the treacherous waters on Newfoundland's southernmost tip, a cast-iron lighthouse was built in 1851 by English engineers who, not having experienced a Newfoundland winter, planned that the lightkeeper would live inside the tower. He, poor man, abandoned the idea within months and moved to a nearby construction shack for the remainder of the winter. Next summer a house was built for him.

FLORENCE: American brig., Capt. Rose, lost at Cape Race, August 9, 1840, with the first mate and 49 passengers, the latter being all German immigrants bound for New York.

S.S *ANGLO SAXON:* Lost near Cape Race, April 27, 1863; 307 drowned.

TOBIN, MRS.: Widow of L. Tobin, died at Witless Bay, October 24, 1868, being survived by 14 children, 125 grandchildren, 51 great grandchildren — 190 descendants.

CLAM COVE: Near Cape Race, scene of loss of French brig., with all her crew except a boy, Sept. 21, 1877.

COSTELLO, W.: Lightkeeper at Ferryland, killed by falling over a cliff Feb. 13, 1905.

S.S. *FLORIZEL:* of Red Cross Line; first arrived in Newfoundland Jan. 18, 1908; wrecked near Renews Feb. 26, 1918; 94 lives lost.

CHAPTER 18

Placentia

The southeast coast of the island, from St. John's and the Avalon Peninsula westward to Placentia, was, though not physically reminiscent of the green hills of Ireland, certainly Irish green in culture, Roman Catholic religion, and native tongue.

Before the famine of the 1840s drove thousands of starving Irish across the Atlantic, many thousands more had already found a new home in Newfoundland. By the 1820s there were, according to geographer John Mannion, "probably more Irish in Newfoundland than in any other [part of] North America."

They had been arriving since the seventeenth century. And though the fishery was still migratory and settlement discouraged by every possible means, some Irish wintered over, as did a few Englishmen. In many cases the decision was made for them, since their masters wanted men on hand to protect their premises. By the 1780s, Irish immigrants were landing on Britain's island colony at the rate of over 5,000 a year. Nearly all came from Waterford, Ireland. That immigration continued through the 1800s as West Country fishing vessels regularly stopped in Ireland en route to Newfoundland to pick up provisions and "youngsters" (an Irish term having nothing to do with age, but rather with status as a labourer, normally unmarried). By the 1830s, the British majority in Newfoundland became aware that 35,000 Irish had come to their island in the three previous decades. They began to sit up with alarm and take notice, fearing for their power and their comfortable majority.

By mid-eighteenth century, one third of the entire Irish population of Newfoundland resided in the Placentia area. But before the lilt of the Irish was heard there, the area had been coveted for centuries — first by Basques who, lured from the south of France and north of Spain in the early 1500s in the crusade for cod, named the site (it appears on the Kallard map of 1547 as Isle de Plazienca, meaning a harbour "within a womb of hills") and built a church, their presence still remembered on tombstones of that early date. Soon thereafter, Placentia, with a harbour encircled by mountains, and deep waters that could accommodate hundreds of ships, was sought after by the French. From

FACING PAGE:

Tombstones of early settlers, Placentia.

183

Presentation Convent,
opened in 1864.

1662, when Louis XIV claimed the area and the French fishery there, Placentia (also then called Plaisance) was known as the French capital of Newfoundland. The town was fortified as a defence against its historic enemy, the English, and as a point from which to attack St. John's. The Récollet Fathers from Quebec established a parish and ordered the construction of a church to serve the French garrison.

With the arrival of the British in 1714 (after the signing of the Treaty of Utrecht), everything changed. Our Lady of Lourdes was replaced by St. Luke's Anglican Church, and for the next fifty-one years, Catholics were forbidden to practise their faith. When religious freedom returned, Catholic churches were built, and from then until now, Catholics and Protestants in Placentia have lived together with little discord. This happy development was due in part to the efforts of two Irish Catholics, both of whom arrived in 1785, just one year after the official establishment of the Roman Catholic Church in Newfoundland. The first was Edmund Burke, a priest and Dominican, who upon his arrival built a "very neat" chapel and, in spite of attracting a substantial number of converts from the Church of England, managed to co-exist in relative harmony with the Protestant authorities. (Burke may well have been related to British statesman and essayist Edmund Burke [1729–97], who, although himself a Protestant, was born in Dublin and throughout his life supported Irish causes.) In 1864, nearly a century after Burke's appointment to Placentia, the Presentation Convent was opened. It is the only stone building remaining in the town.

The other Irishman to change the face of Placentia was no labourer, but a rarity, an Irishman of the merchant class. He was Pierce Sweetman, whose prosperous family in Wexford had provided its share of recruits to the upper echelons of the Catholic Church in Ireland. When Sweetman and Burke landed in Placentia, the port was then the busiest on the south shore of Newfoundland. Sweetman went to work as an agent for Thomas Saunders, a relative by marriage. After only four years, Sweetman had become a partner, and the firm was renamed Saunders and Sweetman, with offices in Poole, Dorset (in effect, its head office), and in Waterford, Ireland, where it obtained the bulk of its migrant labour. The company had already been in the fish-trading business in Placentia for two generations, but Pierce was the first of the Sweetman family to actually visit the place, even though his maternal grandfather, Richard Welsh, had been one of the island's leading merchants during the eighteenth century. Pierce Sweetman's stay was not to be long, but like Edmund Burke, he left a lasting mark.

Sweetman first came to oversee the firm's extensive business concerns. Although by the 1780s most fishermen were "livyers" and overwintering servants, about one third of the labourers still came from the British Isles. Sweetman's biographer, John Mannion, writes that, unlike other Newfoundland merchants, Saunders and Sweetman preferred to hire Irishmen, particularly for work on shore. "For hard labour," claimed Saunders, "one Irish youngster is worth a dozen [English]." The firm consequently encouraged many Irish families to settle in Placentia — and generations later, they are still there.

By 1789, Placentia was in its heyday, and larger than St. John's. Saunders and Sweetman had nineteen shallops at sea, and the firm was transporting dried cod to France, Spain and Portugal, and to St. John's for the West Indies

PLACENTIA: Died, of putrid sore throat, within the last 3 weeks; Elizabeth Kempt, aged 18 years; Anastasia Kempt, 15; Ellen Kempt, 12; Peter Kempt, 10; John Kempt, 8; children of Patrick Kempt, ferryman at the Gut of Great Placentia. July 27, 1858.

DANTIE, THOMAS: Lost with his three brothers and his son in Western Boat on St. Mary's Bay, June 8, 1894.

ST. BRIDE'S: Fishermen belonging to St. Bride's caught a codfish that weighed 130 pounds before it was split, July 20, 1905.

Home of Mary Sweetman Verran and her son, Harry.

trade. In 1791, Pierce Sweetman married Juliet Forstall in Waterford, Ireland. It is unlikely that she ever ventured to Newfoundland, but if so, it was not for long. By 1796 the young couple and their growing family had settled permanently in Wexford, and it was from there that Sweetman managed his flourishing commercial affairs. He became and remained a highly successful businessman, one of Newfoundland's "most respectable merchants."

Pierce and Juliet Sweetman became parents of five children, two sons and three daughters. (Two of the daughters eventually entered a convent in Ireland.) Pierce Sweetman died at his home, Blenheim Lodge, Waterford, in 1841. His surviving son, Roger, ran the company first from Waterford, then from Placentia, until his death in 1862.

It was Roger Sweetman's only child, a daughter, Mary Josephine, who carried on the family story in Placentia. Educated in Ireland at the convent school where her two aunts taught, she returned to Placentia to pursue the same vocation, teaching in the convent school there until she met Harry Thomas Verran.

Verran, a mining engineer, had come to the area to conduct mineral prospecting for Cyrus Field of Atlantic Cable fame. Verran and Mary Sweetman were married in 1859. He died ten years later on his way to Africa, once again on a mission to seek out mineral deposits for Cyrus Field. Mary was left to raise their three children, Alicia, Minnie and Harry. She lived on in Placentia for another forty-two years, and after her death, the property was inherited by her son.

The Sweetman family is recalled by two buildings still standing in Placentia. The first, Verran House, was built in 1893 (perhaps by Mary Sweetman

Verran, who died in 1911, or possibly by her son, Harry Verran Jr.). It is a pleasant, well-proportioned Second Empire style house, with finely crafted exterior trim and three nicely detailed dormers projecting from its mansard roof. The second building is the cable office, erected following the formation of the Anglo-American Telegraph Company. The company's first office, however, was housed in Blenheim House, which was built shortly after Pierce Sweetman arrived in Placentia, its components brought, it is said, piece by piece from Ireland. The offices were moved to the present site (according to Shane O'Dea in *Ten Historic Towns*) "after Roger Sweetman's widow sold the [telegraph] company the land in about 1873." The company, financed by Cyrus Field, operated five Atlantic cables, six that connected Newfoundland to the mainland, and one between Prince Edward Island and Nova Scotia.

Cable office.

CHAPTER 19

Grand Bank

Although the town of Grand Bank had a long and significant history dating back to the 1600s, it was in the late 1800s that the site began to stir with increasingly intense activity — men and women busily cleaning and sorting codfish for salting and drying, their working tables and storage sheds laden with fish — visible evidence that prosperity had arrived. But there was one unusual aspect to this picture, something that could be seen in few (if any) Newfoundland outports — acres and acres of fish laid out to dry, not on flakes but on beaches. As the Bank fishery expanded, over one hundred acres of artificial beaches had been extended inland from the town's long natural beach to accommodate the huge catches being brought in daily from the Grand Banks. Many local merchants had their own section of beach, with their own crews of men and women, all taking advantage of their recent good fortune. The "Bank fishery" was bringing welcome affluence to Grand Bank, and it was largely due to the efforts of one man   Samuel Harris.

Until Harris brought this unaccustomed activity to Grand Bank, the community on the western coast of the Burin Peninsula, in Fortune Bay, had been an inshore fishing station. Oddly enough, the town's name had nothing to do with the Grand Banks, the renowned fishing banks that stretch from Newfoundland to the waters off Nantucket Island and Cape Cod, but instead referred to the harbour's forty-foot-high embankment on which the community was built — a Grand Banc, as the French called it.

The town, originally a migratory fishing station, had for many years been part of France's territory in the New World. In fact, the name appeared in a 1687 census that listed an odd assortment of residents, buildings and other items, including three married men, two married women, one female child, thirty-nine servants, three houses, one church and eighteen muskets. The French presence is still evident today in small communities scattered all along Newfoundland's south coast, many of which bear their original French name — St. Jacques, Cape La Hune, Rencontre East and West, Bay d'Espoir, Bay de

Captain Sam Piercy's store.

L'Eau, Cinq Cerf Bay, La Poile, Isle aux Morts, Channel-Port aux Basques.

Under the 1713 Treaty of Utrecht, the French lost all their territory in Newfoundland, including the lucrative south shore fishery, but they did retain exclusive fishing rights along the north shore from Cape Bonavista to Cape Riche — now known as the French Shore. The Seven Years' War saw France reclaim many settlements in Newfoundland, including St. John's. Then in 1763 the Treaty of Paris returned much of this territory to Britain. France retained its lucrative fishing rights on the French Shore, and was also awarded the small islands of St. Pierre and Miquelon, just twelve miles southwest of the Burin Peninsula. The English residents of Saint Pierre were forced to relocate, most moving to sites around Fortune Bay. Grand Banc became Grand Bank, an English settlement.

There were about sixty-four people living in Grand Bank that summer, but two years later, when Captain James Cook surveyed this part of the coast, Grand Bank's population had soared to 448 — the largest settlement, Cook noted, in Fortune Bay. The little community continued to grow as British vessels with settlers from the West Country arrived and local fishing boats set out in ever-increasing numbers to pursue the thriving cod, lobster, herring and salmon fisheries.

But it was another hundred years or so before Grand Bank really came into its own. By the last decade of the nineteenth century and for the first half of the twentieth, the town was a major supply centre for the southwest coast. Those halcyon days had their beginning in 1881, when Samuel Harris first sailed his seventy-ton schooner to the renowned Grand Bank, southeast of Newfoundland, and the largest of four nearby banks — a vast continental shelf

Captain John Thornhill's Queen Anne home, built in 1917. It is now a hotel.

equal in area to that of France. It had been discovered by western European fishermen centuries before, but Harris was the first man from the town of Grand Bank to venture so far afield.

Born in Grand Bank in 1850, Harris had been orphaned at eight, and within two years was working in the inshore fishery. By the time he reached twenty, the ambitious Harris had taken command of his first vessel, and in 1881 he was able to buy his own ship, which he renamed the *George C. Harris*, after his young son, who was then two years old. Soon Harris was building more "bankers" (large, specially built schooners) and many tern schooners (locally called "three masters") that carried dried cod to markets in Europe and South America. In time his fleet numbered more than thirty vessels, many of which, with true British patriotism, he named after war heroes. Thus, sailing off to foreign ports from Grand Bank went the *General Allenby*, the *General Byng*, the *General Smuts* and, curiously, the *General Ironsides*.

By the time Harris's three children had reached marriageable age, he was a wealthy man, worth an estimated four million dollars. He was easily able to provide his two sons and a daughter with generous wedding gifts, and this he did — each was given a large, roomy house in which to begin married life. All three houses were similar in style. In the ensuing years, daughter Emily's house was demolished, while the home of the second son, Garfield, became a combined residence and office building. But the 1908 house given to the older son, George C. Harris, has fared best, having survived the financial problems of its owner and a near-fatal fire.

George C. Harris did not have to overcome the hurdles that his orphaned father had encountered as a boy. He attended Mount Allison

GRANDS BANKS
DISASTER: 300 French
fishermen died May 31,
1858.

BLACKBURN,
HOWARD: Got astray
from his schooner, the
Grace L. Fears, of
Gloucester, on Burgeo
banks, Jan. 25, 1883;
his dory mate, Thomas
Welch, a Newfoundlander,
died of exposure after
a couple of nights;
Blackburn, though badly
frostbitten held on for five
days and nights and
finally got to safety at
Little River.

University, returned to Grand Bank to work in the family firm, and then married Charlotte Pratt (known as Lottie), a talented artist. Lottie was a sister of Edwin John Pratt, a distinguished professor and critic, and Canada's foremost poet during the first half of the twentieth century. The children of a Methodist minister, Lottie and her brother grew up in a succession of Newfoundland outports. E. J. Pratt's poetry, with its realistic, unsentimental approach, reflected his Newfoundland background. He wrote of heroic Canadian historical themes in "The Titanic," "Brébeuf and His Brethren," and "Towards the Last Spike."

The house into which the newlyweds moved was very much a Newfoundland merchant's house — spacious, solid, and straightforward, with little surface ornamentation other than the rather restrained pilasters on the façade, and diminutive brackets under the eaves. A belvedere on the roof offered a splendid view of the town and Fortune Bay. The Harris house shows a New England influence, which comes, notes Grand Bank historian Randell Pope, "from the close contact that merchants of Newfoundland's south coast had with Nova Scotia and the New England States." Stately and colourful, but not ostentatious, the house seemed to reflect in some subtle way the character of the island's people. It was, quite obviously, the home of a family of substance, but other than by its size, it made little attempt to impress.

In 1914, when Samuel Harris was sixty-four, he turned over the reins of his flourishing business concerns to his son George, who took over as managing director. George, then thirty-five, began to expand the business — perhaps too quickly. He purchased properties at Hermitage, northwest of Grand Bank, and at Change Islands, far to the north, near Fogo. But his timing was poor. Randell Pope writes that "This over-expansion, coupled with the decline in fish prices after World War One and unfavourable government fishery regulations were the main factors which led to the firm's bankruptcy in 1922. [The firm reorganized as the Samuel Harris Export Company, then reorganized again as Grand Bank Fisheries Ltd.] At the time it was said to be the largest bankruptcy in . . . Newfoundland. George C. was devastated; he shouldered the blame and left with nothing." For a while Harris tried politics — surely an equally risky business — but he was determined to change fishery regulations. He ran for office, won once when the government of John R. Bennett took office, but was defeated a year later when another election was called. Harris retired from politics in 1924, two years before his father's death.

George and Lottie Harris had no children. When they died in 1954, their house was sold to Hazen Russell, who used it as a staff house for his fish-processing business. In 1930 the Harris house had a brush with disaster when a fire levelled buildings along the waterfront, damaging the house in the process. Then, years later, when the house was converted to a duplex, a splendid staircase that turned a hundred and eighty degrees was removed and windows were drastically changed. Fortunately, in 1993, the Grand Bank Heritage

Society undertook a major restoration of the Harris house. The staircase was reconstructed with careful attention to detail, and accomplished without the original plans to serve as a guide. The house is now a source of pride to the community, its original handsome visage once more gracing the streets of Grand Bank.

Among the seafaring men who sailed on Samuel Harris's vessels was the enterprising Captain Sam Piercy. Wooed away from St. John's, where he had worked for Sir John Crosbie, Piercy started out in Grand Bank working for Harris, and by 1898 was in command of Harris's banker, the *Mary Harris*. Then, due to that unbeatable combination of enterprise, a gambler's instincts, and an advantageous marriage (his wife was Lucy Forward, a descendant of Ambrose Forward, one of the town's earliest settlers), Piercy was able to purchase his own vessels, which were sometimes chartered by Harris. He began shipping salt cod to ports in Europe and around the Mediterranean, soon earning accolades for his speed, with a record twelve-day Atlantic crossing from Oporto, Portugal, to Grand Bank. In 1910 he gave up "foreign going," bought the fishing premises previously owned by the Forwards and the Lovells (another of the town's early families), and concentrated on his mercantile business.

One section of Piercy's small frame store, still part of his premises, dates from the Forward and Lovell period, and another from Piercy's ownership, with recent extensions. Now, with assistance from federal and local heritage programs, the building (at 18 Water Street) has been restored to the 1918 period, when the Piercy and Harris families, the Forwards, Lovells and others were helping to build the busy town that was soon acknowledged to be the Bank-fishing capital of Newfoundland.

SQUID-JIGGIN'
GROUND

Oh, this is the place
  where the fishermen
  gather
With oilskins and boots
  and Cape-Anns battened
  down.
All sizes of figures with
  squid lines and jiggers,
They congregate here on
  the squid-jiggin' ground.
. . .
There's men from the
  Harbour and men from
  the Tickle,
In all kinds of motor
  boats, green, gray and
  brown;
There's a red-headed Tory
  out here in a dory,
A runnin' down Squires
  on the squid-jiggin'
  ground.

A. R. Scammel

THE FRENCH SHORE

CHAPTER 20

Bay of Islands, Corner Brook and Port au Port Peninsula

In 1924 an instant town appeared in a strikingly beautiful wilderness where the Long Range Mountains (an extension of the Appalachians) and the sea nestled together at the Bay of Islands, where the beaches, strewn with large boulders, resembled a moonscape, and where salmon swam to their spawning grounds up the long Humber Arm.

Bay of Islands was part of the French Shore. There, France and England had been at loggerheads for much of the eighteenth century. When the Treaty of Utrecht ended hostilities in 1713, Britain was given authority over all French colonies and fishing territories in Newfoundland — except for an area along the northern and western shores. Britain, in return, was not to allow settlement near the fishing grounds. France gave up its colony in Placentia and fishing rights on the south shore, but was permitted to fish during the season all along the lucrative north and western shores from Cape Bonavista to Point Riche, part of the long arm of the Northern Peninsula. This became known as the French Shore. Conflict persisted with treaty violations on both sides. In 1763, the Treaty of Paris confirmed the division, and added St. Pierre and Miquelon to the French holdings. But conflict and encroachments continued. Next, the 1783 Treaty of Versailles extended the French Shore boundaries to Cape Ray, thus preserving French rights to the northwest fishery. It was again agreed that settlement would be forbidden — though Newfoundlanders, independent as always, determinedly ignored this provision. And still there was conflict.

It wasn't until the mid-nineteenth century, therefore, that there were many permanent settlers on the French Shore. Ongoing disputes over fishing rights had made the area unsuitable for settlement. Those at Bay of Islands built mostly along the well-protected Humber Arm and earned their living by fishing, farming, hunting and trapping. But there were two other resources at

FACING PAGE:
Glynmill Inn, Corner Brook, named after Sir Glyn West, chairman of Armstrong-Whitworth, a British armament company.

PREVIOUS PAGE:
Lobster Cove Head lighthouse at sunset.

197

Our Lady of Mercy.

PORT AUX BASQUES: George Harvey and his young daughter (afterwards Mrs. C. Guillam) rescued 152 of the passengers and crew of the brig. *Dispatch,* wrecked on Dead Island in June 1828; were presented with a medal and a purse of £100 by Governor Cochrane, Sept. 29, 1830.

ST. GEORGE'S BAY: In the spring of 1868, shortly after sailing from Greenock, six boy stowaways were found on board a vessel in the Canada trade; the ship was driven into St. George's Bay in the ice and, when within eight miles of the land, the captain gave the boys a cake of bread each, put them on the ice and told them to walk ashore. Only four got to safety — one was drowned, and as night fell, one dropped exhausted and perished of cold. The captain was arrested on his return to Greenock, when his crew laid information against him, and the British authorities cabled out instructions and the four surviving boys were taken to Halifax.

hand — the forest of black spruce that surrounds the Bay of Islands, and the natural harbour in the Humber Arm, accessible to ocean-going vessels for three quarters of the year, and only twenty-five miles from the Gulf of St. Lawrence.

It was a man named Gay Silver who, with the help of a few carpenters and lumberers brought in from Nova Scotia and New Brunswick, first exploited these natural advantages by building a sawmill in 1864 at the little settlement of Corner Brook, at the mouth of the Humber River. The second owner was the Halifax firm of Burns and Murray. They took over in 1871, by which time the mill was producing a respectable three to five million feet of lumber a year. The third owner was another Nova Scotian, Christopher Fisher. He bought the mill in 1881 and ran it for forty years, selling in 1923 to the newly formed Newfoundland Power and Paper Company, a government project that resulted mainly from the efforts of Prime Minister Sir Richard Squires. A majority of the shares for this $20-million undertaking were held by the British armament company, Armstrong-Whitworth, which had undertaken to build a power house, mill and town. Squires made certain that things shifted into high gear.

Shift into high gear they did, and within two years, a town was born. The residential section of the community was called (unimaginatively but certainly descriptively) Townsite. It boasted ninety-seven houses, sewage and water facilities, roads, medical facilities, and even an automated telephone system — the first of its kind in either Newfoundland or Canada. But for the people who lived there, the town might well have been named Mudsite. Millions of tons of fill had been dumped on the tidal flat and bog land to form a base for the mill, the docks, and Townsite. Harold Horwood, in *Corner Brook: A Social*

Interior, Our Lady of Mercy.

History of a Paper Town, writes that, "People who were present during the construction all speak of the . . . sea of mud. Conditions were such as would now be thought intolerable." Most of the year, getting around the place was almost impossible. Everyone had to wear knee-length rubber boots, and often lost those. Once some heavy machinery fell into the mud and was never recovered. "But the air of optimism, the certainty that here was Newfoundland coming of age, leaping into the twentieth century, made men and women content to put up with working in mire among swarms of black flies and mosquitoes for exhaustingly long hours with little time to eat or sleep. . . . Corduroy duckwalks laid over the mud made it possible to get round the site. One woman who worked there as a cook reports that as she walked over the slatted boards she could look down between them and see rats scuttling along underneath."

On either side of Townsite, smaller and unregulated villages sprang up, communities with cheaper buildings, built on cheaper land, and not under the company's control. Corner Brook East and Corner Brook West had no building codes, no roads and no sanitary requirements. As a result of raw sewage in the area, typhoid broke out. But despite these difficulties and a host of other problems caused by frantic growth, interruptions of the wood and power supply, marketing glitches, and endless financial problems, within six years or so the population had soared to nearly 10,000. Eventually these towns, along with Townsite and Curling (initially the largest of the four, and one of the oldest communities on the west coast), were amalgamated into the city of Corner Brook.

The project had materialized with unbelievable speed. By June 1925, the machines were rolling. One hundred and sixty enthusiastic dignitaries made

Interior, Our Lady of Mercy.

the nineteen-hour train trip from St. John's to toast the first run of paper from the mill. Prime Minister Munroe spoke to the excited crowd, as did Henry D. Reid of the Reid Newfoundland Company. Squires, now in the parliamentary opposition due to a political scandal, was on hand but declined (or wasn't asked) to speak.

No doubt the visiting dignitaries were housed at the splendid Glynmill Inn, named after Sir Glyn West, the chairman of Armstrong-Whitworth. A spacious, half-timbered structure, it had been built by the company as staff quarters during construction of the mill and Townsite, but it was turned into a hotel in time for the grand opening. It stands today, a reminder of that two-year period when, against all odds, the impossible was achieved.

Only a year after the mill at Corner Brook went into production, its owners were looking for a buyer, thanks to poor markets and ongoing financing problems. In England, Armstrong-Whitworth was in trouble, and both the British and Newfoundland governments, who had guaranteed the bonds, were anxious to sell. It sold twice within the next thirteen years, first to the International Paper Company of New York and then to Bowater-Lloyd, a British company, the present owner.

Southwest of the Bay of Islands is the Port au Port Peninsula, the name either of French or Basques derivation (the Basques *portu* means harbour). Either way, the name tells the story of settlement on the 300-mile-long peninsula, as do the names of some of the towns, Petit Jardin, Grand Jardin, Grand'Terre, De Grau and — a reminder that this is, after all, Newfoundland — Jerry's Nose.

Here, before either Basques or French occupied the peninsula, Dorset Inuit and, later, Newfoundland Beothuk looked out over Port au Port Bay. Jacques Cartier is thought to have landed there in 1534. The peninsula gradually became predominantly French, as families from France, Acadians from Nova Scotia, and settlers from Saint Pierre built homes there. They farmed, raised livestock, and fished for lobster and herring along this strikingly beautiful coastline. (The initial magnet had been that seemingly endless supply of cod, but by the late 1800s it had all but disappeared.)

The twentieth century saw various activities — from lead mining, limestone quarrying, and logging, to scallop fishing, rabbit canning and fox farms, but with limited success. Gradually one industry after another failed, fish stocks declined, and many people were forced to leave in search of work. But somehow the French flavour survived. Port au Port is today the largest enclave of French-speaking people in Newfoundland, its unique culture symbolized by a church, the towering Our Lady of Mercy, that dominates Port au Port West, at Aguathuna. It was built in 1925 by a devout and optimistic people — people who felt that the population of Port au Port would grow to fill its church, the largest wooden church on the island. They could look north to booming Corner Brook, then just coming into its own, so perhaps it was not an unreasonable expectation. Sadly, it was not to be.

CHAPTER 21

Lobster Cove Head Lighthouse

A t a rather large meeting I attended in Bonne Bay," wrote G. C. Fearn, a local politician, "an old and feeble man stood up, and spoke of the great need of this light, and while the tears rolled off his cheeks, he recounted with a husky voice, how he often spent sleepless nights as the wind moaned around the house, because his brave sons were on the banks, and no light to guide them home."

The year was 1889 and there was agitation for a lighthouse on the west coast at Bonne Bay, south of the Straits of Belle Isle. It would help ships identify their position, warn them that deadly rocks lay ahead, and guide them safely into port. Lobster Cove Head, a fishing village on a windswept promontory near Rocky Harbour at the entrance to Bonne Bay, seemed to be the ideal spot. For years before the lighthouse arrived, every family with men at sea had been donating a pint of oil each week to ensure that one house, in a location that was fairly visible, could keep a light going all night in the window. The situation was so desperate, Fearn wrote, that "a stately old dame has offered to keep the light house (when erected) free of salary and, said she, 'You may be sure, it will always be burning, for I have my three boys on the banks.'"

When responsible government arrived in 1855 there were enough people settled on the French Shore to allow for a representative in the House of Assembly in St. John's. In the 1860s and 1870s the growing herring and lobster fisheries prompted even more settlement on the French Shore, so that by 1888 there were twenty-nine English and four French canning factories scattered along the coast, and countless fishermen in frail boats on treacherous seas. Little wonder that demands for lighthouses grew more strident. And yet, until the late 1880s, the coast from Twillingate west and south to Port aux Basques was dark to navigation — another tragic result of centuries of French-English animosity.

But while lighthouses were their responsibility, colonial administrators were not anxious to spend scarce funds on facilities in French territory. The only lights on the western side of the island, those at Point Riche and Cape

FACING PAGE:
Lobster Cove Head light, built in 1897.

*Home to William Young
and his son George. They
and their families tended
the light for sixty-eight
years.*

Norman, were built in 1871 by the Canadian government to light ocean-going ships sailing through the Strait of Belle Isle, one of the most hazardous passages in world shipping lanes. Only fifteen miles wide, it is, for about half the year, iced in and impossible. For much of the other half it is fogbound.

By the early years of the twentieth century, ten lights were marking the coast all along the French Shore. Among the first was the light at Lobster Cove Head at Bonne Bay. It was followed by others, until, by 1913, Newfoundland's forbidding shores were finally fully marked by lighthouses — one hundred years and countless deaths after Fort Amherst became operational.

When the beacon at Lobster Cove Head sent out its first warning light in the spring of 1898, a fisherman, Robert Lewis, was hired as lightkeeper. A native of Dorset, and a Master Mariner, he had recently retired, but his later years were anything but leisurely. Lewis, about sixty-eight years old when the lighthouse became operational, was the father of fourteen children, the youngest of whom was then only eleven. Four others, still in their teens, may then have been living at home as well. Lewis (described by a descendant as "right tall and thin," and his wife as "right big and short") was paid $504 per year.

Lewis served as a watchman while the light was under construction and supervised the arrival of the twenty-five-foot circular cast-iron tower, which was produced in St. John's and equipped with a lantern made in England. Completed in late 1897, the lighthouse stood on a concrete foundation, 115 feet above the high-water level. Its light, which began operation the following year, could be seen for sixteen miles (weather permitting) and flashed every one and a quarter seconds.

Just below the tower was the lightkeepers' house, a pleasant two-storey structure with a saltbox roof, sheathed in clapboard, its twelve-paned windows placed seemingly at random. It too was painted white. A covered walkway led

up from the house to the tower. House, tower and a storage shed stood snug-
ly anchored to the rocky outcropping, but each on a different level — because,
at the time they were built, Newfoundland lacked the heavy equipment necessary to level such a remote site.

Lewis tended the new light until his death in 1902, and then William
Young took over. Young and his wife, Esther Burridge, were, at the time, parents of five children. Another five were to follow. George, the third of their
four sons, succeeded his father in the job. Together they kept the light for a
total of sixty-eight years — William for thirty-nine, and George for another
twenty-nine. Their duties were constant and included not only watching the
light but keeping a daily record of the wind currents and weather, winding up
the light and filling it with kerosene. (In 1931 this type of light was replaced
by a compressed-air mantle, which needed seventy pounds of air pumped into
the mantle to keep it burning all night.) The Youngs also learned the international signals code in order to communicate with ships, kept the grounds
clean, gave the lighthouse a coat of fresh white paint every two years, and
raised all the nautical flags for display on holidays.

When the Youngs came to the light in 1902, they moved into the house
that had been home to the Lewis family. The Youngs' children and two succeeding generations were raised there. Families living in such an isolated spot
learned to be self-reliant. The lightkeeper's wife became adept at tending the
machinery so that if, for whatever reason, he was unable to work, she could
take over. Most chores were shared. Children invented their own games, with
outdoor play closely supervised by their cautious parents or older siblings
because of the dangerous terrain.

Many years after she had left the lighthouse, the Youngs' third daughter,
Annie Walters, spoke of what it had been like to grow up at Lobster Cove Head:

> I was only six years old when dad took over. . . . We were frightened to death
> to come to the lighthouse, afraid we'd never see Santa again: that he would-
> n't know where to find us. [At Christmas] Dad wouldn't leave the lighthouse
> very often . . . so the older people around Rocky Harbour came to the light-
> house. There were no flashlights or lights then, but they all had lanterns.
> We'd go upstairs and look though the window and see them leaving Lobster
> Cove with their lanterns, coming along the shore. People came throughout
> the whole twelve days of Christmas. They'd sing songs, tell stories, and have
> a step-dance.
>
> You used to have to light the lamp every night — a great big long
> chimney. Pop used to have to blow it out by his breath . . . there was no way
> to stop it. That got wore out, and they put in a light that used to wind up
> like a clock. It'd go for six hours. . . . More than once Pop used to have to
> come to meet us [coming home from school in Rocky Harbour] to see that
> we wasn't smothered [by a storm]. . . . We wore dresses, there was no pants
> then, and skin boots most of the time. . . . We wouldn't think about putting

NEVILLE, MRS. L.:
Gave birth to triplets —
three sons — at Bonne
Bay, Jan. 15, 1887; two of
the children survived; the
mother died Jan. 20,
1887.

WRECK OF THE STEAMSHIP ETHIE

Come all you true
    country men, come
    listen to me,
A story I'll tell you of the
    S.S. *Ethie*,
She being the steamboat
    employed on our shore,
To carry freight, mail and
    passengers down on the
    Labrador.

The orders went round to
    preserve for their life,
For the ship she is
    doomed and it's perish
    we might;
But still there is hope;
    there is one brave man
    on board
Who says he can guide
    her safely on to the
    shore.

Walter Young has been
    our purser, as you may
    understand
Volunteered for to guide
    her safely in to the land;
John Gullage, our first
    mate, bravely took to the
    wheel;
Captain English gave
    orders and all worked
    with a will.

Up off Martin's Point
    about one o'clock
Through bravery and
    courage she escaped
    every rock,
And the people on the
    shore saw the ship in
    distress;
All rushed to the spot for
    to help do their best.

on a pair of pants, that wasn't in a girl's line at all. . . . Mom was a good singer. Pop used to get time off every now and then to go in the country . . . if he was gone a week, we had to stay up all night long, well, we'd have a nap in the day. [Mom would] sing songs all night long, to keep us woke. She never had to sing one over twice. She knew over 250 songs. . . . I learned all my songs from Mom."

Young's great-granddaughter, Karen Nicolle, also recalled her great-grandfather's life before he took over as lightkeeper:

He was captain of a ship, *Sailors Home,* that had been trading between Halifax and Bonne Bay. His ship was wrecked and he was out of business . . . . As a light keeper [he] kept a constant watch, saving many lives. One incident occurred in 1914. A ship, the USS *Potomac,* had left Boston to go to Bay of Islands to cut out American schooners that were blocked with ice. [The ship had drifted off course into Bonne Bay and was caught in ice]. My great-grandfather sighted her, gathered a group of men, went to Berry Head Point and lit a bonfire to let them know how close to shore they were. By the time the crew walked ashore one member had one of his feet frozen. The crew were taken in by locals, my great-grandfather being one of them.

A grateful crew member, M. S. Brainard, described William Young in his journal: "Mr. Young is a native Newfoundlander and as fine a man as one could ever meet. He is well over six feet, well built, and as jolly and kind hearted as he is large. I think every one of the crew and most people of Newfoundland will bear me out in the statement that Bill Young is a MAN. I am sure that our gang shall never forget the great kindness that he and Mrs. Young offered us."

Four years later, Walter Young (another of this prolific Bonne Bay family) was involved in an equally dramatic rescue. The story appeared in the *Western Star* in 1927, reprinted from an earlier Newfoundland *Boston-Weekly*:

The loss of the ill-fated steamer *Ethie,* belonging to the Reid Newfoundland Co., occurred in December 1918. . . . When the *Ethie* left Port Saunders on her fateful last trip, the glass indicated that a storm was brewing, with a distance of 60 or 70 miles between, before she could make Bonne Bay, the next safe harbour . . . she made fair progress for a time, until the gale increased to such an extent that in spite of all efforts, she began to drift toward the rocks. The passengers and crew were now ordered to put on life-belts and with captain Edward English and Walter Young (a native of Bonne Bay) in command, she was beached in the only place where there was any possibility of saving the lives of those on board. . . . Immediately after running ashore a line was made fast to a buoy and sent ashore toward the group of men who had assembled on the beach. Several attempts were made to get hold of the buoy but without success, owing to the heavy sea that was running, making it impossible to launch a boat. Finally, one of the men — Reuben Decker, sent out his Newfoundland dog, which brought the buoy safely ashore. . . . Then rigging a "bo'sn's chair" on the line the first passenger to be sent ashore was a baby in a mail bag, followed by the other passengers and the crew. The wreck of the *Ethie,* and the methods adopted by the men of the West Coast is another instance of the resourcefulness of Newfoundland in time of danger and disaster.

O, what of the fright, the
  exhaustion and cold,
The depth of my story
  will never be told!
And all you brave fellows
  gets shipwrecked on the
  sea,
You thinks of the fate of
  the S.S. *Ethie.*

Words from Maude
Simmonds, 1920

George Young, Lobster Cove Head's third and last keeper, was born five years after the family's move to the lighthouse, and spent most of his life there. He and his wife, Mildred, interviewed after their lightkeeper duties abruptly ended, spoke with mixed emotions about their life at the light. George remembered the two-and-a-half-mile trek to school, when he "cursed more than God will ever forgive me for. Days you would plow right to your backside in snow, get up there soaking wet, and all you'd have for your dinner then was a bit of molasses bread." Asked about church on Sunday, he replied, "When you plowed through snow all week going to school, you didn't want to go back in on Sunday. The only time you'd go Sundays was to go see a girl. That was when I got older." Nor was life much easier when, after his father's death, George took over as lightkeeper, and his own family began to grow up. "Twas pretty bleak then," he said, "no one else . . . lots of wind, plenty of it. I was there twice that the chimney pots blew off the house, right through the roof. . . . It wasn't very nice for the family there and small children. . . . We never had no roads then. All supplies and food I'd get . . . by dory or by boat. . . . Or otherwise lug it on your back." In the Depression it was "not too bad, because I was getting a salary — $72 a month, with 6 children, so you knows how I lived."

On the odd occasion George would take time off — always during the day — his favourite pastime being shooting. Gulls were a main part of the family diet, along with vegetables from the family garden. But what his granddaughter, Karen Nicolle, remembered was the endless confinement: "He had to sit and watch the light all night. The lamp was a two wick system with a smaller circular wick inside the original wick that had to be watched continuously. Local people, understanding this confinement, always went to the lighthouse."

So, for the Youngs, it was in many ways a good job — that is until 1970, when federal authorities decided to install an automatic light at Lobster Head Cove. "When your time is up," said Young, "they give you a kick in the ass and out you go." When they left, George, then sixty-two, and Mildred kept a watchful eye on the new light from a house in Rocky Harbour Pond. In an interview many years later, George stoutly maintained that the automatic light had gone out several times since it was installed, adding proudly that "the light never went out once when I worked there."

Today the lightkeepers' house, now more than a century old, is under the authority of Gros Morne Park and open to the public.

THE NORTHERN PENINSULA

CHAPTER 22

Sir Wilfred Grenfell and the
St. Anthony Mission

He was known as Grenfell of Labrador. He became an international hero for his work in saving the lives and improving the livelihoods of the men and women who lived on the forbidding coasts of the northernmost point of Newfoundland and the long, breathtaking coast of Labrador.

Wilfred Thomason Grenfell was twenty-seven, a recent graduate of the London Hospital Medical School, and a convert to the evangelism of American missionary Dwight Moody, when he first encountered the desperate conditions of the people who lived along the northern reaches of Newfoundland and Labrador. Their plight became the inspiration for his life's work. Grenfell had joined the Royal National Mission to Deep Sea Fishermen, and at its request headed to Newfoundland and Labrador to observe conditions in the fishery. The first sight to greet him on his arrival were the smouldering ruins of St. John's — he had arrived just after the Great Fire of July 1892 had destroyed most of that city.

Sailing north along the coast he was horrified to discover thousands of fishermen and their families and native people existing in conditions of appalling hardship. Poverty and sickness were the lot of the seemingly limitless numbers of stationers, "livyers" and Inuit, who had been receiving only an annual visit from one government doctor. That journey changed Grenfell's life and the lives of thousands of others. He spent the summer travelling as far as Hopedale, Labrador, providing medical care to nearly one thousand people (records are incomplete and the numbers could well be much higher). His reputation spread quickly throughout Newfoundland, and in St. John's, people began to raise money for a hospital.

Returning to England, Grenfell made the first of countless fund-raising tours, soon securing enough money for two hospitals. He returned to Labrador, and with assistance from others, opened hospitals at Battle Harbour

FACING PAGE:
Home of the complex and controversial Wilfred Grenfell, who brought modern medicine to Labrador and the remote outports of Newfoundland.

PREVIOUS PAGE:
Newfoundland dory.

ST. ANTHONY:
Methodist Church blown
down in great storm
November 21, 1894.

STRATHCONA: Hospital
steamship used along the
Labrador coast by the
International Grenfell
Association, presented to
the Mission by Lord
Strathcona, 1900;
foundered north of
Seldom Come By, Oct. 2,
1922.

SOP'S ARM, WHITE
BAY: Dynamite explosion
in old gold mine, April
27, 1905; Cornelius
Ricketts blown to pieces.

LAPLANDERS: Four
Lapps arrived at St. John's
Nov. 7, 1908, enroute to
St. Anthony to take
charge of Dr. Grenfell's
herd of reindeer.

and Indian Harbour. Grenfell performed what came to be seen as medical miracles. He also took aim at the truck system, which he saw as binding fishermen to merchant in interminable, unrelieved debt. So he started a fishermen's co-operative at Red Bay.

What followed was phenomenal. Grenfell arranged for construction of a mission hospital at his headquarters in St. Anthony. He built another mission hospital (the fourth) at Harrington, opened six nursing stations along the coasts, recruited other doctors and medical personnel to work in his hospitals, and raised £3,000 for the *Strathcona,* a well-equipped hospital ship. (There had been other hospital ships, but the *Strathcona* was the first to be purpose-built.) With an eye on his other goal, the improvement of living conditions, he initiated local industrial works projects, co-operatives, and handicraft industries, all designed to promote independence from the truck system. He imported Lapland reindeer to provide meat and milk, opened a sawmill, started an orphanage and school in St. Anthony, and made continuous fund-raising tours. He was the author of seven books.

Was Grenfell praised? He became a legend. Was he criticized? Of course. The challenge of fund-raising plagued him throughout his mission and took him away from his patients. People complained about his frequent absences. His involvement in the local economy and crusade for better working conditions was called interference, and a distraction from his mission work. His vast number of projects led to accusations of empire-building. His school (breaking with Newfoundland tradition) was non-denominational. For this he was also criticized. The growing friction with the mission led to the formation in 1912 of the International Grenfell Association, after which the practical medical work was carried on by dedicated, if autocratic, doctors. Grenfell kept on with fund-raising.

One thing for which he had not been criticized was his choice of a wife. Anna Elizabeth Caldwell MacClanahan was twenty-three and Grenfell forty-four when they married in November 1909. Anne, as she was called, was a graduate of Bryn Mawr with a degree in politics and economics. A highly organized, motivated, and independently wealthy woman, she was described as "dignified, handsome, well dressed and very tall" — an inch or so taller than Grenfell, who found this somewhat discomfiting. After a fashionable wedding in Chicago, the couple left for St. Anthony and their newly completed house built on the bedrock behind the hospital.

Robert Rompkey, in *Grenfell of Labrador: a Biography*, described the arrival of the bride and groom aboard the *Prospero* on January 10, 1910:

> The men of St. Anthony had built a traditional arch of spruce boughs, hung with a large banner that proclaimed "WELCOME TO OUR NOBLE DOCTOR AND HIS BONNIE BRIDE," and a komatik [a long sled adopted in northern Newfoundland and Labrador for winter travel and

Wilfred Grenfell.

hauled by dogs] had been decorated with cushions and red and white streamers, ready to convey the couple ashore. . . . Guns went off along the shore, and bonfires blazed. Fireworks rose and burst aloft, drawing shrieks from the children, who had not witnessed such a spectacle before.

[Their house] stood out among the more conventional dwellings of the region as it took shape in January 1910. . . . As it filled up with clutter, it did become distinctively Grenfellian, with its reindeer and caribou antlers, furs, prints of the British Isles, snowshoes, dog whips, hunting and fishing gear, Indian clubs, boxing gloves. . . . The living-room, its walls covered with green burlap, featured a huge fireplace with irregular pieces of gleaming Labradorite set into the grey stone. By contrast, the dining-room walls provided a dark red background for the mahogany furniture. On the second floor were the bedrooms, and on the third a den fitted out with shelves and cupboards where Grenfell could work.

*Grenfellian memorabilia
in the living room.*

JOHNNY CAKES IN
LABRADOR:
Dr. Grenfell Says People
Eat Cornmeal Formerly
Given Dogs.
Dr. Wilfred Grenfell
yesterday addressed
the girls at Miss
Chamberlain's school. . . .
One of the principal
features of the doctor's
work is teaching the
people the heat values of
certain foods. The people
there have been
accustomed to use white
flour almost exclusively
for which they have to
pay $7 to $10 a barrel.
Dr. Grenfell equipped
what he called a Johnny
Cake missionary, who
went about showing the
much greater economy of
using cornmeal. Hitherto
the people have fed
cornmeal to their dogs.
He hopes to substitute
reindeer for dogs, and has
made great progress in
this direction. Sheep have
also been introduced, and
wherever a family have
taken a loom into the
house it has proved of
great educational as well
as economic value.
The Daily News.
St. John's. December 9,
1910.

The house, now open to the public in the summer months, is owned and operated by the Grenfell Historical Society. It has been restored to the busy 1930 period, when the three Grenfell children, Wilfred Thomason Jr., Kinloch Pascoe, and Rosamond Loveday, were teenagers. (The children spent much of their childhood away at school, the boys at Groton and Rosamond at Havergal College in Toronto.)

Of the many legends surrounding Wilfred Grenfell, two stand out. The first, a stirring account of the time he was trapped on a drifting ice pan, began on Easter Sunday 1908. Accompanied by his pet spaniel, Jack, Grenfell set off in a komatik pulled by seven of his best dogs on a fifty-mile trek to see a patient who was facing a possible leg amputation from blood poisoning. He headed out over the ice, planning to stay with friends that night, then proceed to his tilt in Hare Bay the next day. There he intended to rendezvous with another team before resuming his journey. But wind, rain and heavy seas assaulted him, and he found himself stranded on an ice pan, a slushy mess that was sinking fast. The dogs stayed on the ice while Grenfell, his dry clothing and supplies, sank into the slob ice (a heavy, slushy, densely packed mass of ice fragments, snow, and freezing water). As he heaved himself from the icy sea, dragging himself and his dogs from pan to sinking pan, he realized that the wind and tide were taking them out to open sea. Aware that he could never survive the night in his wet gear, he took the only course to save his life — he killed three of the dogs and wrapped himself in their carcasses. He lay there all night, fully expecting to sink into the sea again. But the next day he was sighted, and a crew of five courageous men pushed and rowed their way through the slob ice to save him. When they reached Grenfell, his rescuers barely recognized him. He was suffering from frostbite and exposure, "his face was drained, and the dehydration had given him the appearance of a much older man. They burst into tears." Grenfell's recovery took some time. He was in pain, and depressed about his dogs. He never forgot them. A plaque on the wall in his home reads "To The Memory of Three Noble Dogs, Moody, Watch, and Spy, Whose lives were given for mine on the ice April 21, 1908."

Three years later, Grenfell was in St. John's to witness the realization of a dream — the creation of a seamen's hostel there. The hostel, a respectable alternative to the city's many rowdy taverns, would provide a swimming pool, games room, barber shop, auditorium and other facilities — and it would cost a hefty $175,000. Land for the building was donated by Sir Edgar Bowring. Grenfell, always a forceful speaker and a splendid publicist, had set off on another fund-raising tour in England and Canada. The tour was a success.

The cornerstone was laid in a highly imaginative ceremony that captured world attention. It took place on June 22, 1911, to coincide with the coronation of England's George V. An electrical connection was made between a room in Buckingham Palace and the hostel's Water Street location in St. John's. The king was to return to the palace directly after the coronation ceremonies and press a button that would send a signal through the Atlantic cable, whereupon, far across the Atlantic, the building's cornerstone would be lowered. As the designated moment approached, anxious residents of St. John's stood waiting in breathless anticipation, with their hats raised "in honour of His Majesty." At the appointed hour of 4:00 P.M. in London (12:30 in Newfoundland), King George touched the button and, in a British colony across the ocean, amid the ecstatic cheers of onlookers, the cornerstone slowly

Interior, the Grenfell house.

Door, the Grenfell house.

fell into place. Grenfell received welcome publicity around the world — and additional funding.

Wilfred Grenfell was knighted in 1927, the year that he and Anne retired to Vermont. Theirs had been a life of denial and dedication, with Grenfell honoured worldwide for his truly outstanding humanitarian achievements. Yet he was a driven and complex man who had come, as historian Michael Bliss has pointed out, "right out of the pages of Kipling." Grenfell was "wilful, disorganized, childish, authoritarian, enthusiastic and genuine, a son of the nineteenth century." Sadly, his legacy is not celebrated today as it should be.

Lady Grenfell died in 1938, after a lifetime devoted to her husband and to the Mission. The following summer, Grenfell returned to St. Anthony with her ashes and buried them on the hill behind the hospital. At the end of August he sailed from St. Anthony for the last time. He died at Charlotte, Vermont, on October 9, 1940. His ashes were buried beside those of his beloved Anne.

LABRADOR

◆

CHAPTER 23

Labrador

The coast of Labrador was described in various ways by the European explorers and fishermen who ventured there following the landing of the Vikings in about A.D. 1000. A Portuguese lavrador — a "landholder" cum explorer — called it Tiera de Lavrador. A fellow countryman described it succinctly (if not too accurately) as a "land that was very cool with big trees." But it was Jacques Cartier who, in 1534, offered the most graphic description, saying "This must be the land God gave to Cain . . . being composed of stones and frightful rocks and uneven places [with] not one cart load of earth, though I landed in many places."

And there are also the "desolate-treeless-grey-coloured-bleak-yet-sublime" descriptions sometimes given to this land. This portrayal, of course, completely fails to convey the variety and astonishing colour and life to be found along expanses of the coast and in the interior — waist-high grass on Baffin Island, lupins and several varieties of sub-arctic plants, and trees suitable for use as construction timber farther north, in the Port Hope Simpson area. Perhaps *National Geographic* said it best in its October 1993 issue, describing Labrador as "separated from Newfoundland by rough seas and temperament . . . awash in hard-edged beauty . . . [and] barely rippled by time."

Barely rippled by time it may seem, but in spite of its isolation and forbidding terrain, the Labrador coast has been occupied for thousands of years. At the L'Anse Amour burial site, evidence of Maritime Archaic occupation dating back to 7000 B.C. has been discovered. These people were displaced four thousand years later by the Palaeoeskimos from the Arctic, who were later displaced by ancestors of today's Innu and Inuit. Later, at Red Bay, along the northeast coast of the Strait of Belle Isle, Basque fishermen established a major whaling station, even before an unimpressed Cartier visited in the sixteenth century. The Portuguese came, the British and French, of course, and a few Scandinavians, but permanent settlement was sporadic until later in the eighteenth century when Christian missionaries arrived to convert Labrador's native people.

FACING PAGE:
Moravian mission, Nain.

PREVIOUS PAGE:
Great Northern Peninsula.

Jens Haven, a Dane, established the first mission on the northern coast of Labrador in August 1771. He knew the land, and its forbidding character. Haven belonged to a group known as Moravians, formed in Poland in 1722 by people of various cultural backgrounds. They had in common a zeal for missionary work. Haven had been stationed at their Greenland mission, and made his exploratory visit to Labrador in 1764 in full knowledge of the hazards of settlement. He knew the tragic story of the first group of Moravians who, twelve years earlier, had come to set up a mission station on the rugged coast. They had only meagre supplies, a prefabricated dwelling, and a few seeds. The effort ended in disaster when the pilot and six crew members died — either murdered, as some thought, by native people, or due to hunger and exposure.

Haven, however, was successful, and armed with a land grant from the British government, established a mission at Nain (Labrador's most northerly community, though still far south of its northernmost tip). Their leader was Christopher Brasen, a surgeon. The missionaries, sympathetic to the Inuit, had decided that efforts to convert them to Christianity should not include forcing them to adopt other languages or customs. With respect for the traditions of their potential converts, they decided that no missionary could preach until he had learned the Inuit language by working in the mission store and conversing with the natives. To begin with, only Hansen and fellow Greenland missionary, Christian Drachardt, spoke the Inuit language, and they alone preached in it.

The Nain mission became a trading operation as well, their wish being to keep the Inuit at home, far from the contaminating influences offered by white men to the south, not the least of which was free-flowing rum. They hoped that trade would make the mission self-sufficient. Among the brethren were skilled carpenters and tinsmiths who passed on their skills to the Inuit. And so dwellings were built, and furniture and utensils made. Converts, however, were another matter. They did not come quickly — in fact, not until six years after the missionaries arrived. The first convert, according to Reverend Peacock, "Kingminguse by name, was baptized Peter and was faithful to his baptismal vows for 13 years." Until, that is, he took a trip south where temptation lurked. He acquired a new boat and a second wife as well — a logical acquisition, he explained, since he needed her to "man" his new craft.

The Moravians, undeterred, expanded their missions until a dozen or so small communities dotted the coast. South of Nain, at Hopedale, they erected a sawmill, from which came the lumber for the beautiful church they built in 1782 (now in the possession of Parks Canada), and where, in accordance with their desire not to force a foreign language on the native people, they translated the Old Testament into the Inuit language. North of Nain, at Okak and Hebron, they built (in spite of the scarcity of wood) self-sufficient communities with churches, lodging houses, wash houses, bake houses, smoke houses, and smithies, in which the Inuit learned how to forge hunting weapons. These communities are now ghost towns.

On the southern coast of Labrador, just north of the Strait of Belle Isle, is Battle Harbour, one of several fishing stations established by the British in the latter part of the eighteenth century. Situated on tiny Battle Island, Battle Harbour was once headquarters for the legendary John Slade's Labrador operations.

Slade first came to Newfoundland in 1748, and after successfully developing his trade in the northern areas around Fogo and his main base at Twillingate, he and other merchants ventured to the coast of Labrador in the 1760s with the blessings of Governor Palliser, who was anxious to encourage English activities there. These merchants established thriving cod, seal and salmon fisheries as well as a furring business, and the coast teemed with activity during the summer months. But the American Revolution and roving privateers caused grief for Slade. One of his ships was captured near Labrador in 1779. Twillingate was raided and then Battle Harbour, where a sloop with twenty-two tons of seal oil was captured and goods from Slade's premises were destroyed. Slade died in Poole, England, in 1792, and his brother's four sons took over the business. His nephew John became the Poole-based head of John Slade and Co., while another nephew, Robert, was in charge of the Labrador operations — seven stations all told. By 1848 there were more than four hundred registered vessels in the Labrador fishery, many of which belonged to the Slades.

The premises at Battle Harbour constitute Newfoundland's last intact complex of early mercantile buildings. These structures date either from Robert Slade's management or, if built post 1871, when the complex was sold, from the era of the new owners, Baine, Johnston and Company. Among the buildings are pork, herring, flour, salt, salmon, and seal stores. In 1955, Earle Freighting Service of Carbonear purchased the complex, and in 1991 that firm generously donated the premises to the Battle Harbour Historic Trust.

A small house that belonged to fishermen George and Isaac Smith has been standing in Battle Harbour since those years when the Slades were wielding their considerable influence. Built sometime between 1830 and 1850, it was typical of countless small houses that were put up throughout Newfoundland, their style a result of strong cross-cultural links with Ireland and West County England. Virtually all were built of timber. The Smith house is a storey and a half, with centre stairs and a storage room, or linhay, at the rear. Due to the ravages of wind and weather, few of these early cottages survive. Battle Harbour is fortunate to have one of the oldest in the province.

Another architectural treasure at Battle Harbour is the historic St. James the Apostle Anglican church, commissioned in 1852 and consecrated five years later. The Moravians had by then been bringing the Christian message to Labrador's people for close to a century, but Bishop Feild of Newfoundland felt it was time for the Church of England to have its say, and he set about creating additional missions throughout the colony. The neo-Gothic St. James was

Interior, mission church at Nain.

LABRADOR: Terrific gales swept the coast between October 12th and 15th, 1885; eighty schooners and 300 lives lost and 2,000 people destitute.

INGRAHAM: Steam tug arrived at St. John's July 24, 1919, with six Flat Islands men, arrested on Labrador on charge of moonshining at their home town.

Home is where you hang your hat.

Slade premises, Battle Harbour.

based on plans by the Honourable Reverend William Grey, a noted ecclesiastical English architect. It is the second-oldest wooden Anglican church in the province.

Battle Harbour is where the energetic Wilfred Grenfell opened his first small hospital in 1893 (it was the gift of Walter Baine Grieve of Baine, Johnston and Company), offering to bring to the people in the remote regions of Newfoundland and Labrador, "advice and counsel in the cause of religion,

Home of George and Isaac Smith, Battle Harbour.

St. James the Apostle Anglican Church, Battle Harbour, consecrated in 1857.

temperance, and well-being." With funds raised around the world he did just that, building other hospitals, nursing stations, an orphanage, and the first co-operative in Newfoundland. The small storey-and-a-half Doctors' Cottage, built in 1904, housed a succession of physicians who followed Grenfell's lead in bringing medical help to the native people and the fishermen of Labrador. As well as staff doctors, medical students and nurses often worked at the hospital during the summers, without pay and having paid their own expenses.

Wilfred Grenfell's cottage, built in 1904. Battle Harbour.

Moravian Mission of Labrador, Hopedale, founded in 1752.

Although the tiny settlement of Battle Harbour was known by name to those who followed the career of Wilfred Grenfell, it was Robert Peary who brought the place to the entire world's attention. Heading south from his triumphant, if controversial, journey to the North Pole, Peary stopped first at Indian Harbour to send a brief wire to his wife ("Don't let any Cook's lies disturb you. I have him nailed.") and more lengthy messages to the Associated Press and the *New York Times* ("[Cook] has simply handed the world a gold

Moravian mission, Hopedale.

brick."). Peary's claim, writes Wally Herbert in *The Noose of Laurels*, was "one of the most sensational items in the history of journalism."

By the time that Peary reached Battle Harbour on September 16, 1909, the world press was waiting for him. Three whaleboat loads of journalists descended on the *Roosevelt* ("like so many boarding parties of pirates," as one of them wrote) for a brief encounter with the great man, who promised to hold a lengthier interview later. This took place that same afternoon in the loft of the salt store, in space belonging to fish trader and merchant agent John Edgar Croucher. Peary was enthroned on a pile of nets with Captain Bob Bartlett and Captain Dickson of the *Tyrian* (one of the journalists' ships) on either side. A Labrador gale, "uncanny in the brilliant sunlight, whistled and groaned and snarled with wolfish howls at the eaves." Inside the crowded store, there was considerable snarling as well, as the journalists, eager for the story, pounced on Peary. They queried him relentlessly about his claim to be first at the pole, and the claim by his rival, Dr. Frederick Cook, then heading for a hero's welcome in New York. "I repeat what I have said," snapped Peary, ". . . Dr. Cook has not been at the Pole. . . . Now I do not propose to answer that any further or to produce my proof until there is a properly authorized statement by Dr. Cook himself before a reliable disinterested party." Far from laying to rest the doubts of a waiting world, the interview added fuel to the fires of a controversy that continued to rage for the better part of a century — eighty years, as the *Washington Post Book World* has remarked, of "lies, puffery and propaganda."

After ten hectic days, Peary, Bartlett and the *Roosevelt* sailed from Battle Harbour. The little fishing community, after its brief brush with fame, returned to a less exciting existence. Gradually, the Labrador fishery declined,

225

Moravian mission,
Hopedale.

the Grenfell mission relocated to St. Mary's River (later known as St. Mary's Harbour), and then, in 1930, fire destroyed the Grenfell hospital complex. Rural resettlement to more centralized areas was the impetus for the end of year-round settlement at Battle Harbour, but some stayed on, and many descendants of the island's early residents return to their homes each summer. Now nearly twenty buildings in the mercantile complex have been restored by the Battle Harbour Historic Trust — a priceless contribution to the province's fascinating architectural and social history.

Sadly, few of Labrador's early Moravian buildings remain. Built at such cost by the brethren, they have fallen victim to the unrelenting weather, their demise hastened as one community after another was abandoned due to the gradual decline in the number of Inuit whom the missionaries served so devotedly for so long. Many died from contracting European diseases to which they had no immunity. (In 1848, many Inuit died when a measles epidemic swept the Moravian missions.) Early in the twentieth century, government relocation programs consolidated the outport communities, and the Moravians moved their headquarters to Happy Valley, near Goose Bay. Their humble, rough buildings, the few that remain in lonely Labrador outposts, serve as a reminder of a resilient people and a little-known chapter in our history.

Acknowledgments

I t was typical of Newfoundland's warm hospitality. Our work exploring early settlement in Canada, focussing on early homes and their builders, had led us to that historic province. We were seeking homes with a story to tell. Two books published by the Newfoundland Historic Trust had caught our attention — *Ten Historic Towns* and *A Gift of Heritage*. Shane O'Dea, architectural historian, and professor in the Centre for Material Culture Studies at Memorial University of Newfoundland (MUN), had written of the architectural development of town and outport in both. One contact led to a meeting in his office, a driving tour of the city to see the wealth of its architecture, another get-together in the beautiful outport town of Brigus, and a trip to the opening of the Avondale Railroad Station Museum.

During the four years of our work, Shane was always willing to be consulted about Newfoundland's architectural legacy. We are grateful to him for this and for introducing us to two men at MUN who gave us freely of their time and insight and helped two "mainlanders" to understand the history of their island. Professor Gordon Handcock, author, and an authority on the history of Trinity, talked of Poole merchants, and of settlement patterns that were unique to Newfoundland. We were fortunate to meet the late George Story, professor of English at MUN, editor of the best-selling *Dictionary of Newfoundland English*, and a man who was a veritable gold mine of information about Newfoundland's cultural history.

On that first visit we were contacted by Maudie Whelan, then with the CBC in St. John's, who interviewed us about our project. The link that we established then continued through the years of research and writing. Maudie, who loves the often amusing and poignant personal details that emerge from people's stories, helped us by interviewing members of the Earle, Cantwell and Garrett families, whose recollections gave life to the buildings with which they were connected.

Local historians helped us as we made our way around the province. In Bonavista, we are indebted to James T. Swyers, owner of Bridge House, and Robert Strathie, descendant of Alexander Strathie, who built much of Bonavista. In Trinity, Rupert Morris shared the pride and knowledge of those who live in this harbour town that saw so much of the early explorers and merchants. On the west coast we were guided by Anne Marceau, Interpretative Planner at Gros Morne Park, and Karole Pittman, both authorities not only on Lobster Cove Head lighthouse but on the settlement pattern of the western shore.

There were many knowledgeable people in St. John's who guided us through the available resources there. In the Centre for Newfoundland Studies Archives, Bert Riggs, archivist, and Linda White gave us invaluable advice. David Bradley of the Maritime History Archive at MUN identified areas in that important collection that would be of most use to us.

Our thanks to the staff of the Provincial Archives of Newfoundland and Labrador, who were always ready to be of assistance, whether it was in our search for sources of material, or for the archival photographs that we felt were essential, particularly those of the men and women around whom our story revolved. Ann Devlin-Fischer, Head, Still and Moving Images Collection at PANL, assisted us in our search for some of these archival photographs, as did Calvin Best, Head, Reference Services.

We were anxious that our work be read by authorities on each area, and were very fortunate that George Chalker, Executive Secretary of the Heritage Foundation of Newfoundland and Labrador, agreed to read the St. John's sections. He was, as well, a patient listener to our frequent queries. In Grand Bank, local historian Randell Pope offered us the fruits of his research on the Harris house, and read that section, giving welcome advice.

For the history of Labrador, Joyce Yates, Researcher and Interpretative Planner, Battle Harbour Historic Trust, read our manuscript and gave us assistance on our work with Battle Harbour.

James E. Candow, Project Historian with Parks Canada in its Atlantic Regional Office in Halifax, Nova Scotia, shared his extensive research on the Ryan premises in Bonavista, read the Bonavista section, and introduced us to the research report done by M. Dawe on the Bonavista lighthouse. Elaine Dunham, also with Parks Canada, guided us through the large picture collection housed in their offices in the Historic Properties, and helped us in our selection of archival photos.

Archival newspapers can bring the past to life again, providing a lively look at local events of the day. In this area we owe a great debt to the work of H. M. Mosdell, whose careful study of the St. John's *Royal Gazette* to 1922 resulted in the publication of *When Was That? A Chronological Dictionary of Important Events in Newfoundland Down to and Including the Year 1922*. As Mosdell noted, "The compilation of this work, while tedious and trying in the process, yet revealed to the Compilor much of the romance and tense drama that attaches to the history of the country." Many excerpts taken from *When Was That?* are found throughout this book. Others, from different sources, are identified as such.

We are deeply indebted to eminent Canadian artist David Blackwood, a Newfoundlander from Wesleyville and descendant of a prominent sealing captain, whose work embodies the spirit of the island, the tragedy of death at sea, and the stoicism and deep family bonds of its people. David talked to us about sealing and his childhood in Wesleyville, allowed us to use some photos from his personal archival picture collection, and graciously gave us permission to use his work entitled *Wesleyville: Cyril's Kite Over Blackwood's Hill* for the cover of our book.

John de Visser, who took the outstanding photographs for *True Newfoundlanders*, has captured Canada on film in forty-five previous books. He knows Newfoundland and Labrador as few who are not natives can claim. His previous work there has taken him to sites that reward the adventurous soul who is willing to take any turn in a road. To his artistic talents he adds the instinct of an explorer and the insight of one who knows that the past is ever present, particularly in Newfoundland and Labrador.

Select Bibliography

Barbour, Job. *Forty-Eight Days Adrift*. London 1932. St. John's 1981

The Canadian Biographical Dictionary and Portrait Gallery of Eminent and Self-Made Men. Toronto 1880

Dent, J. D. *The Canadian Portrait Gallery and Biographical Review*. Boston 1900

Dictionary of Canadian Biography. Vols. 1–13. Toronto 1966–94

Galgay, Frank. *The Life and Times of Sir Ambrose Shea*. St. John's 1986

Gentilcore, R. Louis, ed., and Geoffrey J. Matthews, cartographer/designer. *Historical Atlas of Canada*. Vols. 1–2. Toronto 1987, 1993

Halpert, Herbert, and G. M. Story, eds. *Christmas Mumming in Newfoundland: Essays in Anthropology, Folklore and History*. Toronto 1969

Handcock, W. Gordon. *Soe longe as there comes noe women: Origins of English settlement in Newfoundland*. St. John's 1989

Harris, Michael. *Rare Ambition: The Crosbies of Newfoundland*. Toronto 1992

Herbert, Wally. *The Noose of Laurels: Robert E. Peary and the Race for the North Pole*. New York 1989

Hibbs, R. *Who's Who In and From Newfoundland*. St. John's 1927

Hiller, J. K., and Peter Neary. *Newfoundland in the 19th Century*. Toronto 1980

Horwood, Harold. *Corner Brook: A Social History of a Paper Town*. St. John's 1986

Horwood, Harold, and John de Visser. *Historic Newfoundland*. Toronto 1986

Kent, Rockwell. *N by E*. New York 1930

Mannion, John. *The Peopling of Newfoundland: Essays in Historical Geography*. St. John's 1977

Manuel, Edith. *St. Peter's Anglican Church, Twillingate*. St. John's 1970

Mitchell, Elaine. *Placentia: Built Heritage and Forgotten Sites*. St. John's 1986

Morgan, Henry J. *Types of Canadian Women, Past and Present*. Toronto 1903

Mosdell, H. M. *When Was That? A Chronological Dictionary of Important Events in Newfoundland Down to and Including the Year 1922*. St. John's 1923

Murrin, Florence. *Newfoundland: Now and Then*. St. John's 1985

Neary, Peter, and Patrick O'Flaherty. *Part of the Main: An Illustrated History of Newfoundland and Labrador*. St. John's 1983

Newfoundland Historic Trust. *A Gift of Heritage*. St. John's 1975

———. *Ten Historic Towns*. St. John's 1978

Nevin, David. *The Pathfinders: The Epic of Flight*. Vol. 2. Time-Life Books. Virginia n.d.

O'Neill, Paul. *Breakers.* St John's 1982

———. *The Oldest City: The Story of St. John's Newfoundland.* Erin, Ontario, 1975

———. *A Seaport Legacy.* Erin, Ontario, 1976

Prowse, D. W. *History of Newfoundland.* London 1895, Belleville 1972

Rayburn, Alan. *Naming Canada.* Toronto 1994

Rompkey, Ronald. *Grenfell of Labrador.* Toronto 1991

Rowe, Frederick W. *A History of Newfoundland and Labrador.* Toronto 1980

Ryan, Shannon, and Martha Drake. *Seals and Sealers.* St. John's 1987

Rybczynski, Witold. *Home: A Short History of an Idea.* New York 1986

Saunders, Frank. *Sailing Vessels and Crews of Carbonear.* St. John's 1981

Smallwood, Joseph R. *Newfoundland Miscellany.* St. John's 1978

Smallwood, Joseph R., ed. *Encyclopedia of Newfoundland and Labrador.* 5 vols. St. John's 1981–

Story, George M., W. J. Kirwin and J. D. A. Widdowson, eds. *Dictionary of Newfoundland English.* Toronto 1982

Wakeham, P. J. *Princess Sheila.* St. John's 1987

Wardle, Arthur C. *Benjamin Bowring and His Descendants.* London 1938

Witney, Dudley. *The Lighthouse.* Toronto 1975

MAGAZINES, PAMPHLETS and SCHOLARLY PAPERS

Barbour, Carlson C. M. "The Exploits and Anecdotes of the Barbours of Bonavista Bay." St. John's 1973

Blackwood, David. "Chapel of St. John the Baptist Wesleyville." Port Hope 1993

Bruce, Harry. "Keepers of the Light." *Imperial Oil Review.* Toronto, spring 1991

Candow, James. "Signal Hill's Hospitals 1870–1920." Research Bulletin 121. Parks Canada, Halifax

———. "A Short History of James Ryan Ltd." Parks Canada, Atlantic Regional Office, Halifax

Candow, James and Daniel Widley Prowse. "The Origin of Cabot Tower." Research Bulletin 155. Parks Canada

Carbonear Heritage Society. "Rorke's Stone Jug." Carbonear. n.d.

Carter, Owen. Carter family, unpublished papers. Toronto

Coutts, Sally. "Lobster Cove Head Lightstation, Gros Morne National Park." Federal Heritage Buildings Review Office, Informal Building Report No. 89-44. Gros Morne National Park

Cullen, Mary. "Mallard Cottage, Quidi Vidi, St. John's Newfoundland." n.d.

Dawe, M. "Cape Bonavista Lighthouse." Newfoundland Historic Resources, Department of Culture, Recreation, and Youth, Government of Newfoundland, St. John's

English, L. E. F. "Historic Newfoundland and Labrador." St. John's 1955

Fox, C. J. "'A Glorified Stall': Newfoundlanders rant and roar over Confederation etc. 1946–48." *The Beaver: Exploring Canadian History.* Winnipeg, August/September 1996

Handcock, W. Gordon. "Trinity: A Brief History of Its Development up to the 19th Century." Memorial University of Newfoundland. St. John's n.d.

Heritage Foundation of Newfoundland and Labrador. Heritage Structure Inventory. St. John's

Jenness, Stuart E. "Conflicts and Adversities: The Southern Party of the Canadian Arctic Expedition, 1913–1916." *The Beaver.* August/September 1996

Kermode, Lloyd Edward. "The Spirit of Adventure: John Cabot, the Merchants of Bristol and the Re-discovery of America." *The Beaver.* October/November 1996

Matthews, Keith. "Lectures on the History of Newfoundland 1500–1830." Maritime History Group. Memorial University of Newfoundland. St. John's 1973.

McGhee, Robert. "First Arrivals: Who Were the First Canadians?" *Canadian Heritage.* Toronto, May 1981

Naftel, William. "The Brethren in Labrador." *Canadian Heritage.* October/November 1983

O'Dea, Shane. "Simplicity and Survival: Vernacular Response in Newfoundland Architecture. Society for the Study of Architecture in Canada." Bulletin. June 1983

———. "The Domestic Architecture of Old St. John's." Newfoundland Historical Society. Pamphlet 2. 1974

Osmond, Roy. "Families of the South Arm of Bonne Bay 1800's–1930's." Woody Point. 1990

Pocius, Gerald L. "Architecture on Newfoundland's Southern Shore: Diversity and the Emergence of New World Forms. Society for the Study of Architecture in Canada." Bulletin. June 1983.

Pittman, Karole. Interviews with the Young Family of Lobster Cove Head Lighthouse. Bonne Bay. 1987

Pope, Randell. "A History of the George C. Harris House." Grand Bank. n.d.

Ricketts, Shannon. "Ryan Premises." Federal Heritage Buildings Review Office. Architectural History Branch. n.d.

Robinson, Cyril and Louis Jaques. "Dynasty of Lighthouse Keepers." *Weekend Magazine* 7 no. 22. 1957

Tulloch, Judith. "Lobster Cove Head Lighthouse." Canadian Parks Service. Atlantic Regional Office. n.d.

Walwyn, Lady Eileen Mary. Unpublished journals. n.d.

Yates, Joyce. "Backgrounder: Battle Harbour Historic Trust." Halifax 1996

Photo Credits

With the following exceptions, all photographs are by John de Visser.

Introduction
Early fishing boat 1630. National Archives of Canada (NAC) 69713. C. W. Jeffreys pen-and-ink drawing.

Chapter 1
The following four photographs from the Ryan Collection are included with the kind permission of Miss Ena Marie Ryan, London, England.
James Ryan. Parks Canada, Atlantic Regional Office, Halifax, Nova Scotia. Ryan Collection.
Ryan house, Bonavista. Ryan Collection.
James Ryan, standing by fish flakes. Ryan Collection.
Mrs. James Ryan and housekeeper, Bonavista. Ryan Collection.

Chapter 4
Benjamin Lester. Provincial Archives of Newfoundland and Labrador (PANL) B15-29.
John Bingley Garland home in Trinity. PANL A41-59.
Early Anglican church, Trinity. PANL B16-156.
The third St. Paul's Church, Trinity, 1895. PANL A12-151.

Chapter 5
Bowrings' sea captains. PANL C4-9.

The following eight photographs are from the personal collection of David Blackwood.
Seabird in St. John's harbour, 1930s.
Governor Sir Humphrey Walwyn, visiting the Winsor house in Wesleyville, 1937, greeted by sea captains.
Annie Winsor Bishop.
S.S. *Imogene* arriving in St. John's, April 7, 1933.
Governor Sir David Murray Anderson, Eric Bowring and Captain Blackwood on the S.S. *Imogene.*
Captain and Mrs. A. L. Blackwood, 1937.
Barbour's *Neptune.*

Chapter 7
Sealing Steamers in the Ice. Harbour Grace. *Dominion Illustrated Weekly* 2, March 16, 1889. PS 173 Metropolitan Toronto Reference Library.
Loading Fish for Market. Harbour Grace. *Dominion Illustrated Weekly* 2, March 30, 1889. PS 205.
Aviator Mabel Bell. PANL VA 28-173.

Chapter 8
Transatlantic cable laying. Heart's Content, Newfoundland. NAC C66507.

Chapter 9
Bob Bartlett, circa 1900. Parks
    Canada, Atlantic Regional Office,
    Halifax, Nova Scotia 401-10-2-
    900-0233 ARO 2538-01.
Bob Bartlett and parents aboard the
    Morrissey. Parks Canada, Atlantic
    Regional Office, Halifax, Nova
    Scotia 401-10-2-920-0136 ARO
    2558-P2.

Chapter 11
St. Thomas' Church, St. John's. NAC
    C5578.

Chapter 12
Governor Thomas Cochrane. PANL
    VA27-37B.
Governor John Harvey. PANL VA27-
    39A.
Governor John Le Marchant. PANL
    VA27-40A.
Governor Alexander Bannerman.
    PANL VA27-43A.
Governor Anthony Musgrave. PANL
    VA27-44.

Chapter 13
Winterton. Photo by the authors.
Sir James Winter. PANL B3-218.
Elizabeth Bond, mother of Robert
    Bond. PANL A26-124.
Robert Bond. PANL A12-149.
Charlotte Bowring. PANL A23-117.
Codfish drying at mercantile premises,
    possibly Crosbies'. PANL B4-39
    NA 1942.

Chapter 14
Laying of the cornerstone, Cabot
    Tower. June 24, 1897.
    Newfoundland Collection,
    Provincial Reference and
    Resource Library, Arts and

Culture Centre, St. John's.
    C136/PA277.
St. John's after the fire (1892). PANL
    B15-99
Scenes des massacres de Scio; familles
    grecques attendant la mort ou
    l'esclavage. Salon de 1824.
    Eugene Delacroix. Louvre,
    Department des Peintures.

Chapter 15
Preparing for the Race: Quidi Vidi.
    Dominion Illustrated Weekly 2,
    April 20, 1889. PS 249.

Chapter 16
Notice to mariners announcing inau-
    guration of Cape Spear light,
    1836. PANL. Parks Canada,
    Atlantic Regional Office, Halifax,
    Nova Scotia 401-01-2-836-0017.
Marconi and his assistants with Mr.
    Cantwell outside Cabot Tower,
    circa 1901. PANL B1-95.

Chapter 22
Wilfred Grenfell, 1908. PANL A28-8.

Chapter 23
Slade premises. Tom Paddon, North
    West River, Labrador.
Home of George and Isaac Smith.
    Gordon C. Slade.
St. James the Apostle Anglican
    Church. Tom Paddon, North
    West River, Labrador.
Wilfred Grenfell's cottage. Gordon C.
    Slade.

Ferryland Lighthouse. George Gilmour,
    1995.

Index

239